IMMANUEL KANT:
GROUNDWORK OF THE METAPHYSIC OF MORALS
in focus

Groundwork of the Metaphysic of Morals is one of the most important works of moral philosophy ever written, and Kant's most widely read work. It attempts to demonstrate that morality has its foundation in reason and that our wills are free from both natural necessity and the power of desire. It is here that Kant sets out his famous and contro-versial 'categorical imperative', which forms the basis of his moral theory.

This book is an essential guide to the *Groundwork* and the many important and profound claims that Kant raises. The book combines an invaluable introduction to the work offering an exploration of these arguments and setting them in the context of Kant's thinking, along with the complete H.J. Paton translation of the work, and a selection of six of the best contemporary commentaries. It is the ideal companion for all students of Kantian ethics and anyone interested in moral philosophy.

Contributors: Henry Allison, Thomas Hill Jr, Hud Hudson, Christine Korsgaard, Onora O'Neill, Andrews Reath.

Lawrence Pasternack is Assistant Professor in the Department of Philosophy at Oklahoma State University.

IMMANUEL KANT: *GROUNDWORK OF THE METAPHYSIC OF MORALS*
in focus

Edited by
Lawrence Pasternack

London and New York

First published 2002
by Routledge
11 New Fetter Lane, London EC4P 4EE

Simultaneously published in the USA and Canada
by Routledge
29 West 35th Street, New York, NY 10001

Routledge is an imprint of the Taylor & Francis Group

© 2002 selection and editorial matter Lawrence Pasternack;
individual chapters, respective contributors

Groundwork of the Metaphysic of Morals © 1948 H.J. Paton

Typeset in Galliard by
Florence Production Ltd, Stoodleigh, Devon
Printed and bound in Great Britain by
TJ International Ltd, Padstow, Cornwall

British Library Cataloguing in Publication Data
A catalogue record for this book is available from the British Library

Library of Congress Cataloging in Publication Data
A catalog record for this book has been requested

ISBN 0–415–26064–7 hbk
ISBN 0–415–26065–5 pbk

CONTENTS

ACKNOWLEDGMENTS

Permission to reprint was kindly granted by the authors and the publishers of the six essays included in this volume: Thomas Hill Jr, 'Kant's Theory of Practical Reason', *Monist*, 72, 1989, 363–83; Christine Korsgaard, 'Kant's Analysis of Obligation: The Argument of *Foundations* I', *Monist*, 72, 1989, 311–40; Onora O'Neill, 'Consistency in Action' in Nelson Potter and Mark Timmons (eds) *Universality and Morality: Essays on Ethical Universalizability*, Dordrecht: D. Reidel, 1985, pp. 158–86; Henry Allison, 'Morality and Freedom: Kant's Reciprocity Thesis', *Philosophical Review*, 95, 1986, 393–425; Andrews Reath, 'Kant's Theory of Moral Sensibility: Respect for the Moral Law and the Influence of Inclination', *Kant-Studien*, 80, 1989, 284–302; Hud Hudson, 'Kant's Third Antinomy and Anomalous Monism' from Hud Hudson, *Kant's Compatibilism*, Ithaca, New York: Cornell University Press, 1994, with some material originally appearing in '*Wille, Willkür*, and the Imputability of Immoral Actions', *Kant-Studien*, 82, 1991, 179–96.

I wish to thank also the general editor of the Philosophers in Focus series, Stanley Tweyman, and my colleagues Scott Gelfand, John Shook and Mike Taylor.

LIST OF CONTRIBUTORS

Henry Allison is Professor of Philosophy at Boston University. Among his many books are *Kant's Transcendental Idealism* (Yale University Press, 1983), *Kant's Theory of Freedom* (Cambridge University Press, 1990), and *Idealism and Freedom: Essays on Kant's Theoretical and Practical Philosophy* (Cambridge University Press, 1996).

Thomas Hill Jr is Keenan Professor of Philosophy at the University of North Carolina, Chapel Hill. Many of his papers on Kantian ethics have been collected in *Autonomy and Self-Respect* (Cambridge University Press, 1991), *Dignity and Practical Reason in Kant's Moral Theory* (Cornell University Press, 1992), and *Respect, Pluralism and Justice: Kantian Perspectives* (Oxford University Press, 2000).

Hud Hudson is Professor of Philosophy at Western Washington University. He is the author of *Kant's Compatibilism* (Cornell University Press, 1994) and the editor of *Kant's Aesthetics* (Ridgeview, 1991), and has contributed to *Kant-Studien, Noûs, Pacific Philosophical Quarterly, Philosophical Studies* and *Philosophy and Phenomenological Research*.

Christine Korsgaard is Professor of Philosophy at Harvard University. She is the author of *The Sources of Normativity* (Cambridge University Press, 1996), which stems from her 1992 Tanner Lectures at Cambridge University, and *Creating the Kingdom of Ends* (Cambridge University Press, 1996), in which many of her most important papers have been collected.

Onora O'Neill [Nell] is Professor of Philosophy and Principal of Newnham College, Cambridge University. Her books include *Acting on Principle* (Columbia University Press, 1975), *Constructions of Reason: Explorations of Kant's Practical Philosophy* (Cambridge

University Press, 1989) and *Towards Justice and Virtue* (Cambridge University Press, 1996).

Lawrence Pasternack is Assistant Professor of Philosophy at Oklahoma State University. He has contributed to *Kant-Studien*, *Religious Studies* and *Idealistic Studies*.

Andrews Reath is Professor of Philosophy at the University of California, Riverside. He has contributed to *Kant-Studien*, *Pacific Philosophical Quarterly*, *Monist*, *Noûs* and *Journal of the History of Philosophy*.

INTRODUCTION

Immanuel Kant wrote nearly a dozen books and shorter monographs which deal with ethics. Many of them have garnered ample critical attention, but it is the *Groundwork of the Metaphysic of Morals* that has been and continues to be the most widely read.

As the title suggests, the *Groundwork* does not offer a complete account of Kant's ethical vision, but rather lays the foundation for it. The *Metaphysics of Morals*, published some twelve years later, sets out the principal categories of our rights and duties, discusses their derivation from more fundamental principles, and explores some of their more concrete applications. The *Groundwork*, on the other hand, offers a few illustrations of our duties, but its focus is on the foundations.

Kant tells us in the *Groundwork*'s Preface that 'the sole aim of the present Groundwork is to seek out and establish *the supreme principle of morality*'.[1] This principle, as we come to discover, is the categorical imperative: 'act only on that maxim which you can will to become a universal law'. In other words, moral principles (maxims) are those which ought to be followed without exception.

As the *Groundwork* progresses, it moves from an examination of the categorical imperative and the various formulations it can take to an exploration of the will: how to understand the relationship between reason, inclination and freedom. With each step, Kant introduces innovative theses and challenging arguments that have made his ethical theory not only of historical importance, but one that continues to guide many contemporary philosophers.

The essays collected in this volume are suitable for advanced students as well as those more familiar with Kant and ethical theory. Each selection is from a leading contemporary Kant scholar and addresses issues central to Kantian ethics. Thomas Hill Jr's 'Kant's Theory of Practical Reason' provides an excellent study of Kant's account of practical deliberation and the authority of reason. Each of the next three essays –

1

Christine Korsgaard's 'Kant's Analysis of Obligation: The Argument of *Groundwork* I', Onora O'Neill's 'Consistency in Action' and Henry Allison's 'Morality and Freedom: Kant's Reciprocity Thesis' – may be read as a commentary on the *Groundwork*'s three chapters. Andrews Reath's 'Kant's Theory of Moral Sensibility: Respect for the Moral Law and the Influence of Inclination' addresses one of the most difficult and important of Kant's theses: how, aside from all affective desires, can we be motivated to act morally. Finally, there is Hud Hudson's 'Kant's Third Antinomy and Anomalous Monism', which he generously wrote for this volume and is based upon his book *Kant's Compatibilism*. It endeavours to explain how Kant is able to reconcile the seemingly contradictory claims that our wills are free and yet causal determinism is true. As such, it provides a reading of the 'two standpoints' discussed in the *Groundwork*'s third chapter.

The remainder of this Introduction offers a brief account of the historical background to the *Groundwork* and then discusses some of its key themes.[2]

Wolff and the *Inquiry* of 1764

Kant's thoughts about ethics began to appear in print during a period when the doctrines of the British moralists dominated the philosophical scene. They were very much motivated by sceptical concerns about the possibility of having any knowledge beyond our representational content and rejected the possibility of finding for morality any foundation beyond the outpourings of our natural sentiments. So, according to the sentimentalists, if a state of affairs prompts a feeling of approval, it is deemed good; and if it meets with our disapproval, it is deemed bad.[3]

Although Kant eventually came to oppose this approach, in some of his earliest writings on ethics, most notably, his *Inquiry Concerning the Distinctness of the Principles of Natural Theology and Morality* (1764), he saw sentimentalism as offering at least a partial solution to the problem of moral knowledge. The main aim of the *Inquiry* is to compare our knowledge of mathematics, metaphysics and theology, on the one hand, with ethics, on the other. Though he believed we can gain certainty with respect to the former disciplines, he was much more doubtful about whether this is possible in ethics. After distinguishing between cognition as 'the faculty of representing the *true*' and feeling as 'the faculty of experiencing the *good*',[4] he states that our judgments of the good are, at root, 'an immediate effect of the consciousness of the feeling of pleasure combined with the representation of the object'.[5]

He found in this doctrine an advantage that the competing theory of Christian Wolff lacks. Whereas the sentimentalists rest their judgments about morality on feelings, Wolff maintained that formal principles of reason, specifically the principle of perfection, ground morality.[6] What troubled Kant about Wolff's approach was that he could not see how it could serve as a guide to action. He admits that perfection can serve as a 'formal ground' of duty, but a substantive account of what constitutes perfection is still needed. On its own, the rule of perfection, viz. 'perform the most perfect action in your power', does not determine in any specific instance how to act.[7] Some years later, Kant puts this point as follows: 'the comprehensive concept of perfection is not understandable in terms of itself and no practical judgment can be derived from it'.[8] To overcome this weakness, what counts as 'perfect' must be articulated, something that Wolff failed to do.

However, Kant did not completely reject Wolff. In fact, he, like Wolff, held that moral prescriptions express ends which are necessary in themselves,[9] and so was not satisfied by the approach taken by the British moralists. Sentiments can tell us what ends to adopt, but they cannot offer the sort of warrant for them that would establish their necessity.[10] Only reason can provide this necessity, but Kant was not yet able to see how it could do so while also being able to give us specific rules to guide our action.

So, by the end of the *Inquiry*, Kant had a dilemma on his hands: if he were to follow the British moralists, morality could have action-guiding content, but not necessity; if he were to follow Wolff, morality could have necessity but not action-guidingness. This is why Kant ends the *Inquiry* by stating that 'practical philosophy is even more defective than speculative philosophy, for it has yet to be determined whether it is merely the faculty of cognition, or whether it is feeling ... which decides its first principles'.[11]

Kant and Rousseau

Through much of the 1760s Kant continued to express interest in sentimentalism.[12] But also, during these years, he began to be influenced by Rousseau's writings, especially *Émile* and *Of the Social Contract*. Many of Kant's essays and *Reflexionen* from 1763–65 display his preoccupation with Rousseau and indicate that he was highly stimulated by Rousseau's view that the motivational underpinnings of human behaviour are much more malleable than many others believed.

In contrast to the psychological egoism of Hobbes, Rousseau held that human nature, particularly in its conjectural pre-social state, is fundamentally good. The state of nature is not, according to Rousseau, one of fear, competition and love of glory. Rather, it is our membership in society that twists our otherwise benign natural self-interest into *amour propre*; and this transformation cuts much more deeply than does the shift out of the state of nature in Hobbes. For Hobbes, psychological egoism applies just as much within society as it does without it. By contrast, Rousseau thought that society radically transforms our passions and that, through a proper education, a further transformation is possible which can emancipate us from the vanities inculcated by society.[13]

Kant was deeply moved by these affirmations of our natural goodness and in a well-known reflection from 1764/65, he expresses how dramatically he was affected by them:

> I am an inquirer by inclination. I feel a consuming thirst for knowledge, the unrest which goes with the desire to progress in it, and satisfaction at every advance in it. There was a time when I believed this constituted the honor of humanity, and I despised the people, who know nothing. Rousseau set me right about this. This binding prejudice disappeared. I learned to honor humanity, and I would find myself more useless than the common laborer if I did not believe that this attitude of mine can give worth to all others in establishing the rights of humanity.[14]

But beyond this relatively nebulous affirmation of Rousseau's egalitarian view Kant was even more deeply impacted by the possibility that our nature can be so intensely shaped by social forces.

On this point, Kant ponders: 'Everything goes past in flux; the changing tastes, the diverse forms of humanity make the whole play of things uncertain and deceptive. Where can I find the firm point of nature that man cannot overthrow and that can offer him the markers to the shore that will sustain him?'.[15] And, apparently in response, he writes: 'The question is whether I shall find the fulcrum point outside this world or in this world, in order to set the affects in motion. In answer: I find it in the state of nature, that is, of freedom'.[16]

Viewed together, these *Reflexionen* suggest that among the things that Kant took from Rousseau was a conception of freedom that goes beyond the view of the British moralists that whatever we choose is a product of the clash between various desires. If we accept the malleability of human nature, then what desires we have are also malleable. For Kant, this brought to light an enriched conception of freedom, as well as a new problem: how to choose which desires to adopt.

On various occasions, he tried to draw out the moral significance of freedom by relating it to the stoic ideal of mastering inclination in order to achieve a certain repose.[17] This was taken as the 'subordination of everything to free will',[18] and was given a value by virtue of the tranquility it is supposed to bring. But Kant was not satisfied by this account of how freedom and morality are related since it treats our willing in isolation from the will of others. Such an account may be sufficient when considering the conjectural state of nature; but, as we find ourselves living in a society, a more adequate explanation of how one's will relates to the wills of others is needed.

This led Kant, on other occasions, to consider Rousseau's notion of the general will. But he was still troubled. Of the general will, Kant writes: 'this will contains now the merely personal will as well as the universal will, in other words, man contemplates himself in consensus with the universal will'.[19] The general will did offer Kant something of an advance beyond the preceding view, but he was concerned that conformity to the general will was merely of instrumental value as the means for the will to maximize its own freedom. The general will might offer a way to endorse justice and equality, but not because they are of intrinsic worth. Rather, their value would stem from their promotion of the harmonious exercise of different wills within society.

What comes out of these reflections on freedom and the general will is a vision of the conformity of wills which is compatible with the free reign of each. There are here the beginnings of the categorical imperative, but the normative ground of this imperative is not yet pure practical reason. Instead, the value of freedom remained tangled up with the value of tranquility and so Kant's interest in the general will was still connected to an interest in gaining tranquility amid the discordant aims of multiple wills.[20] Likewise, Kant's conception of freedom was not yet fully developed. It may be at this stage likened to the so-called 'negative freedom' mentioned at the beginning of the *Groundwork*'s third chapter, but it still lacks the *Groundwork*'s 'positive freedom' of rational self-legislation. Nevertheless, by making freedom the 'fulcrum point' he was seeking, he took an important step towards overcoming the dilemma between sentimentalism and Wolffian rationalism.

From the *Inaugural Dissertation* to the *Critique* of Pure Reason

In the years following his encounter with Rousseau, we can find in Kant's *Reflexionen* and correspondence a renewed hope for moral philosophy. It is also during these years that he began to envision a metaphysics of morals.[21] Although struggling with how this is possible, Kant resolved that morality should be viewed as a system of pure concepts and so he no longer wavered in his repudiation of the sentimentalist position:

> *Moral Philosophy*, therefore, in so far as it furnishes the first *principles of judgement*, is only cognized by the pure understanding and itself belongs to pure philosophy. Epicurus, who reduced its criteria to the sense of pleasure and pain, is very rightly blamed, together with certain moderns, who have followed him to a certain extent from afar, such as Shaftesbury and his supporters.[22]

Of course, his firmer commitment to morality as a system of pure concepts and his clearer abandonment of sentimentalism did not, on their own, free him from the *Inquiry*'s dilemma. He still needed to explain how reason can legislate with necessity while at the same time being action-guiding. In addition, his more steadfast commitment to morality as an enterprise of reason led him to the further problem of how the will can be motivated to act morally without such motivation being reduced to a sentiment.

Throughout the 1770s Kant was at work developing what eventually became the *Critique of Pure Reason*. For a time, he intended the *Critique* to be a study of both theoretical and practical reason,[23] and though it came eventually to be a work devoted primarily to the former it was still written with the purpose of offering some indirect service to the latter.

Among the most crucial developments in the *Critique* for both theoretical and practical reason is the discovery that *a priori* judgments can also be synthetic. For both the British moralists and Wolff, it was thought that if a judgment were *a priori* it must be analytic. Likewise, they thought that if the judgment were to carry with it necessity or universality, it could do so only if it were analytic. For example, Wolff's principle of perfection bears a necessary relation to morality, but does so only analytically. Morality, quite obviously, calls upon us to do the good and avoid the bad. So too do the maxims 'Do the most perfect act in your power' and 'Refrain from doing that which will hinder the most perfect act in your power'.[24] But what is lacking here is any account of the 'most perfect'. The principle is merely formal, unable to inform us about the good. It is, for Kant, merely tautological because it does no more than restate the command to do what is good without amplifying our knowledge of the good.[25]

However, with the introduction of synthetic *a priori* judgments, a judgment might have necessity and universality, but also be able to expand our knowledge. As will eventually be seen in the *Groundwork*, Kant believed that with the categorical imperative he had found a principle of reason that overcomes the problems faced by Wolff's principle of perfection. It is a synthetic *a priori* judgment and as such provides us with an account of the good that is no mere tautological restatement of the prescription to do good.

The categorical imperative did not, however, spontaneously appear in the *Groundwork*, but developed over a number of decades. Even as far back as the *Inquiry*, Kant was attracted to the idea that genuine moral rules must have necessity, and it was not long afterwards that he also began to associate morality with universality.[26] But it still took quite a few years before his characterizations of morality ceased to waver. By 1780, he finally began to characterize morality in ways that closely resemble the *Groundwork*'s formulation of the categorical imperative, and in his lectures of 1780/81, we can find the following:

> The understanding takes account of everything which has a bearing on its rule. It accepts all those things which conform to the rule and opposes those which conflict with it. But immoral actions conflict with this rule; they cannot be made a universal rule. . . . All action ought, therefore to be so constituted that it agrees with the universal form of the understanding; it must be such that it can at all times become a universal rule; if it is so constituted, it is moral.[27]

The last major component of Kant's mature ethical theory to develop beyond its pre-critical formulations is his account of how we are motivated to act morally. During most of the pre-critical period, he generally followed an account of motivation which explains our actions in terms of a struggle between various feelings. Even while under the sway of Rousseau, and with his growing interest in the moral significance of the will's freedom, Kant did not see how we could be motivated to act without the affective power of feelings to move the will.

Despite the fact that by the beginning of the 1780s Kant had come to view morality as having its justificatory ground in reason, he still did not believe that the intellectual recognition of those grounds could have motivational force. In his lectures of 1780/81, he overtly repudiates this possibility, stating: 'Man is not so delicately made that he can be moved by objective grounds'.[28] Instead, what is needed for moral conduct is to bring sensibility in harmony with these objective grounds: 'Moral laws have in themselves no *vim obligatiorium*, but contain only the norm. They contain the objective conditions of judgment, but not the subjective ones of their execution. The latter consists in their agreement with our desire for happiness.'[29] So, in order to be motivated to act morally, we must be trained to experience feelings of aversion towards what reason prohibits and desire towards what reason commands.

The *Critique of Pure Reason* does not offer such a direct repudiation of the claim that reason can motivate us, but it does seem to still tie moral motivation to feeling, though in a more subtle manner. In one of the final sections of the *Critique*, 'The Canon of Pure Reason', it is argued that reason requires happiness to be ultimately distributed in proportion to our worthiness to receive it. But since such perfect justice cannot be realized in the sensible world, Kant postulates the existence of an afterlife as well as a God, as the omniscient judge of our worthiness. Without these postulates, reason would lack the completeness which it needs in order for us to have full confidence in its practical dictates. Furthermore, without the prospect of a future existence, moral principles could be 'objects of approval and admiration, but not springs of purpose and action'.[30]

From this, it appears that the account of motivation in the *Critique* is of a piece with his other comments on motivation from this time. Yet, there are some indications that the position presented in the *Critique* moves slightly closer to that of the *Groundwork*, for Kant writes: 'it is the moral disposition which conditions and makes possible the participation in happiness, and not conversely the prospect of happiness that makes possible the moral disposition. For in the latter case the disposition would not be moral, and therefore would not be worthy of complete happiness'.[31]

The desire for happiness, as one would expect, is distinguished from the 'moral disposition', but the text is quite unclear about the nature of this disposition.

It may be that Kant considered the moral disposition to be the desire *to be worthy* of happiness, as opposed to the desire to be happy. But, even if this were so, we would still need to explain how the desire to be worthy of happiness carries the moral weight to make one worthy. If, for example, an agent's interest in worthiness were no more than an interest in the means to his own happiness, then it would hardly carry moral worth. After all, it is not, Kant tells us, 'the prospect of happiness that makes possible the moral disposition'.

So, despite the fact that the desire for happiness may stimulate the desire to be worthy of happiness, the latter motive must have something not found in the former. But whatever that additional element is, it is not revealed in the *Critique*. There is, it seems, moral worth to the desire to be worthy of happiness which is not present in the desire for happiness, but the motivational theory of the *Critique* was still unable to explain how it carries this worth. However, at some point between 1781 and 1785, Kant finally worked out just where the distinction lies, and in doing so separated the moral motive from its sotereological entanglements.

The *Groundwork*

In the Preface to the *Groundwork*, Kant states that its sole aim 'is to seek out and establish *the supreme principle of morality*', and he pursues this goal through an account of what it means to have a good will. From the premiss that nothing other than the good will is unqualifiedly good, Kant develops the idea of a good will through the distinction between acting from duty versus acting merely in conformity with it. Actions of the latter type, such as holding to a promise in order to avoid harming one's reputation, are done for some reason other than just because they are right. In such cases, the agent is not deserving of moral praise. However, praiseworthy actions, those which express a good will, are those which are done because of the rightness of the action.

In the language of contemporary ethical theory, what Kant is here advocating is known as motivational internalism. Externalists maintain that, at least in the case of moral actions, one's motive for the act is distinct from what justifies it. One example would be a divine command theorist who is also a psychological egoist: it is God's will which establishes what sort of conduct is moral, but we obey God only out of a fear of punishment and/or a hope of reward. By contrast, the internalist holds that, at least in the case of moral actions, one's motive for the act is the same as what warrants it. In 'Kant's Theory of Practical Reason', Thomas Hill Jr deftly characterizes this thesis as follows: 'Kant is an "internalist" about reasons: there are, in addition to reasons for *believing*, reasons for *acting*, and to acknowledge these is (in part) to be disposed to follow them.'[32] Of course, Kant does not claim that all actions carry this connection between warrant and motivation, but at least some, including the morally praiseworthy ones, do. And so, with the adoption of motivational internalism, morality no longer has to be spiced up with the promise of a future reward. Instead, the *Groundwork* announces Kant's commitment to the idea that reason, the justificatory foundation for morality, can also motivate us.

It is worth noting, however, that motivational internalism is not unique to Kant. Even sentimentalists can be viewed as subscribing to a variety of internalism since they maintain that feelings are what establishes an action's value as well as what motivates us to act. But Kantian internalism is different. It does have, as Andrews Reath argues, an 'affective' component like those feelings central to the sentimentalists' account, but it also has a distinctive 'intellectual' side. The former, humility, is a feeling in the more ordinary sense, whose psychological effect is to offset the force of our self-interested desires; and the latter is respect, 'the attitude which it is appropriate to have towards a law, in which one acknowledges its authority and is motivated to act accordingly'.[33]

It is that intellectual side of moral motivation which was eluding Kant in the early 1780s, leaving a gap between the rational foundation for morality and what motivates action. But, with the gap closed, Kant could finally forge a path from freedom to the categorical imperative. Appealing to this commitment to motivational internalism, Christine Korsgaard helps explain Kant's strategy in the first chapter of the *Groundwork*: 'if we can discover why the good-willed person does it [the right thing] we will have *ipso facto* discovered why it is the right thing'.[34] In other words, to know what motivates moral conduct is to know what justifies it.

Notwithstanding that insight, the step from motivational internalism to the categorical imperative is still considerable. There are diverse motivational principles that one might regard as also carrying justificatory authority, and so, to get to the categorical imperative, Kant must also demonstrate that his specific variety of internalism is correct.[35] What he does, albeit in a very sketchy manner, is to eliminate the alternatives by relying upon what he believes to be an essential connection between moral authority and lawfulness. Competing theories fail to establish the necessity and universality of the ground on which they believe moral authority rests. Sentimentalists assume that humanity, by and large, has the same moral feelings. Yet, if our moral sense were different, our sentiments about various actions would be too. So, given that contingency, morality could not carry with it the necessity required for moral authority.[36]

To defend his more fundamental assumption that genuine moral principles must have a lawful character, we must appeal to his theory of agency. Kant signals this in the second chapter of the *Groundwork* with his assertion that 'if there is such a law, it must already be connected (entirely *a priori*) with the concept of the will of a rational being as such'.[37] If humans are the type of being he believes us to be, that is, if we have free will not only in the sense of being causally independent of natural laws, but also in that we are motivationally free from our desires no matter how strong they are, then the question of how we are to go about choosing our actions becomes all the more important. If we choose to act on a feeling, we are taking the feeling to be a suitable basis for action. We are, in effect, adopting a maxim that treats the feeling as a warrant for action. But the question then arises, what is it about the feeling that yields such a warrant? If the answer is that it *feels* a certain way, be it a strong feeling, a pleasant feeling, etc., we can again ask why strength, pleasantness, etc., matter. In effect, if we are rational beings, then we cannot, as Henry Allison puts the point, 'refuse to play the justification game'.[38]

The importance of the categorical imperative can be seen in light of this. For a rational agent's action to be justified, the action must be of that sort which other rational agents would choose in similar circumstances; and maxims which cannot be adopted by all rational agents without generating a contradiction are surely among those maxims that cannot be rationally justified. To illustrate, Kant offers the maxim of making a false promise. If one adopts the maxim 'I will make a false promise in order to get some money when hard pressed', and then considers whether it can be universalized, it should be seen that if everyone were to adopt such a maxim 'there could properly be no promises at all, since it would be futile to profess a will for future action'.[39]

In addition to his application of the categorical imperative to false promises in the *Groundwork*'s first chapter, Kant re-uses this example along with three others in the second chapter. There, he indicates how the categorical imperative establishes a prohibition on suicide, a duty to further one's talents and a duty to be charitable. Although it is not the *Groundwork*'s main goal to delve into the application of the categorical imperative, we can presume, eager to show that the categorical imperative can succeed where Wolffian perfectionism failed. That is, it can serve as a non-trivial guide to action, thereby showing that pure practical reason can provide a criterion to distinguish between moral and immoral conduct.

Ironically, however, one of the most common objections to, as well as one of the first to be uttered against, Kantian ethics is that it is an 'empty formalism'. This objection, most often attributed to Hegel, charges that the categorical imperative is insufficient to distinguish between moral and immoral maxims. When properly tailored, so it is argued, any maxim, even the most reprehensible, could survive the test. It may be that a general maxim of lying whenever it is in my self-interest cannot be universalized, but what about a specific maxim that references particular circumstances such as the one who is lying, the subject matter of the lie, etc.?

Criticisms of this variety tend to focus on the universal law formulation of the categorical imperative. But the formula of humanity, with its exhortation to treat others not merely as means but also as ends, is less formal, and so one might hope that it can somehow supplement the putative limitations of the universal law formulation. Some Kant scholars take that route and connect his anthropology with the formula of humanity in order to more profitably apply Kantian ethics.[40]

As for the limitations attributed to the universal law formulation, many have come to Kant's defence. One of the most fruitful ways to overcome the formalism objection is to clarify the nature of what is being tested. This is among the main goals of O'Neill's 'Consistency in Action'. She takes care to distinguish maxims from the specific intentions that an agent might have and then uses her account of maxims to clarify how the universalizability test operates.

But whichever route one takes to defend Kantian ethics against the various objections which have arisen, it is worth keeping in mind that the *Groundwork* is just that, a groundwork. In fact, Kant offers this caution on numerous occasions. One such instance can be found in the formula of humanity's treatment of suicide where Kant advises the reader against assuming that all the nuances of the issue have been explored: 'A more precise determination of this principle in order to avoid all misunderstanding ... I must here forego: this question belongs to morals proper'.[41]

The final chapter of the *Groundwork* marks a transition from what Kant characterizes as the analytic method of the first two chapters to the synthetic method of the third. The *Groundwork* leads the reader from a discussion of duty, through various formulations of the categorical imperative, and then to an account of what the will must be like in order for it to be capable of acting from duty. If the will lacks the requisite attributes then, Kant writes, morality would be just 'a mere phantom of the brain', and the *Groundwork* will have done little more than explore 'merely a chimerical Idea without truth'.[42] Hence, the task of the *Groundwork*'s third chapter is to respond to that worry with an argument that the will is rational and free from natural causation.

As described by Henry Allison in 'Morality and Freedom: Kant's Reciprocity Thesis', the opening paragraphs of the third chapter develop an argument that freedom and the moral law reciprocally imply one another. Kant begins by arguing that freedom, as a kind of causality, must be governed by some law, which turns out to be the moral law. He then maintains that a rational will must be free, for, if it were not, then it could not be reason but only natural necessity that determines our actions. This does not prove either that we are free or that we are bound by the moral law, but it does set the stage for the argument's next step.

If the reciprocity thesis is correct, we can prove freedom from the moral law and vice-versa. But to avoid circularity, we must still have an independent argument to establish either that we are free or that we are bound by the moral law. Kant tries to escape this circle by offering an argument which attempts to prove that we are free by way of our membership in the 'intelligible world'. Our capacity for theoretical reason, Kant presumes, requires that we have transcendental freedom, at least with respect to this capacity. But he then uses this to confer transcendental freedom to the will, apparently assuming that if one capacity is free in that respect, so is another. He neglects to take seriously the possibility that there are beings who have only the former and not the latter, and he does not provide us with an argument as to why this is not the case.[43] In the *Critique of Practical Reason*, published three years later, Kant again presents the reciprocity thesis, and this time, in what has been called his 'great reversal', does not try to prove the bindingness of the moral law upon us by way of our being free, but rather the reverse. He begins with the bindingness of the moral law as a 'fact of reason' and thereby argues that we are free.[44]

Another key element in the deduction argument is the distinction between things in themselves and appearances. That distinction, which is at the heart of Transcendental Idealism, is used in the *Critique of Pure Reason* and relied upon thereafter to preserve the possibility of freedom in light of causal determinism. The final paper contained in this volume, Hud Hudson's 'Kant's Third Antinomy and Anomalous Monism', takes us beyond the *Groundwork* and the normative issues in Kantian ethics into the metaphysical problem of how freedom can be compatible with causal determinism. In brief, Hudson's strategy is to distinguish between 'determining' and 'nondetermining' descriptions of the same event. Under the former, the event is treated as within the chain of natural causation. Under the latter, it is treated as arising from the will of a free agent. Although some might respond that this can give us, at best, the illusion of freedom, Hudson takes up this objection by rejecting 'bridge laws' between one description type and another. To put the point somewhat differently, for those interpreters of Transcendental Idealism who reject the 'two-worlds' reading of the phenomena–noumena distinction it would be possible to consider the same event at once according to the conditions for possible experience and at the same time as independent of these conditions, while treating neither as illusion.

The chapters forming this volume are presented with the hope that the reader will see the power of Kantian ethics coming not only from his normative doctrines, but from his conception of agency, as well as the intertwining of the two. The theoretical issues in which Kantian ethics are immersed are not, Kant advises us, relevant just to those interested in technical matters, but are of practical significance. We have, he tells us, 'a disposition to quibble with the strict laws of duty, to throw doubt on their validity or at least on their purity and strictness, and to make them, where possible, more adapted to our wishes and inclinations'.[45] And so, even on practical grounds, Kant recommends that we 'take a step into the field of *practical philosophy*', including a critique of our reason in its practical employment.[46] For through this critique we can strengthen our moral resolve by gaining a better understanding of its foundations.

Notes

1 Kant's works will be cited as 'AK' with the volume and page number of *Kants gesammelte Schriften*, 29 vols (Berlin: Walter de Gruyter, 1902–). Exceptions are the *Critique of Pure Reason*, where references follow the standard A and B pagination of the first and second editions, and Paul Menzer (ed.) *Lectures on Ethics*. Immanuel Kant, *Groundwork for the Metaphysics of Morals*, trans. H.J. Paton, p.23 (this volume) [AK 4:392].

2 For more detailed accounts of the development of Kant's ethics, see: Paul Schlipp, *Kant's Pre-Critical Ethics* (Evanston, Il.: Northwestern University Press, 1938); Josef Schmucker, *Die Ursprünge der Ethik Kants* (Meisenheim am Glan: Verlag, 1961); Richard Velkley, *Freedom and the End of Reason: On the Moral Foundations of Kant's Critical Philosophy* (Chicago: University of Chicago Press, 1989); Keith Ward, *The Development of Kant's View of Ethics* (Oxford: Basil Blackwell, 1972).

3 For a discussion of the relationship between scepticism, sentimentalism, and Kant, see J.B. Schneewind, 'Natural Law, Skepticism, and Methods of Ethics', *Journal of the History of Ideas*, vol. 52, 1991, 289–308.

4 Immanuel Kant, *Inquiry Concerning the Distinctness of the Principles of Natural Theology and Morality* (Prize Essay) in *Theoretical Philosophy, 1755–1770* ed. and trans. David Walford (Cambridge: Cambridge University Press, 1992), p. 273 [AK 2:299].

5 Immanuel Kant, *Inquiry*, p. 273 [AK 2:299].

6 See Christian Wolff, *Vernünftige Gedanken von der Menschen Thun und Lassen, zu Beförderung ihrer Glückseligkeit* (1720) in *Gesammelte Werke*, 78 vols (Hildesheim: Verlag, 1964–), I.4, §12.

7 Kant, *Inquiry*, p. 273 [AK 2:299].

8 *Reflexion* 6624 [AK 19:116].

9 Kant, *Inquiry*, pp. 272–3 [AK 2:298–9].

10 See AK 20:49–50.

11 Kant, *Inquiry*, pp. 274–5 [AK 2:300].

12 See, for example, Kant's announcement of his lectures for winter 1765–6 in *Theoretical Philosophy, 1755–1770*, pp. 290–300 [AK 2:303–13].

13 Like Rousseau, Kant viewed society as a corrupting force. *Amour propre* and envy take hold, rendering the self alienated from itself and requiring that the self modulate its relation to others in order to become reconciled to itself. Rather than gaining tranquility through a sort of solipsistic interest, our social involvement transforms us, such that our self-worth must be gained through a comparative relation to others. Some decades later, in *Religion Within the Limits of Reason Alone*, this idea evolved into Kant's doctrine of radical evil. But, at this stage, our unsocial sociability is not taken to be rooted in the inner corruption of human nature. Our nature remains good, and evil is emergent from the interaction of many wills. See, for example, Allen Wood, 'Unsocial Sociability: The Anthropological Basis of Kantian Ethics', *Philosophical Topics*, vol. 19, 1991, 325–51.

14 AK 20:44.

15 AK 20:46.

16 AK 20:56.

17 AK 20:149.

18 AK 20:179.

19 AK 20:145.

20 See AK 20:31.

21 Letter to Moses Mendelssohn, April 8, 1766, AK 10:71.

22 Immanuel Kant, *On the Form and Principles of the Sensible and Intelligible World* (Inaugural Dissertation) in *Theoretical Philosophy, 1755–1770*, p. 388 [AK 2:396].

23 Letter to Marcus Hertz, February 21, 1772, AK 10:129.

24 Immanuel Kant, *Inquiry*, p. 273 [AK 2:299].

25 See AK 19:116.

26 See *Reflexion* 6641 [AK 19:122].

27 Immanuel Kant, *Lectures on Ethics*, trans. Louis Infield (Indianapolis: Hackett, 1981), p. 45.

28 Immanuel Kant, *Lectures on Ethics*, p. 46.

29 *Reflexion* 7097 [AK 19:248].

30 Immanuel Kant, *Critique of Pure Reason*, trans. Norman Kemp Smith (New York: St. Martin's Press, 1929), A813/B841. Also, 'No man can possibly be righteous without having the hope, from the analogy of the physical world, that righteousness must have its reward' (Immanuel Kant, *Lectures on Ethics*, p. 54).

31 Immanuel Kant, *Critique of Pure Reason*, A813–4/B841–2.

32 Thomas Hill Jr, 'Kant's Theory of Practical Reason', p. 101 (this volume).

33 Andrews Reath, 'Kant's Theory of Moral Sensibility: Respect for the Moral Law and the Influence of Inclination', p. 213 (this volume).

34 Christine Korsgaard, 'Kant's Analysis of Obligation: The Argument of *Groundwork* I', p. 138 (this volume).

35 For a more detailed examination of how Kant moves to the categorical imperative from his account of motivation, see Henry Allison, 'On a Presumed Gap in the Derivation of the Categorical Imperative', *Philosophical Topics*, vol. 19, 1991, 1–15.

36 Kant would also regard consequentialist theories to be deficient in this respect since there is no necessary relationship between what an agent wills and the value of the consequences of his action. On this point, Kant writes: 'the moral worth of an action does not depend on the result expected from it, and so too does not depend on any principle of action that needs to borrow its motive from this expected result. For all these results (agreeable states and even the promotion of happiness in others) could have been brought about by other causes as well' (p. 32) [AK 4:401].

37 P. 55 (this volume) [AK 4:426].

38 Henry Allison, 'Morality and Freedom: Kant's Reciprocity Thesis', p. 192 (this volume).

39 P. 34 (this volume) [AK 4:403].

40 See, for example, Allen Wood, *Kant's Ethical Thought* (Cambridge: Cambridge University Press, 1999); and Robert Louden, *Kant's Impure Ethics: From Rational Beings to Human Beings* (Oxford: Oxford University Press, 1999).

41 P. 57 (this volume) [AK 4:429].

42 P. 71 (this volume) [AK 4:445].

43 This objection is developed by Dieter Henrich in 'Die Deduktion des Sittengesetzes' in Alexander Schwan (ed.) *Denken im Schatten des Nihilismus* (Darmstadt: Wissenschaftliche Buchgesellschaft, 1975), pp. 55–112.

44 The more interesting discussions of the fact of reason include: Henry Allison, 'Justification and Freedom in the *Critique of Practical Reason*' in Eckhart Forster (ed.) *Kant's Transcendental Deductions in the Three 'Critiques' and the 'Opus potumum'* (Stanford, Calif.: Stanford University Press, 1989), pp. 114–30; Karl Ameriks, 'Kant's Deduction of Freedom and Morality', *Journal of the History of Philosophy*, 19, 1981, 53–79; Dieter Henrich, 'The Concept of Moral Insight and Kant's Doctrine of the Fact of Reason', in Richard Velkley (ed.) *The Unity of Reason*, trans. Manfred Kuehn (Cambridge, Mass.: Harvard University Press, 1994), pp. 55–88.

45 P. 36 (this volume) [AK 4:405].

46 P. 36 (this volume) [AK 4:405].

GROUNDWORK
OF THE
METAPHYSIC OF MORALS

by
Immanuel Kant

PREFACE

[The different branches of philosophy]

Ancient Greek philosophy was divided into three sciences: *physics*, *ethics*, and *logic*. This division fits the nature of the subject perfectly, and there is no need to improve on it – except perhaps by adding the principle on which it is based. By so doing we may be able on the one hand to guarantee its completeness and on the other to determine correctly its necessary subdivisions.

All rational knowledge is either *material* and concerned with some object, or *formal* and concerned solely with the form of understanding and reason themselves – with the universal rules of thinking as such without regard to differences in its objects. Formal philosophy is called *logic*; while material philosophy, which has to do with determinate ii objects and with the laws to which they are subject, is in turn divided into two, since the laws in question are laws either of *nature* or of *freedom*. The science of the first is called *physics*, that of the second *ethics*. The former is also called natural philosophy, the latter moral philosophy.

Logic can have no empirical, part[1] – that is, no part in which the universal and necessary laws of thinking are based on grounds taken from experience. Otherwise it would not be logic – that is, it would not be a canon for understanding and reason, valid for all thinking and capable of demonstration. As against this, both natural and moral philosophy can each have an empirical part, since the former has to formulate its laws for nature as an object of experience, and the latter for the will of man so far as affected by nature – the first set of laws being those in accordance with which everything happens, the second 388] iii being those in accordance with which everything ought to happen, although they also take into account the conditions under which what ought to happen very often does not happen.

All philosophy so far as it rests on the basis of experience can be called *empirical* philosophy. If it sets forth its doctrines as depending entirely on *a priori* principles, it can be called *pure* philosophy. The latter when wholly formal is called *logic*; but if it is confined to determinate objects of the understanding, it is then called *metaphysics*.

In this way there arises the Idea of a two-fold metaphysic – a *metaphysic of nature* and a *metaphysic of morals*. Thus physics will have its empirical part, but it will also have a rational one; and likewise ethics – although here the empirical part might be called specifically *practical anthropology*, while the rational part might properly be called *morals*.

[The need for pure ethics]

iv All industries, arts, and crafts have gained by the division of labour – that is to say, one man no longer does everything, but each confines himself to a particular task, differing markedly from others in its technique, so that he may be able to perform it with the highest perfection and with greater ease. Where tasks are not so distinguished and divided, where every man is a jack of all trades, there industry is still sunk in utter barbarism. In itself it might well be a subject not unworthy of examination, if we asked whether pure philosophy in all its parts does not demand its own special craftsman. Would it not be better for the whole of this learned industry if those accustomed to purvey, in accordance with the public taste, a mixture of the empirical and the rational in various proportions unknown even to themselves – the self-styled 'creative thinkers' as opposed to the 'hair-splitters' who attend to the purely rational part – were to be warned against carrying on at
v once two jobs very different in their technique, each perhaps requiring a special talent and the combination of both in one person producing mere bunglers? Here, however, I confine myself to asking whether the nature of science does not always require that the empirical part should be scrupulously separated from the rational one, and that (empirical) physics proper should be prefaced by a metaphysic of nature, while practical anthropology should be prefaced by a metaphysic of morals – each metaphysic having to be scrupulously cleansed of everything
389 empirical if we are to know how much pure reason can accomplish in both cases and from what sources it can by itself draw its own *a priori* teaching. I leave it an open question whether the latter business[1] is to be conducted by all moralists (whose name is legion) or only by those who feel a vocation for the subject.

Since my aim here is directed strictly to moral philosophy, I limit my proposed question to this point only – Do we not think it a matter of the utmost necessity to work out for once a pure moral philosophy

completely cleansed of everything that can only be empirical and appro- vi
priate to anthropology?[1] That there must be such a philosophy is already
obvious from the common Idea[2] of duty and from the laws of morality.
Every one must admit that a law has to carry with it absolute necessity
if it is to be valid morally – valid, that is, as a ground of obligation;
that the command 'Thou shalt not lie' could not hold merely for men,
other rational beings having no obligation to abide by it – and similarly with all other genuine moral laws; that here consequently the
ground of obligation must be looked for, not in the nature of man nor
in the circumstances of the world in which he is placed, but solely *a
priori* in the concepts of pure reason; and that every other precept
based on principles of mere experience – and even a precept that may
in a certain sense be considered universal, so far as it rests in its slightest
part, perhaps only in its motive, on empirical grounds[3] – can indeed
be called a practical rule, but never a moral law.

Thus in practical knowledge as a whole, not only are moral laws, vii
together with their principles, essentially different from all the rest in
which there is some empirical element, but the whole of moral philosophy is based on the part of it that is pure. When applied to man it
does not borrow in the slightest from acquaintance with him (in anthropology), but gives him laws *a priori* as a rational being.[1] These laws
admittedly require in addition a power of judgement sharpened by
experience, partly in order to distinguish the cases to which they apply,
partly to procure for them admittance to the will of man and influence
over practice; for man, affected as he is by so many inclinations,[2] is
capable of the Idea of a pure practical reason, but he has not so easily
the power to realise the Idea *in concreto* in his conduct of life.

A metaphysic of morals is thus indispensably necessary, not merely
in order to investigate, from motives of speculation, the source of practical principles which are present *a priori* in our reason, but because 390] viii
morals themselves remain exposed to corruption of all sorts as long as
this guiding thread is lacking, this ultimate norm for correct moral judgement. For if any action is to be morally good, it is not enough that it
should *conform* to the moral law – it must also be done *for the sake
of the moral law*: where this is not so, the conformity is only too contingent and precarious, since the non-moral ground at work will now and
then produce actions which accord with the law, but very often actions
which transgress it. Now the moral law in its purity and genuineness
(and in the field of action it is precisely this that matters most) is to be
looked for nowhere else than in a pure philosophy. Hence pure philosophy (that is, metaphysics[1]) must come first, and without it there can
be no moral philosophy at all. Indeed a philosophy which mixes up

these pure principles with empirical ones does not deserve the name of philosophy (since philosophy is distinguished from ordinary rational knowledge precisely because it sets forth in a separate science what ix the latter apprehends only as confused with other things). Still less does it deserve the name of moral philosophy, since by this very confusion it undermines even the purity of morals themselves and acts against its own proper purpose.

[The philosophy of willing as such]

It must not be imagined that in the propaedeutics prefixed to his moral philosophy by the celebrated *Wolff* – that is, in the 'Universal Practical Philosophy',[1] as he called it – we already have what is here demanded and consequently do not need to break entirely new ground. Precisely because it was supposed to be a universal practical philosophy, it has taken into consideration, not a special kind of will – not such a will as is completely determined by *a priori* principles apart from any empirical motives and so can be called a pure will – but willing as such, together with all activities and conditions belonging to it in this general sense. Because of this it differs from a metaphysic of morals in the same x way as general logic differs from transcendental philosophy, the first of which sets forth the activities and rules of thinking *as such*, while the second expounds the special activities and rules of *pure* thinking – that is, of the thinking whereby objects are known completely *a priori;*[1] for a metaphysic of morals has to investigate the Idea and principles of a possible *pure* will, and not the activities and conditions of human willing as such, which are drawn for the most part from psychology. 391 The fact that in this 'universal practical philosophy' there is also talk (though quite unjustifiably) about moral laws and duty is no objection to what I say. For the authors of this science remain true to their Idea of it on this point as well: they do not distinguish motives which, as such, are conceived completely *a priori* by reason alone and are genuinely moral, from empirical motives which understanding raises to general concepts by the mere comparison of experiences. On the contrary, without taking into account differences in their origin they xi consider motives only as regards their relative strength or weakness (looking upon all of them as homogeneous) and construct on this basis their concept of *obligation*. This concept is anything but moral; but its character is only such as is to be expected from a philosophy which never decides, as regards the *source* of all practical concepts, whether they arise only *a posteriori* or arise *a priori* as well.

[The aim of the Groundwork]

Intending, as I do, to publish some day a metaphysic of morals, I issue this *Groundwork* in advance. For such a metaphysic there is strictly no other foundation than a critique of *pure practical reason*, just as for metaphysics[1] there is no other foundation than the critique of pure speculative reason which I have already published. Yet, on the one hand, there is not the same extreme necessity for the former critique as for the latter, since human reason can, in matters of morality, be easily brought to a high degree of accuracy and precision even in the most ordinary intelligence, whereas in its theoretical, but pure, activity it is, on the contrary, out and out dialectical;[1] and, on the other hand, a critique of practical reason, if it is to be complete, requires, on my view, that we should be able at the same time to show the unity of practical and theoretical reason in a common principle, since in the end there can only be one and the same reason, which must be differentiated solely in its application. Here, however, I found myself as yet unable to bring my work to such completeness without introducing considerations of quite another sort and so confusing the reader. This is why, instead of calling it a '*Critique of Pure Practical Reason*', I have adopted the title '*Groundwork of the Metaphysic of Morals*'.

But, in the third place, since a metaphysic of morals, in spite of its horrifying title, can be in a high degree popular and suited to the ordinary intelligence, I think it useful to issue separately this preparatory work on its foundations so that later I need not insert the subtleties inevitable in these matters into doctrines more easy to understand.

The sole aim of the present Groundwork is to seek out and establish *the supreme principle of morality*. This by itself is a business which by its very purpose constitutes a whole and has to be separated off from every other enquiry. The application of the principle to the whole system would no doubt throw much light on my answers to this central question, so important and yet hitherto so far from being satisfactorily discussed; and the adequacy it manifests throughout would afford it strong confirmation. All the same, I had to forego this advantage, which in any case would be more flattering to myself than helpful to others, since the convenience of a principle in use and its seeming adequacy afford no completely safe proof of its correctness. They rather awaken a certain bias against examining and weighing it in all strictness for itself without any regard to its consequences.

xii

392] xiii

[*The method of the* Groundwork]

xiv The method I have adopted in this book is, I believe, one which will work best if we proceed analytically from common knowledge to the formulation of its supreme principle and then back again synthetically from an examination of this principle and its origins to the common knowledge in which we find its application. Hence the division turns out to be as follows:

1. *Chapter I:* Passage from ordinary rational knowledge of morality to philosophical.
2. *Chapter II:* Passage from popular moral philosophy to a metaphysic of morals.
3. *Chapter III:* Final step from a metaphysic of morals to a critique of pure practical reason.

Chapter I

PASSAGE FROM ORDINARY RATIONAL KNOWLEDGE OF MORALITY TO PHILOSOPHICAL

[The good will]

It is impossible to conceive anything at all in the world, or even out of it, which can be taken as good without qualification, except a *good will*. Intelligence, wit, judgement, and any other *talents* of the mind we may care to name, or courage, resolution, and constancy of purpose, as qualities of *temperament*, are without doubt good and desirable in many respects; but they can also be extremely bad and hurtful when the will is not good which has to make use of these gifts of nature, and which for this reason has the term '*character*' applied to its peculiar quality. It is exactly the same with *gifts of fortune*. Power, wealth, honour, even health and that complete well-being and contentment with one's state which goes by the name of '*happiness*', produce boldness, and as a consequence often over-boldness as well, unless a good will is   2 present by which their influence on the mind – and so too the whole principle of action – may be corrected and adjusted to universal ends; not to mention that a rational and impartial spectator can never feel approval in contemplating the uninterrupted prosperity of a being graced by no touch of a pure and good will, and that consequently a good will seems to constitute the indispensable condition of our very worthiness to be happy.

Some qualities are even helpful to this good will itself and can make its task very much easier.[1] They have none the less no inner uncondi-tioned worth, but rather presuppose a good will which sets a limit to   394 the esteem in which they are rightly held[2] and does not permit us to regard them as absolutely good. Moderation in affections and passions,[3] self-control, and sober reflexion are not only good in many respects: they may even seem to constitute part of the *inner* worth of a person. Yet they are far from being properly described as good without

25

3 qualification (however unconditionally they have been commended by the ancients). For without the principles of a good will they may become exceedingly bad; and the very coolness of a scoundrel makes him, not merely more dangerous, but also immediately more abominable in our eyes than we should have taken him to be without it.

[The good will and its results]

A good will is not good because of what it effects or accomplishes – because of its fitness for attaining some proposed end: it is good through its willing alone – that is, good in itself. Considered in itself it is to be esteemed beyond comparison as far higher than anything it could ever bring about merely in order to favour some inclination or, if you like, the sum total of inclinations. Even if, by some special disfavour of destiny or by the niggardly endowment of step-motherly nature, this will is entirely lacking in power to carry out its intentions; if by its utmost effort it still accomplishes nothing, and only good will is left (not, admittedly, as a mere wish, but as the straining of every means so far as they are in our control); even then it would still shine like a jewel for its own sake as something which has its full value in itself. Its usefulness or fruitfulness can neither add to, nor subtract from, this value. Its usefulness would be merely, as it were, the setting which enables us to handle it better in our ordinary dealings or to attract the attention of those not yet sufficiently expert, but not to commend it to experts or to determine its value.

4

[The function of reason]

Yet in this Idea of the absolute value of a mere will, all useful results being left out of account in its assessment, there is something so strange that, in spite of all the agreement it receives even from ordinary reason, there must arise the suspicion that perhaps its secret basis is merely some high-flown fantasticality, and that we may have misunderstood the purpose of nature in attaching reason to our will as its governor. We will therefore submit our Idea to an examination from this point of view.

395

In the natural constitution of an organic being – that is, of one contrived for the purpose of life – let us take it as a principle that in it no organ is to be found for any end unless it is also the most appropriate to that end and the best fitted for it. Suppose now that for a being possessed of reason and a will the real purpose of nature were his *preservation*, his *welfare*, or in a word his *happiness*. In that case nature would have hit on a very bad arrangement by choosing reason in the creature to carry out this purpose. For all the actions he has to perform with this end in view, and the whole rule of his behaviour, 5 would have been mapped out for him far more accurately by instinct; and the end in question could have been maintained far more surely by instinct than it ever can be by reason. If reason should have been imparted to this favoured creature as well, it would have had to serve him only for contemplating the happy disposition of his nature, for admiring it, for enjoying it, and for being grateful to its beneficent Cause – not for subjecting his power of appetition to such feeble and defective guidance or for meddling incompetently with the purposes of nature. In a word, nature would have prevented reason from striking out into a *practical use* and from presuming, with its feeble vision, to think out for itself a plan for happiness and for the means to its attainment. Nature would herself have taken over the choice, not only of ends, but also of means, and would with wise precaution have entrusted both to instinct alone.

In actual fact too we find that the more a cultivated reason concerns itself with the aim of enjoying life and happiness, the farther does man get away from true contentment. This is why there arises in many, and that too in those who have made most trial of this use of reason, if they are only candid enough to admit it, a certain degree of *misology* – that 6 is, a hatred of reason;[1] for when they balance all the advantage they draw, I will not say from thinking out all the arts of ordinary indulgence, but even from science (which in the last resort seems to them to be also an indulgence of the mind), they discover that they have in fact only brought more trouble on their heads than they have gained in the 396 way of happiness. On this account they come to envy, rather than to despise, the more common run of men, who are closer to the guidance of mere natural instinct, and who do not allow their reason to have much influence on their conduct. So far we must admit that the judgement of those who seek to moderate – and even to reduce below zero – the conceited glorification of such advantages as reason is supposed to provide in the way of happiness and contentment with life is in no way soured or ungrateful to the goodness with which the world is governed. These judgements rather have as their hidden ground the Idea of another and much more worthy purpose of existence, for which, and not for happiness, reason is quite properly designed, and to which, therefore, as a supreme condition the private purposes of man must for the most part be subordinated.

For since reason is not sufficiently serviceable for guiding the will safely as regards its objects and the satisfaction of all our needs (which 7 it in part even multiplies) – a purpose for which an implanted natural instinct would have led us much more surely; and since none the less reason has been imparted to us as a practical power – that is, as one which is to have influence on the *will*; its true function must be to produce a *will* which is *good*, not as a *means* to some further end, but *in itself*; and for this function reason was absolutely necessary in a world where nature, in distributing her aptitudes, has everywhere else gone to work in a purposive manner. Such a will need not on this account be the sole and complete good,[1] but it must be the highest good and the condition of all the rest, even of all our demands for happiness. In that case we can easily reconcile with the wisdom of nature our observation that the cultivation of reason which is required for the first and unconditioned purpose may in many ways, at least in this life, restrict the attainment of the second purpose – namely, happiness – which is always conditioned; and indeed that it can even reduce happiness to less than zero without nature proceeding contrary to its purpose; for reason, which recognises as its highest practical function the establishment of a good will, in attaining this end is capable only of its own peculiar kind of contentment[2] – contentment in fulfilling a purpose which in turn is determined by reason alone, even if this fulfilment should often involve 8 interference with the purposes of inclination.

[The good will and duty]

397 We have now to elucidate the concept of a will estimable in itself and good apart from any further end. This concept, which is already present in a sound natural understanding and requires not so much to be taught as merely to be clarified, always holds the highest place in estimating the total worth of our actions and constitutes the condition of all the rest. We will therefore take up the concept of *duty*, which includes that of a good will, exposed, however, to certain subjective limitations and obstacles. These, so far from hiding a good will or disguising it, rather bring it out by contrast and make it shine forth more brightly.[1]

[The motive of duty]

I will here pass over all actions already recognised as contrary to duty, however useful they may be with a view to this or that end; for about these the question does not even arise whether they could have been done *for the sake of duty* inasmuch as they are directly opposed to it. I will also set aside actions which in fact accord with duty, yet for which men have *no immediate inclination*, but perform them because impelled to do so by some other inclination. For there it is easy to decide whether the action which accords with duty has been done *from duty* or from some purpose of self-interest. This distinction is far more difficult to perceive when the action accords with duty and the subject has in addition an *immediate* inclination to the action. For example,[1] it certainly accords with duty that a grocer should not overcharge his inexperienced customer; and where there is much competition a sensible shopkeeper refrains from so doing and keeps to a fixed and general price for everybody so that a child can buy from him just as well as anyone else. Thus people are served *honestly*; but this is not nearly enough to justify us in believing that the shopkeeper has acted in this way from duty or from principles of fair dealing; his interest required him to do so. We cannot assume him to have in addition an immediate inclination towards his customers, leading him, as it were out of love, to give no man preference over another in the matter of price. Thus the action was done neither from duty nor from immediate inclination, but solely from purposes of self-interest.

On the other hand, to preserve one's life is a duty, and besides this every one has also an immediate inclination to do so. But on account of this the often anxious precautions taken by the greater part of mankind for this purpose have no inner worth, and the maxim of their action is without moral content. They do protect their lives *in conformity with duty*, but not *from the motive of duty*. When on the contrary, disappointments and hopeless misery have quite taken away the taste for life; when a wretched man, strong in soul and more angered at his fate than faint-hearted or cast down, longs for death and still preserves his life without loving it – not from inclination or fear but from duty; then indeed his maxim has a moral content.

To help others where one can is a duty, and besides this there are many spirits of so sympathetic a temper that, without any further motive of vanity or self-interest, they find an inner pleasure in spreading happiness around them and can take delight in the contentment of others as their own work. Yet I maintain that in such a case an action of this kind, however right and however amiable it may be, has still no genuinely moral worth. It stands on the same footing as other inclinations[1] – for example, the inclination for honour, which if fortunate enough to hit on something beneficial and right and consequently honourable, deserves praise and encouragement, but not esteem; for its maxim lacks moral content, namely, the performance of such actions, not from inclination, but *from duty*. Suppose then that the mind of this friend of man were overclouded by sorrows of his own which extinguished all sympathy with the fate of others, but that he still had power to help those in distress,

9

398
10

11

though no longer stirred by the need of others because sufficiently occupied with his own; and suppose that, when no longer moved by any inclination, he tears himself out of this deadly insensibility and does the action without any inclination for the sake of duty alone; then for the first time his action has its genuine moral worth. Still further: if nature had implanted little sympathy in this or that man's heart; if (being in other respects an honest fellow) he were cold in temperament and indifferent to the sufferings of others – perhaps because, being endowed with the special gift of patience and robust endurance in his own sufferings, he assumed the like in others or even demanded it; if such a man (who would in truth not be the worst product of nature) were not exactly fashioned by her to be a philanthropist, would he not still find in himself a source from which he might draw a worth far higher than any that a good-natured temperament can have? Assuredly he would. It is precisely

399 in this that the worth of character begins to show – a moral worth and beyond all comparison the highest – namely, that he does good, not from inclination, but from duty.

To assure one's own happiness is a duty (at least indirectly); for

12 discontent with one's state, in a press of cares and amidst unsatisfied wants, might easily become a great *temptation to the transgression of duty*. But here also, apart from regard to duty, all men have already of themselves the strongest and deepest inclination towards happiness, because precisely in this Idea of happiness all inclinations are combined into a sum total.[1] The prescription for happiness is, however, often so constituted as greatly to interfere with some inclinations, and yet men cannot form under the name of 'happiness' any determinate and assured conception of the satisfaction of all inclinations as a sum. Hence it is not to be wondered at that a single inclination which is determinate as to what it promises and as to the time of its satisfaction may outweigh a wavering Idea; and that a man, for example, a sufferer from gout, may choose to enjoy what he fancies and put up with what he can – on the ground that on balance he has here at least not killed the enjoyment of the present moment because of some possibly groundless expectations of the good fortune supposed to attach to soundness of health. But in this case also, when the universal inclination towards happiness has failed to determine his will, when good health, at least for him, has not entered into his calculations as so necessary, what

13 remains over, here as in other cases, is a law – the law of furthering his happiness, not from inclination, but from duty; and in this for the first time his conduct has a real moral worth.

It is doubtless in this sense that we should understand too the passages from Scripture in which we are commanded to love our neighbour and even our enemy. For love out of inclination cannot be commanded; but kindness done from duty – although no inclination impels us, and even although natural and unconquerable disinclination stands in our way – is *practical*, and not *pathological*, love, residing in the will and not in the propensions of feeling, in principles of action and not of melting compassion; and it is this practical love alone which can be an object of command.

[The formal principle of duty]

Our second proposition[1] is this: An action done from duty has its moral worth, *not in the purpose* to be attained by it, but in the maxim according with which it is decided upon; it depends therefore, not on the realisation of the object of the action, but solely on the *principle* of *volition* 400 in accordance with which, irrespective of all objects of the faculty of desire,[2] the action has been performed. That the purposes we may have in our actions, and also their effects considered as ends and motives of the will, can give to actions no unconditioned and moral worth is clear from what has gone before. Where then can this worth be found if we are not to find it in the will's relation to the effect hoped for from 14 the action? It can be found nowhere but *in the principle of the will*, irrespective of the ends which can be brought about by such an action; for between its *a priori* principle, which is formal, and its *a posteriori* motive, which is material, the will stands, so to speak, at a parting of the ways; and since it must be determined by some principle, it will have to be determined by the formal principle or volition when an action is done from duty, where, as we have seen, every material principle is taken away from it.

[Reverence for the law]

Our third proposition, as an inference from the two preceding, I would express thus: *Duty is the necessity to act out of reverence for the law.* For an object as the effect of my proposed action I can have an *inclination*, but *never reverence*, precisely because it is merely the effect, and not the activity, of a will. Similarly for inclination as such, whether my own or that of another, I cannot have reverence: I can at most in the first case approve, and in the second case sometimes even love – that is, regard it as favourable to my own advantage. Only something which is conjoined with my will solely as a ground and never as an effect – something which does not serve my inclination, but outweighs it or at least leaves it entirely out of account in my choice – and therefore only 15

bare law for its own sake, can be an object of reverence and therewith a command. Now an action done from duty has to set aside altogether the influence of inclination, and along with inclination every object of the will; so there is nothing left able to determine the will except objectively the *law* and subjectively *pure reverence* for this practical law, and therefore the maxim* of obeying this law even to the
401　detriment of all my inclinations.

Thus the moral worth of an action does not depend on the result expected from it, and so too does not depend on any principle of action that needs to borrow its motive from this expected result. For all these results (agreeable states and even the promotion of happiness in others) could have been brought about by other causes as well, and consequently their production did not require the will of a rational being, in which, however, the highest and unconditioned good can alone be found. Therefore nothing but the *idea of the law* in itself, *which admit-*
16　*tedly is present only in a rational being* – so far as it, and not an expected result, is the ground determining the will – can constitute that pre-eminent good which we call moral, a good which is already present in the person acting on this idea and has not to be awaited merely from the result.**

15　*　A *maxim* is the subjective principle of a volition: an objective principle (that is, one which would also serve subjectively as a practical principle for all rational beings if reason had full control over the faculty of desire) is a practical *law*.

16　**　It might be urged against me that I have merely tried, under cover of the word 'reverence', to take refuge in an obscure feeling instead of giving a clearly articulated answer to the question by means of a concept of reason. Yet although reverence is a feeling, it is not a feeling *received* through outside influence, but one *self-produced* by a rational concept, and therefore specifically distinct from feelings of the first kind, all of which can be reduced to inclination or fear. What I recognise immediately as law for me, I recognise with reverence, which means merely consciousness of the *subordination* of my will to a law without the mediation of external influences on my senses. Immediate determination of the will by the law and consciousness of this determination is called 'reverence', so that reverence is regarded as the *effect* of the law on the subject and not as the *cause* of the law. Reverence is properly awareness of a value which demolishes my self-love. Hence there is something which is regarded neither as an object of inclination nor as an object of fear, though it has at the same time analogy with both. The *object* of reverence is the *law* alone – that law which we impose *on ourselves* but yet as necessary in itself. Considered as a law, we are subject to it without any consultation of self-love; considered as self-imposed it is a consequence of our will. In the first respect it[1] is analogous to fear, in the second
17　to inclination. All reverence for a person is properly only reverence for the law (of honesty and so on) of which that person gives us an example. Because we

[The categorical imperative]

But what kind of law can this be the thought of which, even without   402] 17
regard to the results expected from it, has to determine the will if this
is to be called good absolutely and without qualification? Since I have
robbed the will of every inducement that might arise for it as a consequence of obeying any particular law, nothing is left but the conformity
of actions to universal law as such, and this alone must serve the will
as its principle. That is to say, I ought never to act except in such a
way *that I can also will that my maxim should become a universal law.*
Here bare conformity to universal law as such (without having as its
base any law prescribing particular actions) is what serves the will as
its principle, and must so serve it if duty is not to be everywhere an
empty delusion and a chimerical concept. The ordinary reason of
mankind also agrees with this completely in its practical judgements
and always has the aforesaid principle before its eyes.

Take this question, for example. May I not, when I am hard pressed,   18
make a promise with the intention of not keeping it? Here I readily
distinguish the two senses which the question can have – Is it prudent,
or is it right, to make a false promise? The first no doubt can often be
the case. I do indeed see that it is not enough for me to extricate myself
from present embarrassment by this subterfuge: I have to consider
whether from this lie there may not subsequently accrue to me much
greater inconvenience than that from which I now escape, and also –
since, with all my supposed *astuteness*, to foresee the consequences is
not so easy that I can be sure there is no chance, once confidence in
me is lost, of this proving far more disadvantageous than all the ills I
now think to avoid – whether it may not be a *more prudent* action to
proceed here on a general maxim and make it my habit not to give a
promise except with the intention of keeping it. Yet it becomes clear to
me at once that such a maxim is always founded solely on fear of
consequences. To tell the truth for the sake of duty is something entirely
different from doing so out of concern for inconvenient results; for in
the first case the concept of the action already contains in itself a law
for me, while in the second case I have first of all to look around elsewhere in order to see what effects may be bound up with it for me.   19
When I deviate from the principle of duty, this is quite certainly bad;   403
but if I desert my prudential maxim, this can often be greatly to my

regard the developments of our talents as a duty,[1] we see too in a man of talent
a sort of *example of the law* (the law of becoming like him by practice), and
this is what constitutes our reverence for him. All moral *interest*, so-called, consists
solely in *reverence* for the law.

advantage, though it is admittedly safer to stick to it. Suppose I seek, however, to learn in the quickest way and yet unerringly how to solve the problem 'Does a lying promise accord with duty?' I have then to ask myself 'Should I really be content that my maxim (the maxim of getting out of a difficulty by a false promise) should hold as a universal law (one valid both for myself and others)? And could I really say to myself that every one may make a false promise if he finds himself in a difficulty from which he can extricate himself in no other way?' I then become aware at once that I can indeed will to lie, but I can by no means will a universal law of lying; for by such a law there could properly be no promises at all, since it would be futile to profess a will for future action to others who would not believe my profession or who, if they did so over-hastily, would pay me back in like coin;[1] and consequently my maxim, as soon as it was made a universal law, would be bound to annul itself.

20   Thus I need no far-reaching ingenuity to find out what I have to do in order to possess a good will. Inexperienced in the course of world affairs and incapable of being prepared for all the chances that happen in it, I ask myself only 'Can you also will that your maxim should become a universal law?' Where you cannot, it is to be rejected, and that not because of a prospective loss to you or even to others, but because it cannot fit as a principle into a possible enactment of universal law. For such an enactment reason compels my immediate reverence, into whose grounds (which the philosopher may investigate) I have as yet no *insight*,[1] although I do at least understand this much: reverence is the assessment of a worth which far outweighs all the worth of what is commended by inclination, and the necessity for me to act out of *pure* reverence for the practical law is what constitutes duty, to which every other motive must give way because it is the condition of a will good *in itself*, whose value is above all else.

[Ordinary practical reason]

In studying the moral knowledge of ordinary human reason we have now arrived at its first principle. This principle it admittedly does not conceive thus abstractly in its universal form; but it does always have it actually before its eyes and does use it as a norm of judgement. It

404
21   would be easy to show here how human reason, with this compass in hand, is well able to distinguish, in all cases that present themselves, what is good or evil, right or wrong – provided that, without the least attempt to teach it anything new, we merely make reason attend, as Socrates did, to its own principle; and how in consequence there is no

need of science or philosophy for knowing what man has to do in order
to be honest and good, and indeed to be wise and virtuous. It might
even be surmised in advance that acquaintance with what every man
is obliged to do, and so also to know, will be the affair of every man,
even the most ordinary. Yet we cannot observe without admiration the
great advantage which the power of practical judgement has over that
of theoretical in the minds of ordinary men. In theoretical judgements,
when ordinary reason ventures to depart from the laws of experience
and the perceptions of sense, it falls into sheer unintelligibility and self-
contradiction, or at least into a chaos of uncertainty, obscurity, and
vacillation. On the practical side, however, the power of judgement first
begins to show what advantages it has in itself when the ordinary mind
excludes all sensuous motives from its practical laws. Then ordinary
intelligence becomes even subtle – it may be in juggling with conscience
or with other claims as to what is to be called right, or in trying to   22
determine honestly for its own instruction the value of various actions;
and, what is most important, it can in the latter case have as good
hope of hitting the mark as any that a philosopher can promise himself.
Indeed it is almost surer in this than even a philosopher, because he
can have no principle different from that of ordinary intelligence, but
may easily confuse his judgement with a mass of alien and irrelevant
considerations and cause it to swerve from the straight path. Might it
not then be more advisable in moral questions to abide by the judgement of ordinary reason and, at the most, to bring in philosophy only
in order to set forth the system of morals more fully and intelligibly and
to present its rules in a form more convenient for use (though still more
so for disputation) – but not in order to lead ordinary human intelligence away from its happy simplicity in respect of action and to set it
by means of philosophy on a new path of enquiry and instruction?

[The need for philosophy]

Innocence is a splendid thing, only it has the misfortune not to keep
very well and to be easily misled. On this account even wisdom – which   405
in itself consists more in doing and not doing than in knowing – does
require science as well, not in order to learn from it, but in order to
win acceptance and durability for its own prescriptions. Man feels in   23
himself a powerful counterweight to all the commands of duty presented
to him by reason as so worthy of esteem – the counterweight of his
needs and inclinations, whose total satisfaction he grasps under the
name of 'happiness'. But reason, without promising anything to inclination, enjoins its commands relentlessly, and therefore, so to speak,

with disregard and neglect of these turbulent and seemingly equitable claims (which refuse to be suppressed by any command). From this there arises a *natural dialectic* – that is, a disposition to quibble with these strict laws of duty, to throw doubt on their validity or at least on their purity and strictness, and to make them, where possible, more adapted to our wishes and inclinations; that is, to pervert their very foundations and destroy their whole dignity – a result which in the end even ordinary human reason is unable to approve.

In this way the *common reason of mankind* is impelled, not by any need for speculation (which never assails it so long as it is content to be mere sound reason), but on practical grounds themselves, to leave its own sphere and take a step into the field of *practical philosophy.*
24 It there seeks to acquire information and precise instruction about the source of its own principle, and about the correct function of this principle in comparison with maxims based on need and inclination, in order that it may escape from the embarrassment of antagonistic claims and may avoid the risk of losing all genuine moral principles because of the ambiguity into which it easily falls. Thus ordinary reason, when cultivated in its practical use, gives rise insensibly to a *dialectic* which constrains it to seek help in philosophy, just as happens in its theoretical use; and consequently in the first case as little as in the second will it anywhere else than in a full critique of our reason be able to find peace.

PASSAGE FROM POPULAR MORAL PHILOSOPHY TO A METAPHYSIC OF MORALS

[The use of examples]

If so far we have drawn our concept of duty from the ordinary use of our practical reason, it must by no means be inferred that we have treated it as a concept of experience. On the contrary, when we pay attention to our experience of human conduct, we meet frequent and – as we ourselves admit – justified complaints that we can adduce no certain examples of the spirit which acts out of pure duty, and that, although much may be done *in accordance with* the commands of *duty*, it remains doubtful whether it really is done *for the sake of duty* and so has a moral value. Hence at all times there have been philosophers who have absolutely denied the presence of this spirit in human actions and have ascribed everything to a more or less refined self-love. Yet they have not cast doubt on the rightness of the concept of morality. They have spoken rather with deep regret of the frailty and impurity of human nature, which is on their view noble enough to take as its rule an Idea so worthy of reverence, but at the same time too weak to follow   26 it: the reason which should serve it for making laws it uses only to look after the interest of inclinations, whether singly or – at the best – in their greatest mutual compatibility.

In actual fact it is absolutely impossible for experience to establish   407 with complete certainty a single case in which the maxim of an action in other respects right has rested solely on moral grounds and on the thought of one's duty. It is indeed at times the case that after the keenest self-examination we find nothing that without the moral motive of duty could have been strong enough to move us to this or that good action and to so great a sacrifice; but we cannot infer from this with certainty that it is not some secret impulse of self-love which has actu-ally, under the mere show of the Idea of duty, been the cause genuinely determining our will. We are pleased to flatter ourselves with the false claim to a nobler motive, but in fact we can never, even by the most strenuous self-examination, get to the bottom of our secret impulsions; for when moral value is in question, we are concerned, not with the actions which we see, but with their inner principles, which we cannot see.

27   Furthermore, to those who deride all morality as the mere phantom of a human imagination which gets above itself out of vanity we can do no service more pleasing than to admit that the concepts of duty must be drawn solely from experience (just as out of slackness we willingly persuade ourselves that this is so in the case of all other concepts); for by so doing we prepare for them an assured triumph. Out of love for humanity I am willing to allow that most of our actions may accord with duty; but if we look more closely at our scheming and striving, we everywhere come across the dear self, which is always turning up; and it is on this that the purpose of our actions is based – not on the strict command of duty, which would often require self-denial. One need not be exactly a foe to virtue, but merely a dispassionate observer declining to take the liveliest wish for goodness straight away as its realisation, in order at certain moments (particularly with advancing years and with a power of judgement at once made shrewder by experience and also more keen in observation) to become doubtful whether any genuine virtue is actually to be encountered in the world. And then nothing can protect us against a complete falling away from our Ideas of duty, or can preserve in the soul a grounded reverence for its law, except the clear conviction that even if there never have been actions springing
408] 28 from such pure sources, the question at issue here is not whether this or that has happened; that, on the contrary, reason by itself and independently of all appearances commands what ought to happen; that consequently actions of which the world has perhaps hitherto given no example – actions whose practicability might well be doubted by those who rest everything on experience – are nevertheless commanded unrelentingly by reason; and that, for instance, although up to now there may have existed no loyal friend, pure loyalty in friendship can be no less required from every man, inasmuch as this duty, prior to all experience, is contained as duty in general[1] in the Idea of a reason which determines the will by *a priori* grounds.

It may be added that unless we wish to deny to the concept of morality all truth and all relation to a possible object, we cannot dispute that its law is of such widespread significance as to hold, not merely for men, but for all *rational beings as such* – not merely subject to contingent conditions and exceptions, but *with absolute necessity*.[2] It is therefore clear that no experience can give us occasion to infer even the possibility of such apodeictic laws. For by what right can we make what is perhaps valid only under the contingent conditions of humanity into an object of unlimited reverence as a universal precept for every rational nature? And how could laws for determining *our* will be taken as laws for determining the will of a rational being as such – and only because of this for determining ours – if these laws were merely empirical and did not have their source completely *a priori* in pure, but practical, reason?

What is more, we cannot do morality a worse service than by seeking to derive it from examples. Every example of it presented to me must first be judged by moral principles in order to decide if it is fit to serve as an original example – that is, as a model: it can in no way supply the prime source for the concept of morality. Even the Holy One of the gospel must first be compared with our ideal of moral perfection before we can recognise him to be such. He also says of himself: 'Why callest thou me (whom thou seest) good? There is none good (the archetype of the good) but one, that is, God (whom thou seest not)'. But where do we get the concept of God as the highest good? Solely from the *Idea* of moral perfection,[1] which reason traces *a priori* and conjoins inseparably with the concept of a free will. Imitation has no place in morality, and examples serve us only for encouragement – that is, they set beyond doubt the practicability of what the law commands; they make perceptible what the practical law expresses more generally; but they can never entitle us to set aside their true original, which resides in reason, and to model ourselves upon examples.

[Popular philosophy]

If there can be no genuine supreme principle of morality which is not grounded on pure reason alone independently of all experience, it should be unnecessary, I think, even to raise the question whether it is a good thing to set forth in general (*in abstracto*) these concepts which hold *a priori*, together with their corresponding principles, so far as our knowledge is to be distinguished from ordinary knowledge and described as philosophical. Yet in our days it may well be necessary to do so. For if we took a vote on which is to be preferred, pure rational knowledge detached from everything empirical – that is to say, a metaphysic of morals – or popular practical philosophy, we can guess at once on which side the preponderance would fall.

It is certainly most praiseworthy to come down to the level of popular thought when we have previously risen to the principles of pure reason

29

409

30

and are fully satisfied of our success. This could be described as first
31 *grounding* moral philosophy on metaphysics[1] and subsequently winning
acceptance for it by giving it a popular character after it has been
established. But it is utterly senseless to aim at popularity in our first
enquiry, upon which the whole correctness of our principles depends.
It is not merely that such a procedure can never lay claim to the extremely
rare merit of a truly *philosophical popularity*, since we require no skill
to make ourselves intelligible to the multitude once we renounce all
profundity of thought: what it turns out is a disgusting hotch-potch of
second-hand observations and semi-rational principles on which the
empty-headed regale themselves, because this is something that can be
used in the chit-chat of daily life. Men of insight, on the other hand,
feel confused by it and avert their eyes with a dissatisfaction which,
however, they are unable to cure. Yet philosophers, who can perfectly
410 well see through this deception, get little hearing when they summon
us for a time from this would-be popularity in order that they may win
the right to be genuinely popular only after definite insight has been
attained.

We need only look at the attempts to deal with morality in this
favoured style. What we shall encounter in an amazing medley is at
one time the particular character of human nature (but along with this
also the Idea of a rational nature as such), at another perfection, at
another happiness; here moral feeling and there the fear of God; some-
32 thing of this and also something of that. But it never occurs to these
writers to ask whether the principles of morality are to be sought at all
in our acquaintance with human nature (which we can get only from
experience); nor does it occur to them that if this is not so – if these
principles are to be found completely *a priori* and free from empirical
elements in the concepts of pure reason and absolutely nowhere else
even to the slightest extent – they had better adopt the plan of sepa-
rating off this enquiry altogether as pure practical philosophy or (if one
may use a name so much decried) as a metaphysic* of morals; of
bringing this to full completeness entirely by itself; and of bidding the
public which demands popularity to await in hope the outcome of this
undertaking.

32 * We can, if we like, distinguish pure moral philosophy (metaphysics) from applied
       (applied, that is, to human nature) – just as pure mathematics is distinguished
       from applied mathematics and pure logic from applied logic. By this terminology
       we are at once reminded that moral principles are not grounded on the pecu-
       liarities of human nature, but must be established *a priori* by themselves; and
       yet that from such principles it must be possible to derive practical rules for
       human nature as well, just as it is for every kind of rational nature.

Nevertheless such a completely isolated metaphysic of morals, mixed with no anthropology, no theology, no physics or hyperphysics, still 33 less with occult qualities (which might be called hypo-physical), is not only an indispensable substratum of all theoretical and precisely defined knowledge of duties, but is at the same time a desideratum of the utmost importance for the actual execution of moral precepts. Unmixed with the alien element of added empirical inducements, the pure thought of duty, and in general of the moral law, has by way of reason alone (which first learns from this that by itself it is able to be practical as well as theoretical) an influence on the human heart so much more 411 powerful than all the further impulses* capable of being called up from the field of experience that in the consciousness of its own dignity[1] reason despises these impulses and is able gradually to become their master. In place of this, a mixed moral philosophy, compounded of impulses from feeling and inclination and at the same time of rational 34 concepts, must make the mind waver between motives which can be brought under no single principle and which can guide us only by mere accident to the good, but very often also to the evil.

[Review of conclusions]

From these considerations the following conclusions emerge. All moral concepts have their seat and origin in reason completely *a priori*, and indeed in the most ordinary human reason just as much as in the most highly speculative: they cannot be abstracted from any empirical, and therefore merely contingent, knowledge. In this purity of their origin is to be found their very worthiness to serve as supreme practical principles, and everything empirical added to them is just so much taken away from their genuine influence and from the absolute value of the

---

* I have a letter from the late distinguished Professor *Sulzer*,[1] in which he asks 33 me what it is that makes moral instruction so ineffective, however convincing it may be in the eyes of reason. Because of my efforts to make it complete, my answer came too late. Yet it is just this: the teachers themselves do not make their concepts pure, but – since they try to do too well by hunting everywhere for inducements to be moral – they spoil their medicine altogether by their very attempt to make it really powerful. For the most ordinary observation shows that when a righteous act is represented as being done with a steadfast mind in 34 complete disregard of any advantage in this or in another world, and even under the greatest temptations of affliction or allurement, it leaves far behind it any similar action affected even in the slightest degree by an alien impulse and casts it into the shade: it uplifts the soul and rouses a wish that we too could act in this way. Even children of moderate age feel this impression, and duties should never be presented to them in any other way.

corresponding actions.[1] It is not only a requirement of the utmost necessity in respect of theory, where our concern is solely with speculation,
35 but is also of the utmost practical importance, to draw these concepts and laws from pure reason, to set them forth pure and unmixed, and indeed to determine the extent of this whole practical, but pure, rational knowledge – that is, to determine the whole power of pure practical reason. We ought never – as speculative philosophy[1] does allow and even at times finds necessary – to make principles depend on the special
412 nature of human reason. Since moral laws have to hold for every rational being as such, we ought rather to derive our principles from the general concept of a rational being as such,[2] and on this basis to expound the whole of ethics – which requires anthropology for its *application* to man – at first independently as pure philosophy, that is, entirely as metaphysics[3] (which we can very well do in this wholly abstract kind of knowledge). We know well that without possessing such a metaphysics it is a futile endeavour, I will not say to determine accurately for speculative judgement the moral element of duty in all that accords with duty – but that it is impossible, even in ordinary and practical usage, particularly in that of moral instruction, to base morals on their genuine principles and so to bring about pure moral dispositions and engraft them on men's minds for the highest good of the world.

36 In this task of ours we have to progress by natural stages, not merely from ordinary moral judgement (which is here worthy of great respect) to philosophical judgement, as we have already done,[1] but from popular philosophy, which goes no further than it can get by fumbling about with the aid of examples, to metaphysics. (This no longer lets itself be held back by anything empirical, and indeed – since it must survey the complete totality[2] of this kind of knowledge – goes right to Ideas, where examples themselves fail.) For this purpose we must follow – and must portray in detail – the power of practical reason from the general rules determining it right up to the point where there springs from it the concept of duty.[3]

[Imperatives in general]

Everything in nature works in accordance with laws. Only a rational being has the power to act *in accordance with his idea* of laws – that is, in accordance with principles – and only so has he a *will*. Since *reason* is required in order to derive actions from laws,[4] the will is nothing but practical reason. If reason infallibly determines the will, then in a being of this kind the actions which are recognised to be objectively necessary are also subjectively necessary – that is to say, the will

is then a power to choose *only that* which reason independently of inclination recognises to be practically necessary, that is, to be good. But   37
if reason solely by itself is not sufficient to determine the will; if the will
is exposed also to subjective conditions (certain impulsions) which do
not always harmonise with the objective ones; if, in a word, the will is
not *in itself* completely in accord with reason (as actually happens in
the case of men); then actions which are recognised to be objectively
necessary are subjectively contingent and the determining of such a will
in accordance with objective laws is *necessitation*. That is to say, the
relation of objective laws to a will not good through and through is
conceived as one in which the will of a rational being, although it is
determined[1] by principles of reason, does not necessarily follow these
principles in virtue of its own nature.

The conception of an objective principle so far as this principle is
necessitating for a will is called a command (of reason), and the formula
of this command is called an *Imperative*.

All imperatives are expressed by an *'ought'* (*Sollen*). By this they mark
the relation of an objective law of reason to a will which is not necessarily determined by this law in virtue of its subjective constitution (the
relation of necessitation). They say that something would be good to do
or to leave undone; only they say it to a will which does not always
do a thing because it has been informed that this is a good thing to do.   38
The practically *good* is that which determines the will by concepts of
reason, and therefore not by subjective causes, but objectively – that is,
on grounds valid for every rational being as such. It is distinguished from
the *pleasant* as that which influences the will, not as a principle of reason
valid for every one, but solely through the medium of sensation by purely
subjective causes valid only for the senses of this person or that.*

A perfectly good will would thus stand quite as much under objec-   414] 39
tive laws (laws of the good), but it could not on this account be conceived

---

*   The dependence of the power of appetition on sensation is called an inclina-   38
tion, and thus an inclination always indicates a *need*. The dependence of a
contingently determinable will on principles of reason is called an *interest*. Hence
an interest is found only where there is a dependent will which in itself is not
always in accord with reason: to a divine will we cannot ascribe any interest.
But even the human will can *take an interest* in something without therefore
acting from interest. The first expression signifies *practical* interest in the action;
the second *pathological* interest in the object of the action. The first indicates
only dependence of the will on principles of reason by itself; the second its
dependence on principles of reason at the service of inclination – that is to say,
where reason merely supplies a practical rule for meeting the need of inclination.[1]
In the first case what interests me is the action; in the second case what interests

as *necessitated* to act in conformity with law, since of itself, in accordance with its subjective constitution, it can be determined only by the concept of the good. Hence for the *divine* will, and in general for a *holy* will, there are no imperatives: *'I ought'* is here out of place, because *'I will'* is already of itself necessarily in harmony with the law. Imperatives are in consequence only formulae for expressing the relation of objective laws of willing to the subjective imperative of the will of this or that rational being – for example, of the human will.

[Classification of imperatives]

All *imperatives* command either *hypothetically* or *categorically*. Hypothetical imperatives declare a possible action to be practically necessary as a means to the attainment of something else that one wills (or that one may will). A categorical imperative would be one which represented an action as objectively necessary in itself apart from its relation to a further end.

40 Every practical law represents a possible action as good and therefore as necessary for a subject whose actions are determined by reason. Hence all imperatives are formulae for determining an action which is necessary in accordance with the principle of a will in some sense good. If the action would be good solely as a means *to something else*, the imperative is *hypothetical*; if the action is represented as good *in itself* and therefore as necessary, in virtue of its principle, for a will which of itself accords with reason, then the imperative is *categorical*.

An imperative therefore tells me which of my possible actions would be good; and it formulates a practical rule for a will that does not perform an action straight away because the action is good – whether because the subject does not always know that it is good or because, even if he did know this, he might still act on maxims contrary to the objective principles of practical reason.

A hypothetical imperative thus says only that an action is good for some purpose or other, either *possible* or *actual*. In the first case it is a 415 *problematic* practical principle; in the second case an *assertoric* practical principle. A categorical imperative, which declares an action to be objectively necessary in itself without reference to some purpose – that is, even without any further end – ranks as an *apodeictic* practical principle.

me is the object of the action (so far as this object is pleasant to me). We have seen in Chapter I that in an action done for the sake of duty we must have regard, not to interest in the object, but to interest in the action itself and in its rational principle (namely, the law).

Everything that is possible only through the efforts of some rational   41
being can be conceived as a possible purpose of some will; and consequently there are in fact innumerable principles of action so far as action
is thought necessary in order to achieve some possible purpose which
can be effected by it. All sciences have a practical part consisting
of problems which suppose that some end is possible for us and of
imperatives which tell us how it is to be attained. Hence the latter can in
general be called imperatives of *skill*. Here there is absolutely no question about the rationality or goodness of the end, but only about what
must be done to attain it. A prescription required by a doctor in order
to cure his man completely and one required by a poisoner in order to
make sure of killing him are of equal value so far as each serves to effect
its purpose perfectly. Since in early youth we do not know what ends
may present themselves to us in the course of life, parents seek above
all to make their children learn things *of many kinds*; they provide carefully for *skill* in the use of means to all sorts of *arbitrary* ends, of none
of which can they be certain that it could not[1] in the future become an
actual purpose of their ward, while it is always *possible* that he might
adopt it. Their care in this matter is so great that they commonly neglect
on this account to form and correct the judgement of their children about
the worth of the things which they might possibly adopt as ends.   42

There is, however, *one* end that can be presupposed as actual in all
rational beings (so far as they are dependent beings to whom imperatives apply); and thus there is one purpose which they not only *can*
have, but which we can assume with certainty that they all *do* have by
a natural necessity – the purpose, namely, of *happiness*. A hypothetical imperative which affirms the practical necessity of an action as a
means to the furtherance of happiness is *assertoric*. We may represent
it, not simply as necessary to an uncertain, merely possible purpose,
but as necessary to a purpose which we can presuppose *a priori*
and with certainty to be present in every man because it belongs to his
very being. Now skill in the choice of means to one's own greatest   416
well-being can be called *prudence** in the narrowest sense.[1] Thus an
imperative concerned with the choice of means to one's own happiness

---

*   The word 'prudence' (*Klugheit*) is used in a double sense: in one sense it can   42
have the name of 'worldly wisdom' (*Weltklugheit*); in a second sense that of
'personal wisdom' (*Privatklugheit*). The first is the skill of a man in influencing
others in order to use them for his own ends. The second is sagacity in combining
all these ends to his own lasting advantage.[1] The latter is properly that to which
the value of the former can itself be traced; and of him who is prudent in the
first sense, but not in the second, we might better say that he is clever and astute,
but on the whole imprudent.

43   – that is, a precept of prudence – still remains *hypothetical*: an action is commanded, not absolutely, but only as a means to a further purpose.

Finally, there is an imperative which, without being based on, and conditioned by, any further purpose to be attained by a certain line of conduct, enjoins this conduct immediately. This imperative is *categorical*. It is concerned, not with the matter of the action and its presumed results, but with its form and with the principle from which it follows; and what is essentially good in the action consists in the mental disposition, let the consequences be what they may. This imperative may be called the imperative of *morality*.

Willing in accordance with these three kinds of principle is also sharply distinguished by a *dissimilarity* in the necessitation of the will. To make this dissimilarity obvious we should, I think, name these kinds of principle most appropriately in their order if we said there were either *rules* of skill or *counsels* of prudence or *commands* (*laws*) of morality. For only *law* carries with it the concept of an *unconditioned*,

44   and yet objective and so universally valid, *necessity*; and commands are laws which must be obeyed – that is, must be followed even against inclination. *Counsel* does indeed involve necessity, but necessity valid only under a subjective and contingent condition – namely, if this or that man counts this or that as belonging to his happiness. As against this, a categorical imperative is limited by no condition and can quite precisely be called a command, as being absolutely, although practi-

417   cally,[1] necessary. We could also call imperatives of the first kind *technical* (concerned with art); of the second kind *pragmatic** (concerned with well-being); of the third kind *moral* (concerned with free conduct as such[2] – that is, with morals).

[How are imperatives possible?]

The question now arises 'How are all these imperatives possible?' This question does not ask how we can conceive the execution of an action commanded by the imperative, but merely how we can conceive the necessitation of the will expressed by the imperative in setting us a task.[3] How an imperative of skill is possible requires no special discussion. Who

44   *   It seems to me that the proper meaning of the word '*pragmatic*' can be defined most accurately in this way. For those *Sanctions* are called Pragmatic which, properly speaking, do not spring as necessary laws from the Natural Right of States, but from *forethought* in regard to the general welfare.[1] A *history* is written pragmatically when it teaches *prudence* – that is, when it instructs the world of today how to provide for its own advantage better than, or at least as well as, the world of other times.

wills the end, wills (so far as reason has decisive influence on his actions)   45
also the means which are indispensably necessary and in his power. So
far as willing is concerned, this proposition is analytic: for in my willing
of an object as an effect there is already conceived[1] the causality of
myself as an acting cause – that is, the use of means; and from the
concept of willing an end the imperative merely extracts the concept of
actions necessary to this end. (Synthetic propositions are required in
order to determine the means to a proposed end, but these are concerned, not with the reason for performing the act of will, but with the
cause which produces the object.) That in order to divide a line into two
equal parts on a sure principle I must from its ends describe two inter-
secting arcs – this is admittedly taught by mathematics only in synthetic
propositions; but when I know that the aforesaid effect can be produced
only by such an action, the proposition 'If I fully will the effect, I also will
the action required for it' is analytic; for it is one and the same thing to
conceive something as an effect possible in a certain way through me
and to conceive myself as acting in the same way with respect to it.

If it were only as easy to find a determinate concept of happiness,
the imperatives of prudence would agree entirely with those of skill and   46
would be equally analytic. For here as there it could alike be said 'Who
wills the end, wills also (necessarily, if he accords with reason) the
sole means which are in his power'. Unfortunately, however, the concept   418
of happiness is so indeterminate a concept that although every man
wants to attain happiness, he can never say definitely and in unison
with himself what it really is that he wants and wills. The reason for
this is that all the elements which belong to the concept of happiness
are without exception empirical – that is, they must be borrowed from
experience; but that none the less there is required for the Idea of happiness an absolute whole, a maximum of well-being in my present, and
in every future, state. Now it is impossible for the most intelligent, and
at the same time most powerful, but nevertheless finite, being to form
here a determinate concept of what he really wills. Is it riches that he
wants? How much anxiety, envy, and pestering might he not bring in
this way on his own head! Is it knowledge and insight? This might
perhaps merely give him an eye so sharp that it would make evils at
present hidden from him and yet unavoidable seem all the more frightful,
or would add a load of still further needs to the desires which already   47
give him trouble enough. Is it long life? Who will guarantee that it
would not be a long misery? Is it at least health? How often has infir-
mity of body kept a man from excesses into which perfect health would
have let him fall! – and so on. In short, he has no principle by which
he is able to decide with complete certainty what will make him truly

happy, since for this he would require omniscience. Thus we cannot act on determinate principles in order to be happy, but only on empirical counsels, for example, of diet, frugality, politeness, reserve, and so on – things which experience shows contribute most to well-being on the average. From this it follows that imperatives of prudence, speaking strictly, do not command at all – that is, cannot exhibit actions objectively as practically *necessary*; that they are rather to be taken as recommendations (*consilia*), than as commands (*praecepta*), of reason; that the problem of determining certainly and universally what action will promote the happiness of a rational being is completely insoluble; and consequently that in regard to this there is no imperative possible which in the strictest sense could command us to do what will make us happy, since happiness is an Ideal, not of reason, but of imagination – an Ideal resting merely on empirical grounds, of which it is vain to expect that they should determine an action by which we could attain the totality of a series of consequences which is in fact infinite. Nevertheless, if we assume that the means to happiness could be discovered with certainty, this imperative of prudence would be an analytic practical proposition; for it differs from the imperative of skill only in this – that in the latter the end is merely possible, while in the former the end is given. In spite of this difference, since both command solely the means to something assumed to be willed as an end, the imperative which commands him who wills the end to will the means is in both cases analytic. Thus there is likewise no difficulty in regard to the possibility of an imperative of prudence.

Beyond all doubt, the question 'How is the imperative of *morality* possible?' is the only one in need of a solution; for it is in no way hypothetical, and consequently we cannot base the objective necessity which it affirms on any presupposition, as we can with hypothetical imperatives. Only we must never forget here that it is impossible to settle *by an example*, and so empirically, whether there is any imperative of this kind at all: we must rather suspect that all imperatives which seem to be categorical may none the less be covertly hypothetical. Take, for example, the saying 'Thou shalt make no false promises'. Let us assume that the necessity for this abstention is no mere device for the avoidance of some further evil – as it might be said 'You ought not to make a lying promise lest, when this comes to light, you destroy your credit'. Let us hold, on the contrary, that an action of this kind must be considered as bad in itself, and that the imperative of prohibition is therefore categorical. Even so, we cannot with any certainty show by an example that the will is determined here solely by the law without any further motive, although it may appear to be so; for it is always possible that fear of disgrace, perhaps also hidden dread of other risks, may unconsciously influence the will. Who can prove by experience that a cause is not present? Experience shows only that it is not perceived. In such a case, however, the so-called moral imperative, which as such appears to be categorical and unconditioned, would in fact be only a pragmatic prescription calling attention to our advantage and merely bidding us take this into account.

We shall thus have to investigate the possibility of a *categorical* imperative entirely *a priori*, since here we do not enjoy the advantage of having its reality given in experience and so of being obliged merely to explain, and not to establish, its possibility.[1] So much, however, can be seen provisionally – that the categorical imperative alone purports to be a practical *law*, while all the rest may be called *principles* of the will but not laws; for an action necessary merely in order to achieve an arbitrary purpose can be considered as in itself contingent, and we can always escape from the precept if we abandon the purpose; whereas an unconditioned command does not leave it open to the will to do the opposite at its discretion and therefore alone carries with it that necessity which we demand from a law.

In the second place, with this categorical imperative or law of morality the reason for our difficulty (in comprehending its possibility) is a very serious one. We have here a synthetic *a priori* practical proposition;* and since in theoretical knowledge there is so much difficulty in comprehending the possibility of propositions of this kind, it may readily be gathered that in practical knowledge the difficulty will be no less.

[The Formula of Universal Law]

In this task we wish first to enquire whether perhaps the mere concept of a categorical imperative may not also provide us with the formula containing the only proposition that can be a categorical imperative; for even when we know the purport of such an absolute command, the question of its possibility will still require a special and troublesome effort, which we postpone to the final chapter.

---

* Without presupposing a condition taken from some inclination I connect an action with the will *a priori* and therefore necessarily (although only objectively so – that is, only subject to the Idea of a reason having full power over all subjective impulses to action). Here we have a practical proposition in which the willing of any action is not derived analytically from some other willing already presupposed[1] (for we do not possess any such perfect will[2]), but is on the contrary connected immediately[3] with the concept of the will of a rational being as something which is not contained in this concept.

When I conceive a *hypothetical* imperative in general, I do not know beforehand what it will contain – until its condition is given. But if I conceive a *categorical* imperative, I know at once what it contains. For since besides the law this imperative contains only the necessity that our maxim* should conform[1] to this law, while the law, as we have seen, contains no condition to limit it, there remains nothing over to which the maxim has to conform except the universality of a law as such; and it is this conformity alone that the imperative properly asserts to be necessary.

421

52

There is therefore only a single categorical imperative and it is this: *'Act only on that maxim through[1] which you can at the same time will that it should become a universal law.'*

Now if all imperatives of duty can be derived from this one imperative as their principle, then even although we leave it unsettled whether what we call duty may not be an empty concept, we shall still be able to show at least what we understand by it and what the concept means.

[The Formula of the Law of Nature]

Since the universality of the law governing the production of effects constitutes what is properly called *nature* in its most general sense (nature as regards its form)[2] – that is, the existence of things so far as determined by universal laws – the universal imperative of duty may also run as follows: *'Act as if the maxim of your action were to become through your will a universal law of nature.'*

[Illustrations]

We will now enumerate a few duties, following their customary division into duties towards self and duties towards others and into perfect and imperfect duties.**

53

---

51 * A *maxim* is a subjective principle of action and must be distinguished from an *objective principle* – namely, a practical law. The former contains a practical rule determined by reason in accordance with the conditions of the subject (often his ignorance or again his inclinations): it is thus a principle on which the subject *acts*. A law, on the other hand, is an objective principle valid for every rational being; and it is a principle on which he *ought to act* – that is, an imperative.[1]

53 ** It should be noted that I reserve my division of duties entirely for a future *Metaphysic of Morals* and that my present division is therefore put forward as arbitrary (merely for the purpose of arranging my examples). Further, I understand here by a perfect duty one which allows no exception in the interest of inclination,[1] and so I recognise among *perfect duties*, not only outer ones, but

50

1. A man feels sick of life as the result of a series of misfortunes that has mounted to the point of despair, but he is still so far in posses- 422 sion of his reason as to ask himself whether taking his own life may not be contrary to his duty to himself. He now applies the test 'Can the maxim of my action really become a universal law of nature?' His maxim is 'From self-love I make it my principle to shorten my life if its continuance threatens more evil than it promises pleasure'. The only further question to ask is whether this principle of self-love can become a universal law of nature. It is then seen as one that a system of nature by whose law the very same feeling whose function (*Bestimmung*) is to stimulate the furtherance of life 54 should actually destroy life would contradict itself and consequently could not subsist as a system of nature.[1] Hence this maxim cannot possibly hold as a universal law of nature and is therefore entirely opposed to the supreme principle of all duty.

2. Another finds himself driven to borrowing money because of need. He well knows that he will not be able to pay it back; but he sees too that he will get no loan unless he gives a firm promise to pay it back within a fixed time. He is inclined to make such a promise; but he has still enough conscience to ask 'It is not unlawful and contrary to duty to get out of difficulties in this way?' Supposing, however, he did resolve to do so, the maxim of his action would run thus: 'Whenever I believe myself short of money, I will borrow money and promise to pay it back, though I know that this will never be done.' Now this principle of self-love or personal advantage is perhaps quite compatible with my own entire future welfare; only there remains the question 'Is it right?' I therefore transform the demand of self-love into a universal law and frame my question thus: 'How would things stand if my maxim became a universal law?' I then see straight away that this maxim can never rank as a universal law of nature and be self-consistent, but must necessarily contradict itself. 55 For the universality of a law that every one believing himself to be in need can make any promise he pleases with the intention not to keep it would make promising, and the very purpose of promising, itself impossible, since no one would believe he was being promised anything, but would laugh at utterances of this kind as empty shams.

3. A third finds in himself a talent whose cultivation would make him a useful man for all sorts of purposes. But he sees himself in 423

also inner.[2] This is contrary to the accepted usage of the schools, but I do not intend to justify it here, since for my purpose it is all one whether this point is conceded or not.

comfortable circumstances, and he prefers to give himself up to pleasure rather than to bother about increasing and improving his fortunate natural aptitudes. Yet he asks himself further 'Does my maxim of neglecting my natural gifts, besides agreeing in itself with my tendency to indulgence, agree also with what is called duty?' He then sees that a system of nature could indeed always subsist under such a universal law, although (like the South Sea Islanders) every man should let his talents rust and should be bent on devoting his life solely to idleness, indulgence, procreation, and, in a word, to enjoyment. Only he cannot possibly *will* that this should become a universal law of nature or should be implanted in us as such a law by a natural instinct. For as a rational being he necessarily wills that all his powers should be developed, since they serve him, and are given him, for all sorts of possible ends.

56

4. Yet a *fourth* is himself flourishing, but he sees others who have to struggle with great hardships (and whom he could easily help); and he thinks 'What does it matter to me? Let every one be as happy as Heaven will or as he can make himself; I won't deprive him of anything; I won't even envy him; only I have no wish to contribute anything to his well-being or to his support in distress!' Now admittedly if such an attitude were a universal law of nature, mankind could get on perfectly well – better no doubt than if every-body prates about sympathy and goodwill, and even takes pains, on occasion, to practise them, but on the other hand cheats where he can, traffics in human rights, or violates them in other ways. But although it is possible that a universal law of nature could subsist in harmony with this maxim, yet it is impossible to *will* that such a principle should hold everywhere as a law of nature. For a will which decided in this way would be in conflict with itself, since many a situation might arise in which the man needed love and sympathy from others,[1] and in which, by such a law of nature sprung from his own will, he would rob himself of all hope of the help he wants for himself.

57

[The canon of moral judgement]

These are some of the many actual duties – or at least of what we take to be such – whose derivation from the single principle cited above leaps to the eye. We must *be able to will* that a maxim of our action should become a universal law – this is the general canon for all moral judgement of action. Some actions are so constituted that their maxim cannot even be *conceived* as a universal law of nature without contra-

424

diction, let alone be *willed* as what *ought* to become one. In the case of others we do not find this inner impossibility, but it is still impossible to *will* that their maxim should be raised to the universality of a law of nature, because such a will would contradict itself. It is easily seen that the first kind of action is opposed to strict or narrow (rigorous) duty, the second only to wider (meritorious) duty;[1] and thus that by these examples all duties – so far as the type of obligation is concerned (not the object of dutiful action)[2] – are fully set out in their dependence on our single principle.

If we now attend to ourselves whenever we transgress a duty, we find that we in fact do not will that our maxim should become a universal law – since this is impossible for us – but rather that its opposite should remain a law universally: we only take the liberty of making an *exception* to it for ourselves (or even just for this once) to the advantage of our inclinations. Consequently if we weighted it all up from one and the same point of view – that of reason – we should find a contradiction in our own will, the contradiction that a certain principle should be objectively necessary as a universal law and yet subjectively should not hold universally but should admit of exceptions. Since, however, we first consider our action from the point of view of a will wholly in accord with reason, and then consider precisely the same action from the point of view of a will affected by inclination, there is here actually no contradiction, but rather an opposition of inclination to the precept of reason (*antagonismus*), whereby the universality of the principle (*universalitas*) is turned into a mere generality (*generalitas*) so that the practical principle of reason may meet our maxim half-way. This procedure, though in our own impartial judgement it cannot be justified, proves none the less that we in fact recognise the validity of the categorical imperative and (with all respect for it) merely permit ourselves a few exceptions which are, as we pretend, inconsiderable and apparently forced upon us.

We have thus at least shown this much – that if duty is a concept which is to have meaning and real legislative authority for our actions, this can be expressed only in categorical imperatives and by no means in hypothetical ones. At the same time – and this is already a great deal – we have set forth distinctly, and determinately for every type of application, the content of the categorical imperative, which must contain the principle of all duty (if there is to be such a thing at all). But we are still not so far advanced as to prove a priori that there actually is an imperative of this kind – that there is a practical law which by itself commands absolutely and without any further motives, and that the following of this law is duty.

[The need for pure ethics]

For the purpose of achieving this proof it is of the utmost importance to take warning that we should not dream for a moment of trying to derive the reality of this principle from *the special characteristics of human nature*. For duty has to be a practical, unconditioned necessity of action; it must therefore hold for all rational beings (to whom alone an imperative can apply at all), and *only because of this* can it also be a law for all human wills. Whatever, on the other hand, is derived from the special predisposition of humanity, from certain feelings and propensities, and even, if this were possible, from some special bent peculiar to human reason and not holding necessarily for the will of every rational being – all this can indeed supply a personal maxim, but not a law: it can give us a subjective principle – one on which we have a propensity and inclination to act – but not an objective one on which we should be *directed* to act although our every propensity, inclination, and natural bent were opposed to it; so much so that the sublimity and inner worth of the command is the more manifest[1] in a duty, the fewer are the subjective causes for obeying it and the more those against – without, however, on this account weakening in the slightest the necessitation exercised by the law or detracting anything from its validity.

It is here that philosophy is seen in actual fact to be placed in a precarious position, which is supposed to be firm although neither in heaven nor on earth is there anything from which it depends or on which it is based. It is here that she has to show her purity as the authoress of her own laws – not as the mouthpiece of laws whispered to her by some implanted sense or by who knows what tutelary nature, all of which laws together, though they may always be better than nothing, can never furnish us with principles dictated by reason. These principles must have an origin entirely and completely *a priori* and must at the same time derive from this their sovereign authority – that they expect nothing from the inclinations of man, but everything from the supremacy of the law and from the reverence due to it, or in default of this condemn man to self-contempt and inward abhorrence.

Hence everything that is empirical is, as a contribution to the principle of morality,[1] not only wholly unsuitable for the purpose, but is even highly injurious to the purity of morals; for in morals the proper worth of an absolutely good will, a worth elevated above all price, lies precisely in this – that the principle of action is free from all influence by contingent grounds, the only kind that experience can supply. Against the slack, or indeed ignoble, attitude which seeks for the moral principle among empirical motives and laws we cannot give a warning too strongly or too often; for human reason in its weariness is fain to rest upon this pillow and in a dream of sweet illusions (which lead it to embrace a cloud in mistake for Juno)[2] to foist into the place of morality some misbegotten mongrel patched up from limbs of very varied ancestry and looking like anything you please, only not like virtue, to him who has once beheld her in her true shape.*

Our question therefore is this: 'Is it a necessary law *for all rational* 62 *beings* always to judge their actions by reference to those maxims of which they can themselves will that they should serve as universal laws?' If there is such a law, it must already be connected (entirely *a priori*) with the concept of the will of a rational being as such.[1] But in order to discover this connexion we must, however much we may bristle, take a step beyond it – that is, into metaphysics, although into a region of it different from that of speculative philosophy, namely, the metaphysic of morals.[2] In practical philosophy we are not concerned with accepting 427 reasons for what *happens*, but with accepting laws of what *ought to happen* even if it never does happen – that is, objective practical laws. And here we have no need to set up an enquiry as to the reasons why anything pleases or displeases; how the pleasure of mere sensation differs from taste, and whether the latter differs from a universal approval by reason;[3] whereon feelings of pleasure and displeasure are based; how from these feelings there arise desires and inclinations; and how from these in turn, with the co-operation of reason, there arise maxims. All this belongs to empirical psychology, which would constitute the second part of the doctrine of nature, if we take this doctrine to be the 63 *philosophy of nature* so far as grounded on *empirical laws*.[1] Here, however, we are discussing objective practical laws, and consequently the relation of a will to itself as determined solely by reason. Everything related to the empirical then falls away of itself; for if *reason entirely by itself* determines conduct (and it is the possibility of this which we now wish to investigate), it must necessarily do so *a priori*.

[The Formula of the End in Itself]

The will is conceived as a power of determining oneself to action *in accordance with the idea of certain laws*. And such a power can be

---

* To behold virtue in her proper shape is nothing other than to show morality 61 stripped of all admixture with the sensuous and of all the spurious adornments of reward or self-love. How much she then casts into the shade all else that 62 appears attractive to the inclinations can be readily perceived by every man if he will exert his reason in the slightest – provided he has not entirely ruined it for all abstractions.

found only in rational beings. Now what serves the will as a subjective[2] ground of its self-determination is an *end*; and this, if it is given by reason alone, must be equally valid for all rational beings. What, on the other hand, contains merely the ground of the possibility of an action whose effect is an end is called a *means*.[3] The subjective ground of a desire is an *impulsion* (*Triebfeder*); the objective ground of a volition is a *motive* (*Bewegungsgrund*). Hence the difference between subjective ends, which are based on impulsions, and objective ends, which depend on motives valid for every rational being. Practical principles are *formal* if they abstract from all subjective ends; they are *material*, on the other hand, if they are based on such ends and consequently on certain impulsions.[1] Ends that a rational being adopts arbitrarily as *effects* of his action (material ends) are in every case only relative; for it is solely their relation to special characteristics in the subject's power of appetition which gives them their value. Hence this value can provide no universal principles, no principles valid and necessary for all rational beings and also for every volition[2] – that is, no practical laws. Consequently all these relative ends can be the ground only of hypothetical imperatives.

Suppose, however, there were something *whose existence* has *in itself* an absolute value, something which as *an end in itself* could be a ground of determinate laws; then in it, and in it alone, would there be the ground of a possible categorical imperative – that is, of a practical law.

Now I say that man, and in general every rational being, *exists* as an end in himself, *not merely as a means* for arbitrary use by this or that will: he must in all his actions, whether they are directed to himself or to other rational beings, always be viewed *at the same time as an end*. All the objects of inclination have only a conditioned value; for if there were not these inclinations and the needs grounded on them,[1] their object would be valueless. Inclinations themselves, as sources of needs, are so far from having an absolute value to make them desirable for their own sake that it must rather be the universal wish of every rational being to be wholly free from them.[2] Thus the value of all objects that can *be produced* by our actions is always conditioned. Beings whose existence depends, not on our will, but on nature, have none the less, if they are non-rational beings, only a relative value as means and are consequently called *things*. Rational beings, on the other hand, are called *persons* because their nature already marks them out as ends in themselves – that is, as something which ought not to be used merely as a means – and consequently imposes to that extent a limit on all arbitrary treatment of them (and is an object of reverence). Persons, therefore, are not merely subjective ends whose existence as an object

The margin numbers: 64, 428, 65

of our actions has a value *for us*: they are *objective ends* – that is, things whose existence is in itself an end, and indeed an end such that in its place we can put no other end to which they should serve *simply* as means; for unless this is so, nothing at all of *absolute* value would be found anywhere. But if all value were conditioned – that is, contin- 66
gent – then no supreme principle could be found for reason at all.

If then there is to be a supreme practical principle and – so far as the human will is concerned – a categorical imperative,[1] it must be such that from the idea of something which is necessarily an end for every one because it is an *end in itself* it forms an *objective* principle of the will and consequently can serve as a practical law. The ground of this 429
principle is: *Rational nature exists as an end in itself.* This is the way in which a man necessarily conceives his own existence: it is therefore so far a *subjective* principle of human actions. But it is also the way in which every other rational being conceives his existence on the same rational ground which is valid also for me;* hence it is at the same time an *objective* principle, from which, as a supreme practical ground, it must be possible to derive all laws for the will. The practical imperative will therefore be as follows: *Act in such a way that you always treat humanity,[2] whether in your own person or in the person of any other, never simply[3] as a means, but always at the same time as an* 67
end. We will now consider whether this can be carried out in practice.

[Illustrations]

Let us keep to our previous examples.

First, as regards the concept of necessary duty to oneself, the man who contemplates suicide will ask 'Can my action be compatible with the Idea of humanity *as an end in itself?*' If he does away with himself in order to escape from a painful situation, he is making use of a person merely as *a means* to maintain a tolerable state of affairs till the end of his life. But man is not a thing – not something to be used *merely* as a means: he must always in all his actions be regarded as an end in himself. Hence I cannot dispose of man in my person by maiming, spoiling, or killing. (A more precise determination of this principle in order to avoid all misunderstanding – for example, about having limbs amputated to save myself or about exposing my life to danger in order to preserve it, and so on – I must here forgo: this question belongs to morals proper.)

---

* This proposition I put forward here as a postulate. The grounds for it will be 66
found in the final chapter.[1]

Secondly, so far as necessary or strict duty to others is concerned, the man who has a mind to make a false promise to others will see at once that he is intending to make use of another man *merely as a means* to an end he does not share. For the man whom I seek to use for my own purposes by such a promise cannot possibly agree with my way of behaving to him, and so cannot himself share the end of the action. This incompatibility with the principle of duty to others leaps to the eye more obviously when we bring in examples of attempts on the freedom and property of others. For then it is manifest that a violator of the rights of man intends to use the person of others merely as a means without taking into consideration that, as rational beings, they ought always at the same time to be rated as ends – that is, only as beings who must themselves be able to share in the end of the very same action.*

Thirdly, in regard to contingent (meritorious) duty to oneself, it is not enough that an action should refrain from conflicting with humanity in our own person as an end in itself: it must also *harmonise with this end.* Now there are in humanity capacities for greater perfection which form part of nature's purpose for humanity in our person.[1] To neglect these can admittedly be compatible with the *maintenance* of humanity as an end in itself, but not with the *promotion* of this end.

Fourthly, as regards meritorious duties to others, the natural end which all men seek is their own happiness. Now humanity could no doubt subsist if everybody contributed nothing to the happiness of others but at the same time refrained from deliberately impairing their happiness. This is, however, merely to agree negatively and not positively with *humanity as an end in itself* unless every one endeavours also, so far as in him lies, to further the ends of others. For the ends of a subject who is an end in himself must, if this conception is to have its *full* effect in me, be also, as far as possible, *my* ends.

---

68   *   Let no one think that here the trivial *'quod tibi non vis fieri, etc.'*[1] can serve as a standard or principle. For it is merely derivative from our principle, although subject to various qualifications: it cannot be a universal law[2] since it contains the ground neither of duties to oneself nor of duties of kindness to others (for many a man would readily agree that others should not help him if only he could be dispensed from affording help to them), nor finally of strict duties towards others; for on this basis the criminal would be able to dispute with the judges who punish him, and so on.

[The Formula of Autonomy]

This principle of humanity, and in general of every rational agent, *as an end in itself* (a principle which is the supreme limiting condition of every man's freedom of action) is not borrowed from experience; firstly, because it is universal, applying as it does to all rational beings as such, and no experience is adequate to determine universality; secondly, because in it humanity is conceived, not as an end of man (subjectively) – that is, as an object which, as a matter of fact, happens to be made an end – but as an objective end – one which, be our ends what they may, must, as a law, constitute the supreme limiting condition of all subjective ends and so must spring from pure reason. That is to say, the ground for every enactment of practical law lies *objectively in the rule* and in the form of universality which (according to our first principle) makes the rule capable of being a law (and indeed a law of nature); *subjectively*, however, it lies in the *end*; but (according to our second principle) the subject of all ends is to be found in every rational being as an end in himself. From this there now follows our third practical principle for the will – as the supreme condition of the will's conformity with universal practical reason – namely, the Idea *of the will of every rational being as a will which makes universal law.*

431]70

By this principle all maxims are repudiated which cannot accord with the will's own enactment of universal law. The will is therefore not merely subject to the law, but is so subject that it must be considered as also *making the law* for itself and precisely on this account as first of all subject to the law (of which it can regard itself as the author).

71

[The exclusion of interest]

Imperatives as formulated above – namely, the imperative enjoining conformity of actions to universal law on the analogy of a *natural order* and that enjoining the universal *supremacy* of rational beings in themselves *as ends* – did, by the mere fact that they were represented as categorical, exclude from their sovereign authority every admixture of interest as a motive. They were, however, merely *assumed* to be categorical because we were bound to make this assumption if we wished to explain the concept of duty. That there were practical propositions which commanded categorically could not itself be proved, any more than it can be proved in this chapter generally; but one thing could have been done – namely, to show that in willing for the sake of duty renunciation of all interest,[1] as the specific mark distinguishing a categorical from a hypothetical imperative, was expressed in the very

59

432   imperative itself by means of some determination inherent in it. This is what is done in the present third formulation of the principle – namely, in the Idea of the will of every rational being as *a will which makes universal law.*

72   Once we conceive a will of this kind, it becomes clear that while a will *which is subject to law* may be bound to this law by some interest, nevertheless a will which is itself a supreme law-giver cannot possibly as such depend on any interest; for a will which is dependent in this way would itself require yet a further law in order to restrict the interest of self-love to the condition that this interest should itself be valid as a universal law.[1]

Thus the *principle* that every human will is *a will which by all its maxims enacts universal law** – provided only that it were right in other ways – would be *well suited* to be a categorical imperative in this respect: that precisely because of the Idea of making universal law it is *based on no interest* and consequently can alone among all possible imperatives be *unconditioned.* Or better still – to convert the proposition – if there is a categorical imperative (that is, a law for the will of every rational being), it can command us only to act always on the maxim of such a will in us as can at the same time look upon itself as making universal law; for only then is the practical principle and the

73   imperative which we obey unconditioned, since it is wholly impossible for it to be based on any interest.

We need not now wonder, when we look back upon all the previous efforts that have been made to discover the principle of morality, why they have one and all been found to fail. Their authors saw man as tied to laws by his duty, but it never occurred to them that he is subject only to *laws which are made by himself* and yet are *universal,* and that he is bound only to act in conformity with a will which is his own but has as nature's purpose for it[1] the function of making universal law. For when they thought of man merely as subject to a law (whatever it might be), the law had to carry with it some interest in order to attract

433   or compel, because it did not spring as a law from *his own* will: in order to conform with the law his will had to be necessitated by *something else* to act in a certain way. This absolutely inevitable conclusion meant that all the labour spent in trying to find a supreme principle of duty was lost beyond recall; for what they discovered was never duty, but only the necessity of acting from a certain interest. This interest

72   *   I may be excused from bringing forward examples to illustrate this principle, since those which were first used as illustrations of the categorical imperative and its formula can all serve this purpose here.

might be one's own or another's; but on such a view the imperative was bound to be always a conditioned one and could not possibly serve as a moral law. I will therefore call my principle the principle of   74
the *Autonomy* of the will in contrast with all others, which I consequently class under *Heteronomy.*

[The Formula of the Kingdom of Ends]

The concept of every rational being as one who must regard himself as making universal law by all the maxims of his will, and must seek to judge himself and his actions from this point of view, leads to a closely connected and very fruitful concept – namely, that of *a kingdom of ends.*

I understand by a '*kingdom*' a systematic union of different rational beings under common laws. Now since laws determine ends as regards their universal validity, we shall be able – if we abstract from the personal differences between rational beings, and also from all the content of their private ends – to conceive a whole of all ends in system-atic conjunction (a whole both of rational beings as ends in themselves and also of the personal ends[1] which each may set before himself); that is, we shall be able to conceive a kingdom of ends which is possible in accordance with the above principles.

For rational beings all stand under the *law* that each of them should treat himself and all others, *never merely as a means*, but always *at*   75
the same time as an end in himself. But by so doing there arises a systematic union of rational beings under common objective laws – that is, a kingdom. Since these laws are directed precisely to the relation of such beings to one another as ends and means, this kingdom can be called a kingdom of ends (which is admittedly only an Ideal).

A rational being belongs to the kingdom of ends as a *member*, when, although he makes its universal laws, he is also himself subject to these laws. He belongs to it as its *head*, when as the maker of laws he is himself subject to the will of no other.[1]

A rational being must always regard himself as making laws in a   434
kingdom of ends which is possible through freedom of the will – whether it be as member or as head. The position of the latter he can main-tain, not in virtue of the maxim of his will alone, but only if he is a completely independent being, without needs and with an unlimited power adequate to his will.

Thus morality consists in the relation of all action to the making of laws whereby alone a kingdom of ends is possible. This making of laws must be found in every rational being himself and must be able to   76

61

spring from his will. The principle of his will is therefore never to perform an action except on a maxim such as can also be a universal law, and consequently such *that the will can regard itself as at the same time making universal law by means of its maxim.* Where maxims are not already by their very nature in harmony with this objective principle of rational beings as makers of universal law, the necessity of acting on this principle is practical necessitation – that is, *duty.* Duty does not apply to the head in a kingdom of ends, but it does apply to every member and to all members in equal measure.

The practical necessity of acting on this principle – that is, duty – is in no way based on feelings, impulses, and inclinations, but only on the relation of rational beings to one another, a relation in which the will of a rational being must always be regarded as *making universal law,* because otherwise he could not be conceived as *an end in himself.* Reason thus related every maxim of the will, considered as making universal law, to every other will and also to every action towards oneself: it does so, not because of any further motive or future advan-
77 tage, but from the Idea of the *dignity* of a rational being who obeys no law other than that which he at the same time enacts himself.

[The dignity of virtue]

In the kingdom of ends everything has either a *price* or a *dignity.* If it has a price, something else can be put in its place as an *equivalent;* if it is exalted above all price and so admits of no equivalent, then it has a dignity.

What is relative to universal human inclinations and needs has a *market price;* what, even without presupposing a need, accords with
435 a certain taste – that is, with satisfaction in the mere purposeless play of our mental powers[1] – has a *fancy price (Affektionspreis);* but that which constitutes the sole condition under which anything can be an end in itself has not merely a relative value – that is, a price – but has an intrinsic value – that is, *dignity.*

Now morality is the only condition under which a rational being can be an end in himself; for only through this is it possible to be a law-making member in a kingdom of ends. Therefore morality, and humanity so far as it is capable of morality, is the only thing which has dignity.
78 Skill and diligence in work have a market price; wit, lively imagination, and humour have a fancy price; but fidelity to promises and kindness based on principle (not on instinct) have an intrinsic worth. In default of these, nature and art alike contain nothing to put in their place;[1] for their worth consists, not in the effects which result from them,

not in the advantage or profit they produce, but in the attitudes of mind – that is, in the maxims of the will – which are ready in this way to manifest themselves in action even if they are not favoured by success. Such actions too need no recommendation from any subjective disposition or taste in order to meet with immediate favour and approval; they need no immediate propensity or feeling for themselves; they exhibit the will which performs them as an object of immediate reverence; nor is anything other than reason required to *impose* them upon the will, not to *coax* them from the will – which last would anyhow be a contradiction in the case of duties. This assessment reveals as dignity the value of such a mental attitude and puts it infinitely above all price, with which it cannot be brought into reckoning or comparison without, as it were, a profanation of its sanctity.

What is it then that entitles a morally good attitude of mind – or virtue – to make claims so high? It is nothing less than the *share* which 79
it affords to a rational being *in the making of universal law*, and which therefore fits him to be a member in a possible kingdom of ends. For this he was already marked out in virtue of his own proper nature as an end in himself and consequently as a maker of laws in the kingdom of ends – as free in respect of all laws of nature, obeying only those laws which he makes himself and in virtue of which his maxims can have their part in the making of universal law (to which he at the same time subjects himself). For nothing can have a value other than that 436
determined for it by the law. But the law-making which determines all value must for this reason have a dignity – that is, an unconditioned and incomparable worth – for the appreciation of which, as necessarily given by a rational being, the word *'reverence'* is the only becoming expression. *Autonomy* is therefore the ground of the dignity of human nature and of every rational nature.

[Review of the Formulae]

The aforesaid three ways of representing the principle of morality are at bottom merely so many formulations of precisely the same law, one of them by itself containing a combination of the other two. There is nevertheless a difference between them, which, however, is subjectively rather than objectively practical: that is to say, its purpose is to bring an Idea of reason nearer to intuition (in accordance with a certain analogy) and so nearer to feeling. All maxims have, in short, 80

1. a *form*, which consists in their universality; and in this respect the formula of the moral imperative is expressed thus: 'Maxims must be chosen as if they had to hold as universal laws of nature';

2. a *matter* – that is, an end; and in this respect the formula says: 'A rational being, as by his very nature an end and consequently an end in himself, must serve for every maxim as a condition limiting all merely relative and arbitrary ends';

3. a *complete determination*[1] of all maxims by the following formula, namely: 'All maxims as proceeding from our own making of law ought to harmonise with a possible kingdom of ends as a kingdom of nature'.*

This progression may be said to take place through the categories of the *unity* of the form of will (its universality); of the *multiplicity* of its matter (its objects – that is, its ends); and of the *totality* or completeness of its system of ends.[2] It is, however, better if in moral *judgement*

81   we proceed always in accordance with the strict method and take as our basis the universal formula of the categorical imperative: '*Act on*

437   *the maxim which can at the same time be made a universal law*'. If, however, we wish also to secure acceptance for the moral law, it is very useful to bring one and the same action under the above-mentioned three concepts and so, as far as we can, to bring the universal formula[1] nearer to intuition.

[Review of the whole argument]

We can now end at the point from which we started out at the beginning – namely, the concept of an unconditionally good will. The *will* is *absolutely good* if it cannot be evil – that is, if its maxim, when made into a universal law, can never be in conflict with itself. This principle is therefore also its supreme law: 'Act always on that maxim whose universality as a law you can at the same time will'. This is the one principle on which a will can never be in conflict with itself, and such an imperative is categorical. Because the validity of the will as a universal law for possible actions is analogous to the universal interconnexion of existent things in accordance with universal laws – which constitutes the formal aspect of nature as such[2] – we can also express the categorical imperative as follows: '*Act on that maxim which can at the same time have for its object*[3] *itself as a universal law of nature*'.

82   In this way we provide the formula for an absolutely good will.

Rational nature separates itself out from all other things by the fact that it sets itself an end. An end would thus be the matter of every good

---

80   *   Teleology views nature as a kingdom of ends; ethics views a possible kingdom of ends as a kingdom of nature. In the first case the kingdom of ends is a theoretical Idea used to explain what exists. In the second case it is a practical Idea used to bring into existence what does not exist but can be made actual by our conduct – and indeed to bring it into existence in conformity with this Idea.

will. But in the Idea of a will which is absolutely good – good without any qualifying condition (namely, that it should attain this or that end) – there must be complete abstraction from every end that has to be *produced* (as something which would make every will only relatively good). Hence the end must here be conceived, not as an end to be produced, *but as a self-existent* end. It must therefore be conceived only negatively[1] – that is, as an end against which we should never act, and consequently as one which in all our willing we must never rate *merely* as a means, but always at the same time as an end. Now this end can be nothing other than the subject of all possible ends himself, because this subject is also the subject of a will that may be absolutely good; for such a will cannot without contradiction be subordinated to any other object. The principle 'So act in relation to every rational being (both to yourself and to others) that he may at the same time count in your maxim as an end in himself' is thus at bottom the same as the principle 'Act on a maxim which at the same time contains in itself its own universal validity for every rational being'. For to say that in using   438
means to every end I ought to restrict my maxim by the condition that it should also be universally valid as a law for every subject is just the   83
same as to say this – that a subject of ends, namely, a rational being himself, must be made the ground for all maxims of action, never *merely* as a means, but as a supreme condition restricting the use of every means – that is, always also as an end.

Now from this it unquestionably follows that every rational being, as an end in himself, must be able to regard himself as also the maker of universal law in respect of any law whatever to which he may be subjected; for it is precisely the fitness of his maxims to make universal law that marks him out as an end in himself. It follows equally that this dignity (or prerogative) of his above all the mere things of nature carries with it the necessity of always choosing his maxims from the point of view of himself – and also of every other rational being – as a maker of law (and this is why they are called persons). It is in this way that a world of rational beings (*mundus intelligibilis*) is possible as a kingdom of ends – possible, that is, through the making of their own laws by all persons as its members. Accordingly every rational being must so act as if he were through his maxims always a law-making member in the universal kingdom of ends. The formal principle of such maxims is 'So act as if your maxims had to serve at the same time as a universal   84
law (for all rational beings)'. Thus a kingdom of ends is possible only on the analogy of a kingdom of nature; yet the kingdom of ends is possible only through maxims – that is, self-imposed rules – while nature is possible only through laws concerned with causes whose action is

necessitated from without. In spite of this difference, we give to nature as a whole, even although it is regarded as a machine, the name of a 'kingdom of nature' so far as – and for the reason that – it stands in a relation to rational beings as its ends.[1] Now a kingdom of ends would actually come into existence through maxims which the categorical imperative prescribes as a rule for all rational beings, *if these maxims were universally followed*. Yet even if a rational being were himself to follow such a maxim strictly, he cannot count on everybody else being faithful to it on this ground, nor can he be confident that the kingdom of nature and its purposive order will work in harmony with him, as a fitting member, towards a kingdom of ends made possible by himself – or, in other words, that it will favour his expectation of happiness.[2] But in spite of this the law 'Act on the maxims of a member who makes universal laws for a merely possible kingdom of ends' remains in full force, since its command is categorical. And precisely here we encounter the paradox that without any further end or advantage to be attained the mere dignity of humanity, that is, of rational nature in man – and consequently that reverence for a mere Idea – should function as an inflexible precept for the will; and that it is just this freedom from dependence on interested motives which constitutes the sublimity of a maxim and the worthiness of every rational subject to be a law-making member in the kingdom of ends; for otherwise he would have to be regarded as subject only to the law of nature – the law of his own needs. Even if it were thought that both the kingdom of nature and the kingdom of ends were united under one head and that thus the latter kingdom ceased to be a mere Idea and achieved genuine reality, the Idea would indeed gain by this the addition of a strong motive, but never any increase in its intrinsic worth; for, even if this were so, it would still be necessary to conceive the unique and absolute law-giver himself as judging the worth of rational beings solely by the disinterested behaviour they prescribed to themselves in virtue of this Idea alone. The essence of things does not vary with their external relations; and where there is something which, without regard to such relations, constitutes by itself the absolute worth of man, it is by this that man must also be judged by everyone whatsoever – even by the Supreme Being. Thus *morality* lies in the relation of action to the autonomy of the will – that is, to a possible making of universal laws by means of its maxims. An action which is compatible with the autonomy of the will is *permitted*; one which does not harmonise with it is *forbidden*. A will whose maxims necessarily accord with the laws of autonomy is a *holy*, or absolutely good, will. The dependence of a will not absolutely good on the principle of autonomy (that is, moral necessitation) is *obligation*. Obligation can thus have no reference to a holy being. The objective necessity to act from obligation is called *duty*.

From what was said a little time ago we can now easily explain how it comes about that, although in the concept of duty we think of subjection to the law, yet we also at the same time attribute to the person who fulfils all his duties a certain sublimity and *dignity*. For it is not in so far as he is *subject* to the law that he has sublimity, but rather in so far as, in regard to this very same law, he is at the same time its *author* and is subordinated to it only on this ground. We have also shown above[1] how neither fear nor inclination, but solely reverence for the law, is the motive which can give an action moral worth. Our own will, provided it were to act only under the condition of being able to make universal law by means of its maxims – this ideal will which can be ours is the proper object of reverence; and the dignity of man consists precisely in his capacity to make universal law, although only on condition of being himself also subject to the law he makes.

Autonomy of the will
as the supreme principle of morality

Autonomy of the will is the property the will has of being a law to itself (independently of every property belonging to the object of volition). Hence the principle of autonomy is 'Never to choose except in such a way that in the same volition the maxims of your choice are also present as universal law'. That this practical rule is an imperative – that is, that the will of every rational being is necessarily bound to the rule as a condition – cannot be proved by mere analysis of the concepts contained in it, since it is a synthetic proposition. For proof we should have to go beyond knowledge of objects and pass to a critique of the subject – that is, of pure practical reason – since this synthetic proposition, as commanding apodeictically, must be capable of being known entirely *a priori*. This task does not belong to the present chapter. None the less by mere analysis of the concepts of morality we can quite well show that the above principle of autonomy is the sole principle of ethics. For analysis finds that the principle of morality must be a categorical imperative, and that this in turn commands nothing more nor less than precisely this autonomy.

440

87

88

Heteronomy of the will
as the source of all spurious principles of morality

If the will seeks the law that is to determine it *anywhere else* than in the fitness of its maxims for its own making of universal law – if therefore in going beyond itself it seeks this law in the character of any of its objects – the result is always *heteronomy*. In that case the will does not give itself the law, but the object does so in virtue of its relation to the will. This relation, whether based on inclination or on rational ideas, can give rise only to hypothetical imperatives: 'I ought to do something *because I will something else*'. As against this, the moral, and therefore categorical, imperative, says: 'I ought to will thus or thus, although I have not willed something else'. For example, the first says: 'I ought not to lie if I want to maintain my reputation'; while the second says: 'I ought not to lie even if so doing were to bring me not the slightest disgrace.' The second imperative must therefore abstract from all objects to this extent – they should be without any *influence*[1] at all on the will so that practical reason (the will) may not merely administer an alien interest but may simply manifest its own sovereign authority as the supreme maker of law. Thus, for example, the reason[2] why I ought to promote the happiness of others is not because the realisation of their happiness is of consequence to myself (whether on account of immediate inclination or on account of some satisfaction gained indirectly through reason), but solely because a maxim which excludes this cannot also be present in one and the same volition as a universal law.

Classification
of all possible principles of morality based on the assumption of heteronomy as their fundamental concept

Here, as everywhere else, human reason in its pure use – so long as it lacks a critique – pursues every possible wrong way before it succeeds in finding the only right one.

All the principles that can be adopted from this point of view are either *empirical* or *rational*. The *first* kind, drawn from the principle of *happiness*, are based either on natural, or on moral, feeling. The *second* kind, drawn from the principle of *perfection*, are based either on the rational concept of perfection as a possible effect of our will or else on the concept of a self-existent perfection (God's will) as a determining cause of our will.

[Empirical principles of heteronomy]

Empirical principles are always unfitted to serve as a ground for moral laws. The universality with which these laws should hold for all rational beings without exception – the unconditioned practical necessity which they thus impose – falls away if their basis is taken from the *special constitution of human nature* or from the accidental circumstances in which it is placed. The principle of *personal happiness* is, however, the most objectionable, not merely because it is false and because its pretence that well-being always adjusts itself to well-doing is contradicted by experience; nor merely because it contributes nothing whatever towards establishing morality, since making a man happy is quite different from making him good and making him prudent or astute in seeking his advantage quite different from making him virtuous; but because it bases morality on sensuous motives which rather undermine it and totally destroy its sublimity, inasmuch as the motives of virtue are put in the same   91
class as those of vice and we are instructed only to become better at calculation, the specific difference between virtue and vice being completely wiped out. On the other hand, moral feeling, this alleged special sense* (however shallow be the appeal to it when men who are unable to *think* hope to help themselves out by *feeling*, even when the question is solely one of universal law, and however little feelings, differing as they naturally do from one another by an infinity of degrees, can supply a uniform measure of good and evil – let alone that one man by his feeling can make no valid judgements at all for others) – moral feeling still remains closer to morality and to its dignity in this respect: it does virtue the honour of ascribing to her *immediately* the approval and esteem in which she is held, and does not, as it were, tell her to her face that we are   443
attached to her, not for her beauty, but only for our own advantage.

[Rational principles of heteronomy]

Among the *rational* bases of morality – those springing from reason – the ontological concept of *perfection*[1] (however empty, however in-   92
definite it is, and consequently useless for discovering in the boundless field of possible reality the maximum reality appropriate to us; and however much, in trying to distinguish specifically between the reality

---

*   I class the principle of moral feeling with that of happiness because every empir-   91
    ical principle promises a contribution to our well-being merely from the satisfaction afforded by something – whether this satisfaction is given immediately and without and consideration of advantage or is given in respect of such advantage. Similarly we must with *Hutcheson*[1] class the principle of sympathy for the happiness of others along with the principle of moral sense as adopted by him.

here in question and every other, it shows an inevitable tendency to go round in a circle and is unable to avoid covertly presupposing the morality it has to explain) – this concept none the less is better than the theological concept which derives morality from a divine and supremely perfect will;[2] not merely because we cannot intuit God's perfection and can only derive it from our own concepts, among which that of morality is the most eminent; but because, if we do not do this (and to do so would be to give a crudely circular explanation), the concept of God's will still remaining to us – one drawn from such characteristics as lust for glory and domination and bound up with frightful ideas of power and vengefulness – would inevitably form the basis for a moral system which would be in direct opposition to morality.

Yet if I had to choose between the concept of moral sense and that of perfection in general[3] (both of which at least do not undermine morality, though they are totally incompetent to support it as its foundation), I should decide for the latter; for this, since it at least withdraws the settlement of this question from sensibility and brings it before the court of pure reason, even although it there gets no decision, does still preserve unfalsified for more precise determination the indeterminate Idea (of a will good in itself).

93

[The failure of heteronomy]

For the rest I believe I may be excused from a lengthy refutation of all these systems. This is so easy and is presumably so well understood even by those whose office requires them to declare themselves for one or other of these theories (since their audience will not lightly put up with a suspension of judgement) that to spend time on it would be merely superfluous labour. But what is of more interest to us here is to know that these principles never lay down anything but heteronomy as the first basis of morality and must in consequence necessarily fail in their object.

444

Wherever an object of the will has to be put down as the basis for prescribing a rule to determine the will, there the rule is heteronomy; the imperative is conditioned, as follows: '*If*, or *because*, you will this object, you ought to act thus or thus'; consequently it can never give a moral – that is, a categorical – command. However the object determines the will – whether by means of inclination, as in the principle of personal happiness, or by means of reason directed to objects of our possible volitions generally, as in the principle of perfection – the will never determines itself *immediately* by the thought of an action, but only by the impulse which the anticipated effect of the action exercises on the will: '*I ought to do something because I will something else*.' And

94

the basis for this must be yet a further law in me as a subject, whereby I necessarily will this 'something else' – which law in turn requires an imperative to impose limits on this maxim.[1] The impulsion supposed to be exercised on the will of the subject, in accordance with his natural constitution, by the idea of a result to be attained by his own powers belongs to the nature of the subject – whether to his sensibility (his inclinations and taste) or to his understanding and reason, whose operation on an object is accompanied by satisfaction in virtue of the special equipment of their nature – and consequently, speaking strictly, it is nature which would make the law. This law, as a law of nature, not only must be known and proved by experience and therefore is in itself contingent and consequently unfitted to serve as an apodeictic rule of action such as a moral rule must be, but it is *always merely heteronomy of the will*: the will does not give itself the law, but an alien impulsion does so through the medium of the subject's own nature as tuned for its reception.

95

[The position of the argument]

An absolutely good will, whose principle must be a categorical imperative, will therefore, being undetermined in respect of all objects, contain only the *form* of *willing*, and that as autonomy. In other words, the fitness of the maxim of every good will to make itself a universal law is itself the sole law which the will of every rational being spontaneously imposes on itself without basing it on any impulsion or interest.

How such a synthetic a priori *proposition is possible* and why it is necessary – this is a problem whose solution lies no longer within the bounds of a metaphysic of morals; nor have we here asserted the truth of this proposition, much less pretended to have a proof of it in our power. We have merely shown by developing the concept of morality generally in vogue that autonomy of the will is unavoidably bound up with it or rather is its very basis. Any one therefore who takes morality to be something, and not merely a chimerical Idea without truth, must at the same time admit the principle we have put forward. This chapter, consequently, like the first, has been merely analytic. In order to prove that morality is no mere phantom of the brain – a conclusion which follows if the categorical imperative, and with it the autonomy of the will, is true and is absolutely necessary as an *a priori* principle – we require a *possible synthetic use of pure practical reason*.[1] On such a use we cannot venture without prefacing it by a *critique* of this power of reason itself – a critique whose main features, so far as is sufficient for our purpose, we must outline in our final chapter.

445

96

71

Chapter III

PASSAGE FROM A METAPHYSIC OF MORALS TO A CRITIQUE OF PURE PRACTICAL REASON

The concept of freedom is the key to explain autonomy of the will

Will is a kind of causality belonging to living beings so far as they are rational. *Freedom* would then be the property this causality has of being able to work independently of *determination* by alien causes; just as *natural necessity* is a property characterising the causality of all non-rational beings – the property of being determined to activity by the influence of alien causes.

The above definition of freedom is *negative* and consequently unfruitful as a way of grasping its essence; but there springs from it a *positive* concept, which, as positive, is richer and more fruitful. The concept of causality carries with it that of *laws* (*Gesetze*) in accordance with which, because of something we call a cause, something else – namely, its effect – must be posited (*gesetzt*). Hence freedom of will, although it is not the property of conforming to laws of nature, is not for this reason lawless: it must rather be a causality conforming to immutable laws, though of a special kind; for otherwise a free will would be self-contradictory. Natural necessity, as we have seen, is a heteronomy of efficient causes; for every effect is possible only in conformity with the law that something else determines the efficient cause to causal action. What else then can freedom of will be but autonomy – that is, the property which will has of being a law to itself? The proposition 'Will is in all its actions a law to itself' expresses, however, only the principle of acting on no maxim other than the one which can have for its object[1] itself as at the same time a universal law. This is precisely the formula of the categorical imperative and the principle of morality. Thus a free will and a will under moral laws are one and the same.[2]

98

447

72

Consequently if freedom of the will is presupposed, morality, together with its principle, follows by mere analysis of the concept of freedom. Nevertheless the principle of morality is still a synthetic proposition, namely: 'An absolutely good will is one whose maxim can always have as its content itself considered as a universal law'; for we cannot discover this characteristic of its maxim by analysing the concept of an absolutely 99 good will. Such synthetic propositions are possible only because two cognitions[1] are bound to one another by their connexion with a third term in which both of them are to be found. The *positive* concept of freedom furnishes this third term, which cannot, as in the case of physical causes, be the nature of the sensible world (in the concept of which there come together the concepts of something as cause and of *something else* as effect in their relation to one another). What this third term is to which freedom directs us and of which we have an Idea *a priori*, we are not yet in a position to show here straight away,[2] nor can we as yet make intelligible the deduction of the concept of freedom from pure practical reason and so the possibility of a categorical imperative: we require some further preparation.

Freedom must be presupposed as a property of the will of all rational beings

It is not enough to ascribe freedom to our will, on whatever ground, unless we have sufficient reason for attributing the same freedom to all rational beings as well. For since morality is a law for us only as *rational* 100 *beings*, it must be equally valid for all rational beings; and since it must be derived solely from the property of freedom, we have got to prove that freedom too is a property of the will of all rational beings. It is not enough to demonstrate freedom from certain alleged experiences of human nature (though to do this is in any case absolutely impossible 448 and freedom can be demonstrated only *a priori*):[1] we must prove that it belongs universally to the activity of rational beings endowed with a will. Now I assert that every being who cannot act except *under the Idea of freedom* is by this alone – from a practical point of view – really free; that is to say, for him all the laws inseparably bound up with freedom are valid just as much as if his will could be pronounced free in itself on grounds valid for theoretical philosophy.* And I maintain

---

* This method takes it as sufficient for our purpose if freedom is presupposed 100 merely *as an Idea* by all rational beings in their actions; and I adopt it in order to avoid the obligation of having to prove freedom from a theoretical point of view as well. For even if this latter problem is left unsettled, the same laws as

that to every rational being possessed of a will we must also lend the
101 Idea of freedom as the only one under which he can act. For in such
a being we conceive a reason which is practical – that is, which exercises causality in regard to its objects. But we cannot possibly conceive
of a reason as being consciously directed from outside in regard to its
judgements;[1] for in that case the subject would attribute the determination of his power of judgement, not to his reason, but to an impulsion.
Reason must look upon itself as the author of its own principles independently of alien influences. Therefore as practical reason,[2] or as the
will of a rational being, it must be regarded by itself as free; that is,
the will of a rational being can be a will of his own only under the
Idea of freedom, and such a will must therefore – from a practical point
of view – be attributed to all rational beings.

The interest attached to the Ideas of morality

[Moral interest and the vicious circle]

We have at last traced the determinate concept of morality back to the
Idea of freedom, but we have been quite unable to demonstrate freedom
449 as something actual in ourselves and in human nature: we saw merely
102 that we must presuppose it if we wish to conceive a being as rational
and as endowed with consciousness of his causality in regard to actions
– that is, as endowed with a will. Thus we find that on precisely the
same ground we must attribute to every being endowed with reason
and a will this property of determining himself to action under the Idea
of his own freedom.[1]

From the presupposition of this Idea there springs, as we further saw,
consciousness of a law of action, the law that subjective principles of
action – that is, maxims – must always be adopted in such a way that
they can also hold as principles objectively – that is, universally – and
can therefore serve for our own enactment of universal law. But why
should I subject myself to this principle simply as a rational being and
in so doing also subject to it every other being endowed with reason?
I am willing to admit that no interest *impels* me to do so since this
would not produce a categorical imperative; but all the same I must
necessarily *take* an interest in it and understand how this happens; for
this 'I ought' is properly an 'I will' which holds necessarily for every

would bind a being who was really free are equally valid for a being who
cannot act except under the Idea of his own freedom. In this way we can relieve
ourselves of the burden which weighs upon theory.[1]

rational being provided that reason in him is practical without any hindrance. For beings who, like us, are affected also by sensibility – that is, by motives of a different kind – and who do not always act as reason by itself would act, this necessity is expressed as an 'I ought' and the subjective necessity is distinct from the objective one.[1]   103

It looks as if, in our Idea of freedom, we have in fact merely taken the moral law for granted – that is, the very principle of the autonomy of the will – and have been unable to give an independent proof of its reality and objective necessity. In that case we should still have made a quite considerable gain inasmuch as we should at least have formulated the genuine principle more precisely than has been done before. As regards its validity, however, and the practical necessity of subjecting ourselves to it we should have got no further. Why must the validity of our maxim as a universal law be a condition limiting our action? On what do we base the worth we attach to this way of acting – worth supposed to be so great that there cannot be any interest which is higher? And how does it come about that in this alone man believes himself to feel his own personal worth, in comparison with   450 which that of a pleasurable or painful state is to count as nothing? To these questions we should have been unable to give any sufficient answer.

We do indeed find ourselves able to take an interest in a personal characteristic which carries with it no interest in mere states,[1] but only   104 makes us fit to have a share in such states in the event of their being distributed by reason. That is to say, the mere fact of deserving happiness can by itself interest us even without the motive of getting a share in this happiness. Such a judgement, however, is in fact merely the result of the importance we have already assumed to belong to moral laws (when we detach ourselves from every empirical interest by our Idea of freedom). But on this basis we can as yet have no insight into the principle that we ought to detach ourselves from such interest – that is, that we ought to regard ourselves as free in our actions and yet to hold ourselves bound by certain laws in order to find solely in our own person a worth which can compensate us for the loss of everything that makes our state valuable. We do not see how this is possible nor consequently *how the moral law can be binding.*

In this, we must frankly admit, there is shown a kind of circle, from which, as it seems, there is no way of escape. In the order of efficient causes we take ourselves to be free so that we may conceive ourselves to be under moral laws in the order of ends; and we then proceed to think of ourselves as subject to moral laws on the ground that we have described our will as free. Freedom and the will's enactment of its own

105 laws are indeed both autonomy – and therefore are reciprocal concepts[1] – but precisely for this reason one of them cannot be used to explain the other or to furnish its ground. It can at most be used for logical purposes in order to bring seemingly different ideas of the same object under a single concept (just as different fractions of equal value can be reduced to their simplest expression).

[The two standpoints]

One shift, however, still remains open to us. We can enquire whether we do not take one standpoint when by means of freedom we conceive ourselves as causes acting *a priori*, and another standpoint when we contemplate ourselves with reference to our actions as effects which we see before our eyes.

One observation is possible without any need for subtle reflexion and, we may assume, can be made by the most ordinary intelligence 451 – no doubt in its own fashion through some obscure discrimination of the power of judgement known to it as 'feeling'. The observation is this – that all ideas coming to us apart from our own volition (as do those of the senses) enable us to know objects only as they affect ourselves: what they may be in themselves remains unknown. Consequently, ideas of this kind, even with the greatest effort of attention and clarification 106 brought to bear by understanding, serve only for knowledge of *appearances*, never of *things in themselves*. Once this distinction is made (it may be merely by noting the difference between ideas given to us from without, we ourselves being passive, and those which we produce entirely from ourselves, and so manifest our own activity), it follows of itself that behind appearances we must admit and assume something else which is not appearance – namely, things in themselves – although, since we can never be acquainted with these, but only with the way in which they affect us, we must resign ourselves to the fact that we can never get any nearer to them and can never know what they are in themselves. This must yield us a distinction, however rough, between the *sensible world* and the *intelligible world*, the first of which can vary a great deal according to differences of sensibility in sundry observers, while the second, which is its ground, always remains the same. Even as regards himself – so far as man is acquainted with himself by inner sensation[1] – he cannot claim to know what he is in himself. For since he does not, so to say, make himself, and since he acquires his concept of self not *a priori* but empirically, it is natural that even about himself he should get information through sense – that is, through inner sense – and consequently only through the mere appearance of his own nature

and through the way in which his consciousness is affected. Yet beyond 107
this character of himself as a subject[1] made up, as it is, of mere appearances he must suppose there to be something else which is its ground
– namely, his Ego as this may be constituted in itself; and thus as
regards mere perception and the capacity for receiving sensations[2] he
must count himself as belonging to the *sensible world*, but as regards
whatever there may be in him of pure activity (whatever comes into
consciousness, not through affection of the senses, but immediately)[3] he
must count himself as belonging to the *intellectual world*, of which,
however, he knows nothing further.

A conclusion of this kind must be reached by a thinking man about
everything that may be presented to him. It is presumably to be found 452
even in the most ordinary intelligence, which, as is well known, is always
very much disposed to look behind the objects of the senses for something further that is invisible and is spontaneously active; but it goes on
to spoil this by immediately sensifying this invisible something in its turn
– that is to say, it wants to make it an object of intuition, and so by
this procedure it does not become in any degree wiser.

Now man actually finds in himself a power which distinguishes him
from all other things – and even from himself so far as he is affected 108
by objects. This power is *reason*.[1] As pure spontaneity reason is elevated
even above *understanding* in the following respect. Understanding –
although it too is spontaneous activity and is not, like sense, confined
to ideas which arise only when we are affected by things (and therefore are passive) – understanding cannot produce by its own activity
any concepts other than those whose sole service is *to bring sensuous
ideas under rules* and so to unite them in one consciousness: without
this employment of sensibility it would think nothing at all. Reason, on
the other hand – in what are called 'Ideas' – shows a spontaneity so
pure that it goes far beyond anything sensibility can offer: it manifests
its highest function in distinguishing the sensible and intelligible worlds
from one another and so in marking out limits for understanding itself.[2]

Because of this a rational being must regard himself *qua intelligence*
(and accordingly not on the side of his lower faculties) as belonging to
the intelligible world, not to the sensible one. He has therefore two
points of view from which he can regard himself and from which he
can know laws governing the employment of his powers and consequently governing all his actions. He can consider himself *first* – so far
as he belongs to the sensible world – to be under laws of nature
(heteronomy); and *secondly* – so far as he belongs to the intelligible 109
world – to be under laws which, being independent of nature, are not
empirical but have their ground in reason alone.

As a rational being, and consequently as belonging to the intelligible world, man can never conceive the causality of his own will except under the Idea of freedom; for to be independent of determination by causes in the sensible world (and this is what reason must always attribute to itself) is to be free. To the Idea of freedom there is inseparably attached the concept of *autonomy*, and to this in turn the universal

453 principle of morality – a principle which in Idea[1] forms the ground for all the actions of *rational* beings, just as the law of nature does for all appearances.

The suspicion which we raised above is now removed – namely, that there might be a hidden circle in our inference from freedom to autonomy and from autonomy to the moral law; that in effect we had perhaps assumed the Idea of freedom only because of the moral law in order subsequently to infer the moral law in its turn from freedom; and that consequently we had been able to assign no ground at all for the moral law, but had merely assumed it by begging a principle which well-meaning souls will gladly concede us, but which we could never

110 put forward as a demonstrable proposition. We see now that when we think of ourselves as free, we transfer ourselves into the intelligible world as members and recognise the autonomy of the will together with its consequence – morality; whereas when we think of ourselves as under obligation, we look upon ourselves as belonging to the sensible world and yet to the intelligible world at the same time.

How is a categorical imperative possible?

A rational being counts himself, *qua* intelligence, as belonging to the intelligible world, and solely *qua* efficient cause belonging to the intelligible world does he give to his causality the name of '*will*'. On the other side, however, he is conscious of himself as also a part of the sensible world, where his actions are encountered as mere appearances of this causality. Yet the possibility of these actions cannot be made intelligible by means of such causality, since with this we have no direct acquaintance; and instead these actions, as belonging to the sensible world, have to be understood as determined by other appearances – namely, by desires and inclinations. Hence, if I were solely a member of the intelligible world, all my actions would be in perfect conformity with the principle of the autonomy of a pure will; if I were solely a part of the sensible world, they would have to be taken as in complete conformity with the law of nature governing desires and inclinations –

111 that is, with the heteronomy of nature. (In the first case they would be grounded on the supreme principle of morality; in the second case on

that of happiness.) *But the intelligible world contains the ground of the sensible world and therefore also of its laws;* and so in respect of my will, for which (as belonging entirely to the intelligible world) it gives laws immediately,[1] it must also be conceived as containing such a ground.[2] Hence, in spite of regarding myself from one point of view as a being that belongs to the sensible world, I shall have to recognise that, *qua* intelligence, I am subject to the law of the intelligible world — that is, to the reason which contains this law in the Idea of freedom, and so to the autonomy of the will — and therefore I must look on the laws of the intelligible world as imperatives for me and on the actions which conform to this principle as duties.

454

And in this way categorical imperatives are possible because the Idea of freedom makes me a member of an intelligible world. This being so, if I were solely a member of the intelligible world, all my actions *would* invariably accord with the autonomy of the will; but because I intuit myself at the same time as a member of the sensible world, they *ought* so to accord. This *categorical* 'ought' presents us with a synthetic *a priori* proposition, since to my will as affected by sensuous desires there is added the Idea of the same will,[3] viewed, however, as a pure will belonging to the intelligible world and active on its own account — a will which contains the supreme condition of the former will, so far as reason is concerned. This is roughly like the way in which concepts of the understanding, which by themselves signify nothing but the form of law in general, are added to intuitions of the sensible world and so make synthetic *a priori* propositions possible on which all our knowledge of nature is based.

112

The practical use of ordinary human reason confirms the rightness of this deduction. There is no one, not even the most hardened scoundrel — provided only he is accustomed to use reason in other ways — who, when presented with examples of honesty in purpose, of faithfulness to good maxims, of sympathy, and of kindness towards all (even when these are bound up with great sacrifices of advantage and comfort), does not wish that he too might be a man of like spirit. He is unable to realise such an aim in his own person — though only on account of his desires and impulses; but yet at the same time he wishes to be free from these inclinations, which are a burden to himself. By such a wish he shows that having a will free from sensuous impulses he transfers himself in thought into an order of things quite different from that of his desires in the field of sensibility; for from the fulfilment of this wish he can expect no gratification of his sensuous desires and consequently no state which would satisfy any of his actual or even conceivable inclinations (since by such an expectation the very Idea which elicited the

113

455 wish would be deprived of its superiority); all he can expect is a greater inner worth of his own person. This better person he believes himself to be when he transfers himself to the standpoint of a member of the intelligible world. He is involuntarily constrained to do so by the Idea of freedom – that is, of not being dependent on *determination* by causes in the sensible world; and from this standpoint he is conscious of possessing a good will which, on his own admission, constitutes the law for the bad will belonging to him as a member of the sensible world – a law of whose authority he is aware even in transgressing it. The moral 'I ought' is thus an 'I will' for man as a member of the intelligible world; and it is conceived by him as an 'I ought' only in so far as he considers himself at the same time to be a member of the sensible world.

The extreme limit of practical philosophy

[The antinomy of freedom and necessity]

All men think of themselves as having a free will. From this arise all judgements that actions are such as *ought to have been done*, although they *have not been done*. This freedom is no concept of experience, nor can it be such, since it continues to hold although experience shows

114 the opposite of those requirements which are regarded as necessary[1] under the presupposition of freedom. On the other hand, it is just as necessary that everything which takes place should be infallibly determined in accordance with the laws of nature; and this necessity of nature is likewise no concept of experience, precisely because it carries with it the concept of necessity and so of *a priori* knowledge. The concept of nature is, however, confirmed by experience and must inevitably be presupposed if experience – that is, coherent knowledge of sensible objects in accordance with universal laws – is to be possible. Hence, while freedom is only an *Idea* of reason whose objective reality is in itself questionable, nature is a *concept of the understanding*, which proves, and must necessarily prove, its reality in examples from experience.

From this there arises a dialectic[2] of reason, since the freedom attributed to the will seems incompatible with the necessity of nature; and although at this parting of the ways reason finds the road of natural necessity much more beaten and serviceable than that of freedom for *purposes of speculation*, yet for *purposes of action* the footpath of freedom is the only one on which we can make use of reason in our

456 conduct. Hence to argue freedom away is as impossible for the most

abstruse philosophy as it is for the most ordinary human reason. Reason 115
must therefore suppose that no genuine contradiction is to be found
between the freedom and the natural necessity ascribed to the very
same human actions; for it can abandon the concept of nature as little
as it can abandon that of freedom.

All the same we must at least get rid of this seeming contradiction
in a convincing fashion – although we shall never be able to comprehend how freedom is possible. For if the thought of freedom is
self-contradictory or incompatible with nature – a concept which is
equally necessary – freedom would have to be completely abandoned
in favour of natural necessity.

[The two standpoints]

From this contradiction it would be impossible to escape if the subject
who believes himself free were to conceive himself *in the same sense,*
or *in precisely the same relationship,* when he calls himself free as when
he holds himself subject to the law of nature in respect of the same
action. Hence speculative philosophy has the unavoidable task of
showing at least this – that its illusion about the contradiction rests on
our conceiving man in one sense and relationship when we call him
free and in another when we consider him, as a part of nature, to be 116
subject to nature's laws; and that both characteristics not merely *can*
get on perfectly well together but must be conceived as *necessarily
combined* in the same subject; for otherwise we could not explain why
we should trouble reason with an Idea which – even if it can *without
contradiction* be combined with a different and adequately verified
concept – does yet involve us in a business which puts reason to sore
straits in its theoretical use. This duty is incumbent on speculative philosophy solely in order that it may clear a path for practical philosophy.
Thus it is not left to the discretion of philosophers whether they will
remove the seeming contradiction or leave it untouched; for in the latter
case the theory on this topic becomes *bonum vacans,*[1] of which the
fatalist can justifiably take possession and can chase all morality out of
its supposed property, which it has no title to hold.

Nevertheless at this point we cannot yet say that the boundary of
practical philosophy begins. For practical philosophy has no part in the
settlement of this controversy: it merely requires speculative reason to
bring to an end the dissension in which it is entangled on theoretical 457
questions so that practical reason may have peace and security from
external attacks capable of bringing into dispute the territory it seeks
to cultivate.

117   The lawful title to freedom of will claimed even by ordinary human reason is grounded on a consciousness – and an accepted presupposition – that reason is independent of purely subjective determination by causes which collectively make up all that belongs to sensation and comes under the general name of sensibility. In thus regarding himself as intelligence man puts himself into another order of things, and into relation with determining causes of quite another sort, when he conceives himself as intelligence endowed with a will and consequently with causality, than he does when he perceives himself as a phenomenon in the sensible world (which he actually is as well) and subjects his causality to external determination in accordance with laws of nature. He then becomes aware at once that both of these can, and indeed must, take place at the same time; for there is not the slightest contradiction in holding that a *thing as an appearance* (as belonging to the sensible world) is subject to certain laws of which it is independent *as a thing* or being *in itself*. That he must represent and conceive himself in this double way rests, as regards the first side, on consciousness of himself as an object affected through the senses; as concerns the second side, on consciousness of himself as intelligence – that is, as independent of sensuous impressions in his use of reason (and so as belonging to the intelligible world).

118   Hence it comes about that man claims for himself a will which does not impute to itself anything appertaining merely to his desires and inclinations; and, on the other hand, that he conceives as possible through its agency, and indeed as necessary, actions which can be done only by disregarding all desires and incitements of sense. The causality of such actions lies in man as intelligence and in the laws of such effects and actions as accord with the principles of an intelligible world. Of that world he knows[1] no more than this – that in it reason alone, and indeed pure reason independent of sensibility, is the source of law; and also that since he is there his proper self only as intelligence (while as a human being he is merely an appearance of himself), these laws apply to him immediately[2] and categorically. It follows that incitements from desires and impulses (and therefore from the whole sensible world

458   of nature) cannot impair the laws which govern his will as intelligence. Indeed he does not answer for the former nor impute them to his proper self – that is, to his will; but he does impute to himself the indulgence which he would show them if he admitted their influence on his maxims to the detriment of the rational laws governing his will.

[There is no knowledge of the intelligible world]

By *thinking* itself into the intelligible world practical reason does not overstep its limits in the least: it would do so only if it sought to *intuit or feel itself* into that world. The thought in question is a merely negative one with respect to the sensible world: it gives reason no laws for deter- 119 mining the will and is positive only in this one point, that it combines freedom as a negative characteristic with a (positive) power as well – and indeed with a causality of reason called by us 'a will' – a power so to act that the principle of our actions may accord with the essential character of a rational cause, that is, with the condition that the maxim of these actions should have the validity of a universal law. If practical reason were also to import an *object of the will* – that is, a motive of action – from the intelligible world, it would overstep its limits and pretend to an acquaintance with something of which it has no knowl- edge. The concept of the intelligible world is thus only *a point of view*[1] which reason finds itself constrained to adopt outside appearances *in order to conceive itself as practical*. To conceive itself thus would not be possible if the influences of sensibility were able to determine man; but it is none the less necessary so far as we are not to deny him consciousness of himself as intelligence and consequently as a rational cause which is active by means of reason – that is, which is free in its operation. This thought admittedly carries with it the Idea of an order and a legislation different from that of the mechanism of nature appropriate to the world of sense. It makes necessary the concept of an intelligible world (that is, of the totality of rational beings as things in themselves); but it makes not the slightest pretension to do more 120 than conceive such a world with respect to its *formal* condition – to con- ceive it, that is, as conforming to the condition that the maxim of the will should have the universality of a law, and so as conforming to the auton- omy of the will, which alone is compatible with freedom. In contrast with this all laws determined by reference to an object give us heteronomy, which can be found only in laws of nature and can apply only to the world of sense.

[There is no explanation of freedom]

Reason would overstep all its limits if it took upon itself to *explain how* pure reason can be practical. This would be identical, with the task of explaining *how freedom is possible*. 459

We are unable to explain anything unless we can bring it under laws which can have an object given in some possible experience. Freedom, however, is a mere Idea: its objective validity can in no way be exhibited by reference to laws of nature and consequently cannot be exhibited in any possible experience. Thus the Idea of freedom can never admit of full comprehension, or indeed of insight,[1] since it can never by any analogy have an example falling under it. It holds only as a necessary presupposition of reason in a being who believes himself to be conscious of a will – that is, of a power distinct from mere appetition (a power, namely, of determining himself to act as intelligence and consequently 121 to act in accordance with laws of reason independently of natural instincts). But where determination by laws of nature comes to an end, all *explanation* comes to an end as well. Nothing is left but *defence* – that is, to repel the objections of those who profess to have seen more deeply into the essence of things and on this ground audaciously declare freedom to be impossible. We can only show them that their pretended discovery of a contradiction in it consists in nothing but this: in order to make the law of nature apply to human actions they have necessarily had to consider man as an appearance; and now that they are asked to conceive him, *qua* intelligence, as a thing in himself as well, they continue to look upon him as an appearance in this respect also. In that case, admittedly, to exempt man's causality (that is, his will) from all the natural laws of the sensible world would, in one and the same subject, give rise to a contradiction. The contradiction would fall away if they were willing to reflect and to admit, as is reasonable, that things in themselves (although hidden) must lie behind appearances as their ground, and that we cannot require the laws of their operations to be identical with those that govern their appearances.

[There is no explanation of moral interest]

The subjective impossibility of *explaining* freedom of will is the same 122 as the impossibility of finding out and making comprehensible what 460 *interest** man can take in moral laws; and yet he does in fact take such

---

122 * An interest is that in virtue of which reason becomes practical – that is, becomes a cause determining the will. Hence only of a rational being do we say that he takes an interest in something: non-rational creatures merely feel sensuous impulses. Reason takes an immediate interest in an action only when the universal validity of the maxim of the action is a ground sufficient to determine the will. Such an interest alone is pure. When reason is able to determine the will only by means of some further object of desire or under the presupposition of some special feeling in the subject, then it takes only a mediate interest in the action; and since reason entirely by itself without the aid of experience can discover neither objects for the will nor a special feeling underlying the will, the latter

an interest. The basis of this in ourselves we call 'moral feeling'. Some people have mistakenly given out this feeling to be the gauge of our moral judgements: it should be regarded rather as the *subjective* effect exercised on our will by the law and having its objective ground in reason alone.

If we are to will actions for which reason by itself prescribes an 'ought' to a rational, yet sensuously affected, being, it is admittedly necessary that reason should have a power of *infusing* a *feeling of pleasure* or satisfaction in the fulfilment of duty,[1] and consequently that it should possess a kind of causality by which it can determine sensibility in accordance with rational principles. It is, however, wholly impossible 123 to comprehend – that is, to make intelligible *a priori* – how a mere thought containing nothing sensible in itself can bring about a sensation of pleasure or displeasure; for there is here a special kind of causality, and – as with all causality – we are totally unable to determine its character *a priori*: on this we must consult experience alone. The latter cannot provide us with a relation of cause and effect except between two objects of experience – whereas here pure reason by means of mere Ideas (which furnish absolutely no objects for experience) has to be the cause of an effect admittedly found in experience. Hence for us men it is wholly impossible to explain how and why the *universality of a maxim as a law* – and therefore morality – should interest us. This much only is certain: the law is not valid for us *because it interests us* (for this is heteronomy and makes practical reason depend on sensibility – that is to say, on an underlying feeling – in which case 461 practical reason could never give us moral law); the law interests us because it is valid for us as men in virtue of having sprung from our will as intelligence and so from our proper self; *but what belongs to mere appearance is necessarily subordinated by reason to the character of the thing in itself.*

[General review of the argument]

Thus the question 'How is a categorical imperative possible?' can be 124 answered so far as we can supply the sole presupposition under which it is possible – namely, the Idea of freedom – and also so far as we can have insight into the necessity of this presupposition. This is sufficient for the *practical use* of reason – that is, for conviction of the *validity*

---

interest would be merely empirical, and not a pure rational interest. The logical interest of reason (interest in promoting its own insight) is never immediate, but presupposes purposes for which reason can be employed.

of this imperative, and so too of the moral law. But how this presupposition itself is possible is never open to the insight of any human reason. Yet, on the presupposition that the will of an intelligence is free, there follows necessarily its *autonomy* as the formal condition under which alone it can be determined. It is not only perfectly *possible* (as speculative philosophy can show) to presuppose such freedom of the will (without contradicting the principle that natural necessity governs the connexion of appearances in the sensible world); it is also *necessary*, without any further condition, for a rational being conscious of exercising causality by means of reason and so of having a will (which is distinct from desires) to make such freedom in practice – that is, in Idea – underlie all his voluntary actions as their condition.[1] But *how* pure reason can be practical in itself without further motives drawn from some other source; that is, how the bare *principle of the universal validity*

125 *of all its maxims as laws* (which would admittedly be the form of a pure practical reason) can by itself – without any matter (or object) of the will in which we could take some antecedent interest – supply a motive and create an interest which could be called purely *moral*; or, in other words, *how pure reason can be practical* – all human reason is totally incapable of explaining this, and all the effort and labour to seek such an explanation is wasted.

It is precisely the same as if I sought to fathom how freedom itself is possible as the causality of a will. There I abandon a philosophical basis[1]

462 of explanation, and I have no other. I could, no doubt, proceed to flutter about in the intelligible world, which still remains left to me – the world of intelligences; but although I have an *Idea* of it, which has its own good grounds, yet I have not the slightest *acquaintance* with such a world, nor can I ever attain such acquaintance by all the efforts of my natural power of reason. My Idea signifies only a 'something' that remains over when I have excluded from the grounds determining my will everything that belongs to the world of sense: its sole purpose is to restrict the principle that all motives come from the field of sensibility, by setting bounds to this field and by showing that it does not comprise all

126 in all within itself, but that there is still more beyond it; yet with this 'more' I have no further acquaintance. Of the pure reason which conceives this Ideal, after I have set aside all matter – that is, all knowledge of objects – there remains nothing over for me except its form – namely, the practical law that maxims should be universally valid – and the corresponding conception of reason, in its relation to a purely intelligible world, as a possible efficient cause, that is, a cause determining the will. Here all sensuous motives must entirely fail; this Idea of an intelligible world would itself have to be the motive or to be that wherein reason originally took

an interest. To make this comprehensible is, however, precisely the problem that we are unable to solve.

[The extreme limit of moral enquiry]

Here then is the extreme limit of all moral enquiry. To determine this limit is, however, of great importance in this respect: by so doing reason may be kept, on the one hand, from searching around in the sensible world – greatly to the detriment of morality – for the supreme motive and for some interest, comprehensible indeed, but empirical; and it may be kept, on the other hand, from flapping its wings impotently, without leaving the spot, in a space that for it is empty – the space of transcendent concepts known as 'the intelligible world' – and so from getting lost among mere phantoms of the brain. For the rest, the Idea of a purely intelligible world, as a whole of all intelligences to which we ourselves belong as rational beings (although from another point of view we are members of the sensible world as well), remains always a serviceable and permitted Idea for the purposes of a rational belief, though all knowledge ends at its boundary: it serves to produce in us 127 a lively interest in the moral law by means of the splendid ideal of a universal kingdom of *ends in themselves* (rational beings), to which we can belong as members only if we are scrupulous to live in accordance 463 with maxims of freedom as if they were laws of nature.

Concluding note

The speculative use of reason *in regard to nature* leads to the absolute necessity of some supreme cause of the *world*; the practical use of reason *with respect to freedom* leads also to absolute necessity – but only to the absolute necessity *of the laws of action* for a rational being as such. Now it is an essential *principle* for every use of reason to push its knowledge to the point where we are conscious of its *necessity* (for without necessity it would not be knowledge characteristic of reason). It is an equally essential *limitation* of the same reason that it cannot have insight into the *necessity* either of what is or what happens, or of what ought to happen, except on the basis of a *condition* under which it is or happens or ought to happen. In this way, however, the satisfaction of reason is merely postponed again and again by continual 128 enquiry after a condition. Hence reason unrestingly seeks the unconditionally necessary and sees itself compelled to assume this without any means of making it comprehensible – happy enough if only it can find a concept compatible with this presupposition. Thus it is no discredit to

1 our deduction of the supreme principle of morality, but rather a reproach which must be brought against reason as such, that it cannot make comprehensible the absolute necessity of an unconditional practical law (such as the categorical imperative must be). For its unwillingness to do this by means of a condition – namely, by basing this necessity on some underlying interest – reason cannot be blamed, since in that case there would be no moral law, that is, no supreme law of freedom. And thus, while we do not comprehend the practical unconditioned necessity of the moral imperative, we do comprehend its *incomprehensibility*. This is all that can fairly be asked of a philosophy which presses forward in its principles to the very limit of human reason.

Notes

(The first figure given is the page number of the second German edition, as shown in the margin of the translation. The cross-references also refer to these pages.)

PREFACE

ii, n. 1.   There can, however, be an applied logic; *see* p. 32 footnote.

v, n. 1.   That is, a metaphysic of morals.

vi, n. 1.   Anthropology is roughly equivalent to what we should now call psychology, though the latter title is usually reserved by Kant for theories about the soul as an incorporeal substance.

vi, n. 2.   'Idea' – with a capital I – is a technical term for a concept of the unconditioned (especially of an unconditioned totality or whole), and on Kant's view duty is unconditioned (or absolute). On the other hand, 'idea' – with a small i – is used in the ordinary English sense: it is a translation of the German *Vorstellung*. For 'idea' *see* also the analysis of pp. 127–28. We find 'Idea' used also more loosely, as on page x, for the concept of an organic whole – e.g. a science.

vi, n. 3.   Kant seems to have in mind such a precept as 'Honesty is the best policy'. This commends the universal duty of honesty by an appeal to the empirical motive of self-interest.

vii, n. 1.   But *see* also p. 35. It is only the ultimate principles that require no anthropology.

vii, n. 2.   Inclinations are for Kant *habitual* desires.

viii, n. 1.   That is, a metaphysic of morals – not of nature.

ix, n. 1.   This work by Christian Wolff was published in 1738–39.

x, n. 1.   Kant has in mind his own Transcendental Logic (as set forth in the *Critique of Pure Reason*) – the logic of pure *a priori* knowledge, not of all thinking as such.

xi, n. 1.   Metaphysics is here the metaphysic of nature.

xii, n. 1.   That is to say, it is liable to fall into contradictions (antinomies) and illusions.

CHAPTER I

2, n. 1. This sentence should be noted as it affirms what Kant is commonly supposed to deny.

2, n. 2. That is, these qualities are not good when they are incompatible with a good will.

2, n. 3. An affection (*Affekt*) is a sudden passion like anger and is compared by Kant to intoxication. A passion (*Leidenschaft*) is a lasting passion or obsession like hate and is compared by Kant to a disease.

6, n. 1. The use of the word 'misology' is one of the passages which show the influence of Plato's *Phaedo* on Kant's ethical theory. This was due to the publication in 1767 of Moses Mendelssohn's *Phädon* – a work which is in great part a translation of Plato.

7, n. 1. Kant never claims – as it is too commonly said – that a good will is the sole good.

7, n. 2. Observe Kant's recognition of the 'contentment' found in good action. The view that he regarded this – or even a more mundane satisfaction – as diminishing or destroying the goodness of an action is a pure fabrication.

8, n. 1. Kant's view is always that obstacles make a good will more *conspicuous* – not that a good will is shown only in overcoming obstacles.

9, n. 1. The example refers, not to the preceding sentence, but to the one before that. It is not so easy as Kant suggests to distinguish between actions done from duty and actions done from self-interest – even a grocer may have a conscience. Nevertheless he is right in saying that an action done solely out of self-interest is not commonly regarded as morally good.

9, n. 2. For 'maxim' *see* the footnotes to pp. 15 and 51.

10, n. 1. Strictly speaking, it stands on the same footing as an *action* done from such inclinations as the inclination for honour.

12, n. 1. Happiness, as is indicated immediately below, is the *satisfaction* of all inclinations as a sum.

13, n. 1. It should be noted that Kant has neglected – presumably by an oversight – to state his *first* proposition in a *general* form.

13, n. 2. That is, as Kant indicates below, the controlling maxim must be formal, not material, where an action is done for the sake of duty.

16, footnote, n. 1. Strictly speaking, it is reverence (and not the law) which is analogous to fear and inclination.

17, footnote, n. 1. *See* pp. 55–56.

19, n. 1. This looks like falling back on mere self-interest, but Kant's point is that there could be *no promises at all* if this maxim were universally followed. *See* p. 18 above, also pp. 55 and 49.

20, n. 1. The highest grades of knowledge are for Kant 'insight' and (above insight) 'comprehension'. *See* pp. 120 and 123, and also *K.M.E.*, I 334.

CHAPTER II

28, n. 1.   It should be noted that it is contained as *duty in general* – not as a specific duty.

28, n. 2.   This need not mean that one rule cannot over-ride another.

29, n. 1.   This whole passage again suggests the influence of Plato. For the special point about the concept of God *see* p. 92.

31, n. 1.   Metaphysics is here a metaphysic of morals.

33, n. 1.   Dignity is a technical term for intrinsic value. *See* p. 77.

33, footnote, n. 1.   Professor J. G. Sulzer (1720–79) translated Hume's *Enquiry* into German in 1755.

34, n. 1.   Here again Kant is warning us only against contaminating moral *principles* by the addition of non-moral motives. To do this is to diminish the value of corresponding actions, as when we advocate honesty on the ground that it is the best policy.

35, n. 1.   Speculative or theoretical philosophy has to allow, not only that human reason is discursive (in the sense that its concepts give us no knowledge apart from sensuous intuition), but also that for knowledge it is dependent on pure intuitions of space and time, which may be *peculiar* to human beings.

35, n. 2.   We cannot, however, derive moral principles by mere *analysis* of the concept 'rational being'; *see* p. 50, footnote. For such derivation we require a *synthetic* use of reason; *see* p. 96.

35, n. 3.   Metaphysics is here a metaphysic of morals.

36, n. 1.   In Chapter I.

36, n. 2.   Ideas in a metaphysic of morals (as elsewhere) go to a 'complete totality' such as can never be given in experience.

36, n. 3.   We must pass from subjective principles (or maxims) to conditioned objective principles (hypothetical imperatives), and from them to the unconditioned categorical imperative of duty (especially the imperative of autonomy – pp. 69 ff. – which prepares the way for the concept of freedom). This can be clear only on a second reading.

36, n. 4.   If this 'derivation' were logical deduction, we could hardly infer from it that the will is practical reason. Kant seems to have in mind something more like what Aristotle called a *practical* syllogism – one whose conclusion is not a proposition, but an action.

37, n. 1.   'Determined' here means *'objectively* determined' – not *'subjectively* determined' as it means in a later sentence on this page.

38, footnote, n. 1.   Such a rule is a hypothetical imperative.

40, n. 1.   The word 'its' refers to the will.

41, n. 1.   The edition of the Berlin Academy strikes out the German word equivalent to 'not'.

42, n. 1.   Prudence might perhaps better be described as rational self-love.

42, footnote, n. 1.   This is one of the places where Kant indicates that prudence is concerned, not merely with means, but with the harmonisation of ends.

44, n. 1.   To be practically necessary is to be objectively necessary; compare p. 50 footnote. To be theoretically necessary would be to fall under the necessity of nature, which is something quite different. *See* p. 97.

44, n. 2.   This will become clearer in Chapter III.

44, n. 3.   That is to say, we are concerned, not with finding out the means necessary to an end, but with the obligation to use these means when they are known.

44, footnote, n. 1.   A pragmatic sanction is an imperial or royal decree having the effect of a fundamental law. Examples are the edict of Charles VII of France in 1438 – the basis of the liberties of the Gallican church; and that of the Emperor Charles VI in 1724 determining the Austrian succession. Kant considers such sanctions to be prudential – not as following from the system of natural law which applies to all States as such.

45, n. 1.   We are dealing – as Kant indicates in the next clause – with the *concept* of willing an end. In analytic propositions we have to distinguish sharply between the *concept* of the subject and the subject itself (usually a thing and not a concept).

49, n. 1.   We have to show, not only how a categorical imperative is possible, but also *that* it is possible.

50, footnote, n. 1.   The willing of an action enjoined by a categorical imperative cannot be derived by analysing the concept of willing an end (as is done in the case of a hypothetical imperative).

50, footnote, n. 2.   We shall, however, find in Chapter III – see especially pp. 111–12 – that the *Idea* of such a perfect will is necessary in order to establish the synthetic *a priori* practical propositions of morality.

50, footnote, n. 3.   To say that the categorical imperative connects an action *immediately* with the concept of a rational will is to say that the connexion is not derived from the presupposed willing of some further end. Yet in spite of this *immediate* connexion the proposition remains synthetic: the willing of the action is *not* contained in the concept of a rational will.

51, n. 1.   The maxim in question is a *material* maxim. See T.C.I., pp. 135–36.

51, footnote, n. 1.   An objective principle is an imperative only for finite agents who are imperfectly rational.

52, n. 1.   The use of a preposition here (and elsewhere) may seem an unnecessary complication. Perhaps Kant wishes to emphasise the *interpenetration* of the material and formal maxim. In willing in accordance with a material maxim I will *at the same time* that this maxim should be a universal law. As a material maxim is based on sensuous motives, this formula by itself disposes of the traditional doctrine that in a morally good action a sensuous motive can never, on Kant's view, be present at the same time as the moral motive.

52, n. 2.   When we speak of 'nature', we may take it in a *material* sense as equivalent to the sum total of *phenomena*; or we may take it in a *formal* sense as equivalent to the sum total of the *laws* governing the existence of natural phenomena. This second usage is more akin to popular phrases like 'the nature of man' and 'the nature of the world'. Hence we might say, speaking popularly, that it is the nature of the world to be governed by the law of cause and effect. In spite of this, Kant treats the laws of nature as purposive when he asks if our maxims can be conceived or willed as laws of nature. *See* also pp. 81, 87, and 80, footnote.

53, footnote, n. 1.   *See* my analysis of the argument. In *T.C.I.*, pp. 147–48, I laid too much stress on the over-riding of one duty by another. The main point is the 'latitude' allowed to inclination in imperfect duties.

53, footnote, n. 2.   Outer duties are duties to others; inner duties are duties to myself.

54, n. 1.   Many commentators say that Kant condemns suicide on the ground that if everyone committed suicide there would be no one left to do so! There is clearly no trace of such an argument here (or indeed anywhere else, so far as I know), and the reader should be on his guard against such absurdities.

56, n. 1.   This is put in a prudential way, but Kant's doctrine is not prudential, as can be seen from p. 11 and p. 68, footnote.

57, n. 1.   This distinction is the same as that between perfect and imperfect duties.

57, n. 2.   Kant is dealing only with the four main types of duty (perfect and imperfect, inner and outer). Every type has different kinds of obligation falling under it according as it is concerned with different kinds of object. For example, perfect duties to others include duties not to assail their freedom or steal their property, as well as not to borrow on false pretences. *See* p. 68.

60, n. 1.   Kant is again dealing with degrees of conspicuousness, not with degrees of excellence.

61, n. 1.   The point is that we must not introduce empirical considerations into the *principle of morality*. The moral principle must by itself be sufficient to determine action, but this does not mean that other motives may not be present *at the same time*.

61, n. 2.   By embracing a cloud in mistake for Juno Ixion became the father of the 'mongrel' race of centaurs.

62, n. 1.   The proposition establishing this *a priori* connexion is, however, not analytic but synthetic. *See* p. 50, footnote.

62, n. 2.   Here a metaphysic of morals is taken to include a critique of practical reason. The latter is specially concerned with *justifying* the *a priori* connexion between the moral law and a rational will as such. *See* pp. 87 and 95–96.

62, n. 3.   These differences – between the pleasant, the beautiful, and the good – are discussed in the *Critique of Judgement*, e.g. in §. 5.

63, n. 1.   As we have seen (pp. i–iii), physics (or natural philosophy) must have an empirical, as well as an *a priori*, part. This empirical part is in turn divided into two parts, the first of which is concerned with the world of physical nature, while the second (which is here in question) is concerned with mind.

63, n. 2.   I have here ventured – perhaps rashly – to substitute 'subjective' for 'objective'. 'An objective ground' – if it could mean anything here – would have to mean 'a ground in objects'. This sense is very rare in Kant and would be most confusing in a passage where everywhere else 'objective' means valid for every rational being as such. On the other hand Kant always emphasises that ends (whether objective or subjective) must be subjectively chosen – we can never be compelled to make anything our end. *See*, for example, the use of the word 'subjectively' on p. 70, especially the second use of it.

Every end is a subjective ground of the will's self-determination. If it is given solely by reason, it becomes an objective ground as well.

63, n. 3. A means considered as the ground (or cause) of the possibility of an action seems to be an instrument. Thus, for example, a hammer is (or contains) the ground of the possibility of knocking in a nail. In practice, however, Kant usually treats an action itself as a means (the means enjoined by a hypothetical imperative).

64, n. 1. Compare p. 14.

64, n. 2. If Kant means 'every volition' strictly, he must have in mind universal *principles* only – not particular moral laws.

65, n. 1. We might expect inclinations to be grounded on needs, but Kant appears usually to take the view that needs are grounded on inclinations.

65, n. 2. Kant is not usually so hostile to inclinations. Is his attitude here perhaps due to the influence of the *Phaedo*?

66, n. 1. Here Kant distinguishes clearly between a supreme practical *principle* valid for all rational beings as such and a corresponding categorical *imperative* valid for imperfectly rational agents such as men. This distinction should always be kept in mind where it is not made explicitly.

66, n. 2. Strictly speaking, 'humanity' should be 'rational nature as such', but the only rational nature with which we are acquainted is to be found in man. Kant himself makes this distinction at the beginning of the previous paragraph.

66, n. 3. The word 'simply' is essential to Kant's meaning since we all have to use other men as means.

66, footnote, n. 1. The reference is to pp. 99–100 and 101–2. A rational being can act only under the Idea of freedom, and so must conceive himself as autonomous and therefore as an end in himself.

68, footnote, n. 1. 'Don't do to others what you don't want done to yourself.'

68, footnote, n. 2. It should be observed that here Kant regards a law as universal only if it covers *all* duties and so is an ultimate principle. So far as he uses 'universal law' in this sense, his claim that it is independent of knowledge of human nature is at least not palpably absurd.

69, n. 1. The *purpose* (or *end*) *of nature* for humanity is to be sharply distinguished from *the natural purpose* (or *end*) which all men seek (as in the paragraph immediately following). The first conception supposes nature to have a final end or aim which is not to be found in nature itself. The second rests on observation of nature and can be confirmed by such observation. See *Critique of Judgement*, §. 67.

71, n. 1. Here Kant is not bidding us to renounce all interests: we have, for example, a right, and even an indirect duty, to seek our own happiness. What he is saying is that the categorical imperative cannot be based on any interest: it excludes from its *sovereign authority* 'every admixture of interest as a motive'. Our judgement of duty must in no way be influenced by our interests – this is the only sense in which all interests must be renounced.

72, n. 1. Kant is considering the hypothesis that we are bound to obey moral laws only because of self-interest. He argues that a will bound by self-interest would not always issue in right actions unless it was bound by a *further* law bidding it act on maxims of self-interest *only* when these maxims were capable of being willed as universal laws; *see* also p. 94. Hence a will bound by self-interest could not be a *supreme* law-giver nor would it make *universal* law.

73, n. 1. Although Kant says 'natural purpose' (*Naturzweck*), he must mean 'purpose of nature' (*Zweck der Natur*). *See* n. 1 on p. 69 above.

74, n. 1. Here we are not considering the *content* of personal ends (which has just been excluded). What we are considering is only the *form* of a kingdom of ends composed of persons capable of willing personal ends (whatever be their content) *in conformity with universal law*.

75, n. 1. Could this mean, that unlike us, God as omnipotent is not thwarted by the will of others? Or that He is not subject to State law? Or that as holy He is not under the categorical imperative considered as a divine command?

77, n. 1. This is a reference to Kant's own aesthetic theory. I use the term 'fancy price' (in the absence of a better) to mean a value for fancy or imagination.

78, n. 1. It may seem a moralistic prejudice on Kant's part thus to put moral value so far above aesthetic value. Yet when we consider what we think of men who combine the finest aesthetic taste with fiendish cruelty (as happened in some cases during the war), we may begin to incline towards Kant's view.

80, n. 1. A complete determination combines both form and matter.

80, n. 2. Unity, multiplicity (or plurality), and totality are the three categories of *quantity*, the last of which combines the other two.

81, n. 1. It would be a more natural rendering to say 'bring the *action* nearer to intuition'. But an action is already near to intuition, and what we require to bring nearer to intuition is the universal formula (or the Idea of reason, as on pp. 79–80 above).

81, n. 2. *See* also n. 2 on p. 52.

81, n. 3. It is not clear whether 'object' means object of thought or object (purpose) of will. On p. 98 'object' is apparently equated with 'content', but this again is ambiguous.

82, n. 1. Kant forgets that in the case of imperfect (or wider) duties the end in itself is conceived positively.

84, n. 1. Rational beings are here regarded as the *ends* (*or purposes*) *of nature*. *See* n. 1 on p. 69. This teleological assumption is also made in Kant's use of the universal law of nature as an analogy for the universal law of morality (or freedom).

84, n. 2. The introduction of happiness as a reward for virtue is a trifle crude. It would be more satisfactory to say, as Kant does elsewhere, that without the co-operation of nature the good will could not be successful in realising its ends.

86, n. 1. The reference is to pp. 14 ff., especially to the footnote on pp. 16–17.

88, n. 1. Analysis of concepts seems here to produce synthetic propositions. Does Kant refer to an analytic argument? *See* my analysis of p. xiv.

89, n. 1. This is not the inhuman doctrine that a good man should not be influenced by any desire for objects, but that he should not allow his desire for any object to interfere with his judgement of duty.

89, n. 2. Kant is referring to the reason which is the basis of the categorical imperative. This reason cannot be merely that I happen to be interested in the happiness of others.

91, footnote, n. 1. Francis Hutcheson (1694–1747), Professor of Moral Philosophy in the University of Glasgow, was the leading exponent of the doctrine of moral sense. Kant was himself for some time influenced by this doctrine.

92, n. 1. Kant has in mind the doctrines of Christian Wolff (1679–1754) and his followers. *See* n. 1 on p. ix.

92, n. 2. The reference is primarily to the doctrine of Crusius (1712–76).

92, n. 3. The reference is to the *ontological* concept of perfection mentioned above.

94, n. 1. If any object of will is made the basis for morality, we require (1) a law binding us to pursue this object, and (2) – if the law is to issue always in right actions – a *further* law bidding us act on the maxim of pursuing this object *only* when the maxim is capable of being willed as a universal law. *See* n. 1 on p. 72.

96, n. 1. This passage (together with p. xiv) suggests a connexion between a synthetic argument and synthetic propositions. I do not see how this can be so since the same propositions must appear in both analytic and synthetic arguments. *See* my analysis of the argument of p. xiv and also my note on p. 88.

CHAPTER III

98, n. 1. *See* n. 3 on p. 81.

98, n. 2. A will 'under moral laws' is not a will which always acts according to moral laws, but one which would so act if reason had full control over passion. *See Critique of Judgement*, §. 87 (the long footnote). Even a bad will is under moral laws and is free.

99, n. 1. The two 'cognitions' may be thought of as the subject and the predicate of a synthetic proposition so long as we have in mind only categorical propositions; but we must remember that hypothetical and disjunctive propositions may also be synthetic.

99, n. 2. The Idea in question is made more precise in pp. 111–12, where it is the Idea of my will as belonging to the intelligible world and as active on its own account – that is, as free.

100, n. 1. This parenthesis is obscure in the German text, and, strictly speaking, it is not possible to demonstrate freedom *a priori*: all we can show *a priori* is that a rational agent must necessarily act on the presupposition of freedom.

100, footnote, n. 1. The burden which weighs upon theory is the burden of a task which cannot be carried out: it is impossible to prove freedom theoretically, though we can show from a theoretical point of view that freedom is not incompatible with natural necessity.

101, n. 1. It should be observed that Kant appeals first to *theoretical* reason as a power of judgement.

101, n. 2. It is not clear whether this is merely an inference or whether practical reason has the same insight into its own presuppositions as has theoretical reason.

102, n. 1. *See* n. 1 on p. 66, footnote.

102, n. 2. The German text has 'Ideas' in the plural, but this seems to be a slip.

103, n. 1. Compare pp. 37 and 39.

104, n. 1. 'States' here may cover agreeable 'states of affairs' as well as 'states of feeling'.

105, n. 1. Reciprocal concepts are concepts which have the same denotation (that is, which apply to precisely the same objects). Thus, for example the concept of a three-sided rectilineal figure and the concept of a three-angled rectilineal figure are reciprocal concepts.

106, n. 1. Inner sensation or inner sense may be identified with what is sometimes called 'introspection'.

107, n. 1. A subject here is a subject known – through inner sense – as an *object* of experience.

107, n. 2. Not only as an object of inner sense, but also *as a subject capable of sensing* (and so as an object affected through the senses – p. 117), I must regard myself as belonging to the world of sense.

107, n. 3. To manifest pure activity is to think and act on principles of reason. We know these principles (and so far this activity) immediately – i.e. not through sense.

108, n. 1. Reason is here used in a technical sense as a power of *Ideas*, while understanding is a power of *categories*.

108, n. 2. To mark out the limits of the sensible world is to mark out the limits of understanding; for apart from sensibility understanding can think nothing at all.

109, n. 1. This does not mean that men always act morally, but that they act on the presupposition of freedom and so of a moral law to which they are subject.

111, n. 1. 'Immediately' means independently of sensuous impulsions and their objects.

111, n. 2. That is, a ground of actions and laws in the sensible world. My new version here was suggested by a criticism of Dr. Dieter Henrich (*Philosophische Rundschau*, 2. Jahrgang, Heft 1/2, 35 a.). The discussion in the first two editions of *T.C.I.* was based on a common mistranslation; but the present version confirms its conclusion. For a fuller discussion see the Appendix to Chapter XXIV of the third edition of *T.C.I.*, pp. 250–52.

111, n. 3. *See* n. 2 on p. 99.

114, n. 1. That is, as objectively (not subjectively) necessary. *See* p. 37.

114, n. 2. For dialectic *see* pp. 23–24 and my note on p. xii.

116, n. 1. '*Bonum vacans*' is unoccupied property.

118, n. 1. The extent of this 'knowledge' is considerably curtailed in the following paragraph.

118, n. 2. *See* n. 1 on p. 111 – a passage with which the present statement should be compared.

119, n. 1. To say that the *concept* of the intelligible world is only a point of view is *not* to say that the intelligible world itself is only a point of view; and we must remember that the concept of the sensible world can with equal justification be described as a point of view.

120, n. 1. Observe the distinction between 'comprehension' and 'insight'. To comprehend – *see* p. 123 – is to make intelligible *a priori*. See also n. 1 on p. 20.

122, n. 1. Compare n. 2 on p. 7.

124, n. 1. That is, *as far as reason is concerned. See* pp. 111–12.

125, n. 1. The reference is presumably to natural philosophy or physics in Kant's widest sense.

KANT'S THEORY OF PRACTICAL REASON

Thomas Hill Jr

Contemporary discussions of practical reason often refer vaguely to the Kantian conception of reasons as an alternative to various means–ends theories, but it is rarely clear what this is supposed to be, except that somehow moral concerns are supposed to fare better under the Kantian conception. The theories of Nagel, Gewirth, Darwall, and Donagan have been labelled 'Kantian' because they deviate strikingly from standard preference models, but their roots in Kant have not been traced in detail and important differences may go unnoticed. All this is not surprising, of course, because Kant's conception of practical reason is inseparable from his ideas of freedom, which are notoriously difficult and controversial. It is hard enough to characterize these ideas accurately in Kantian terminology, harder still to explain them in terms of contemporary debates about reasons for action.

Though well aware of these obstacles, I want to present here a summary of some main features of Kant's theory of practical reason, as I have come to see this, indicating along the way how Kant's theory differs from some familiar alternatives. My focus will be primarily on the *Groundwork*, but, unlike some, I do not see the basic theory of the *Groundwork* as radically different from Kant's later writings. What I have to say here is part of a larger project in which, I hope, there will be enough detailed textual analysis to make convincing what I will now present as more or less unargued conclusions. For present purposes, detail will be sacrificed for scope. The main aim is to give a coherent characterization of Kant's idea of practical reason rather than to defend it either on textual grounds or as a tenable theory; but, of course, if as a result the text seems clearer or the Kantian perspective more plausible, I will not be disappointed.

1 Reasoning with hypothetical imperatives

Practical reasoning, in general, is reasoning about what I *ought* to do. This, for Kant, is the same as reasoning about what is *good* for me to do except that 'ought' conveys the sense that, as imperfectly rational and liable to contrary inclinations, I might not do what is good even though I can.[1] The word 'ought' [Sollen], like 'must' and other ways of expressing Kant's imperatives, is supposed to express the sense that something is 'necessary,' whether to achieve an end or to satisfy morality; but the necessity is a practical one posed by 'compelling' reasons, not a logical necessity or a causal or metaphysical inevitability.

The connection between 'ought' and 'good' should not be misunderstood. Kant accepts the traditional equivalence between what one rationally ought to do and what is good to do; but rational choice is prior to goodness.[2] That is, goodness is not a property of acts, experiences, or ends which can be discerned independently of the reasons, or rational considerations, for acting. Thus, though Kant agrees with the tradition that an act is rational if and only if it is good to do (or promotes what is best), he does not hold that an act is rational *because* it is (or promotes) good but rather an act is counted as good (or good producing) *because* rational considerations favor it. What is *good* to do and what one *ought* to do are both determined by what reason prescribes; the difference in the expressions lies in the sense of practical necessity conveyed by the word 'ought.'

The capacity to engage in practical reasoning is a feature of beings with a *will*, and only such beings.[3] At times Kant announces grandly that practical reason *is* the will, but subsequent discussion quickly reveals that the concepts are too complex to maintain the identification.[4] Reason, Kant implies, sometimes 'determines' the will, but sometimes does not. Relations between 'reason' and 'will' are complex and puzzling, but several preliminary points seem clear. First, Kant did not conceive of the reasoning relevant to practical affairs in the way that Hume did: that is, as merely a capacity to discern 'matters of (empirical) fact' and 'relations of ideas.'[5] Hume's picture is that reason is essentially theoretical, a fact-finding and analysing power which may serve to present background information for agents who are then moved to act by their desires. It is this picture that led Hume to deny that there are rational principles of conduct, even governing prudential choices. The only Humean offenses against reason, strictly speaking, are in the formation of beliefs. Kant's attempt to make an essential connection between reason and will represents an important departure from Hume's picture. To have a will is to acknowledge the force of certain rational constraints, even if one's final choice does not always conform to them. And if one engages in the reasoning relevant to practical concerns one could not have a will indifferent to its conclusions. Kant is an 'internalist' about reasons: there are, in addition to reasons for *believing*, reasons for *acting*, and to acknowledge these is (in part) to be disposed to follow them.

A second point stems from Kant's repeated definitions of *will* as a causal power that works in accord with the agent's *idea* of principles or laws.[6] When a being with a will 'makes things happen,' we attribute this to his acceptance of a reason; and this can be partially expressed as his policy, maxim, or principle. We understand the act not merely by reference to a prior cause, e.g., an inner impulse, but by constructing a rationale for it. The rationale, if fully stated, would refer to the agent's ideas about the effects of his act, his goals, his attitude regarding similar cases, and, ultimately, the principle of reason that (we suppose) guided and constrained his choice. Acts are judged rational or not according to how this *rationale* measures up to the standards of rationality and not by trying to see whether the right metaphysical faculty ('Reason' and not 'Sensibility') was operative.[7]

Non-moral practical reasoning is supposed to be guided by hypothetical imperatives.[8] Though the term 'hypothetical imperative' derives from a classification of forms of judgment, it is widely conceded that Kant's basic idea cannot be adequately captured by focus on linguistic form alone. Moral imperatives, supposedly categorical, can be expressed in hypothetical form: for example, 'if you plan to judge a man in law, you ought not to engage in business with him.' And non-moral imperatives, supposedly hypothetical, can be expressed in categorical form: for example, 'You ought to take an aspirin.' Kant's idea of hypothetical imperatives is best understood, I think, when they are seen as 'oughts' which have their rational force entirely from their place in a complex rationale which has the following structure:

(1) Any fully rational agent (necessarily) wills the necessary (and available) means to his ends.
(2) So one ought to will the necessary (and available) means to one's ends. (The Hypothetical Imperative)
(3) M is a necessary (and available) means to E.
(4) So if one wills E, one ought to will M.
(5) P (a person) wills E.
(6) So P ought to will M.

The first premise is, for Kant, an analytic truth about rational agency, and the second simply re-expresses the idea with the word 'ought' (according to Kant's view that 'ought' is merely a way of expressing rational requirements especially appropriate to 'imperfect wills'). The third and fifth premises express beliefs about relevant facts: causal connections and the ends to which the agent is committed. The conclusion is 'hypothetical' in that its rational force is entirely dependent on the facts presupposed in the argument and, further, because one can rationally escape the conclusion by choosing to give up an end to which one was committed. In effect, the rational requirement is always an option: take the means or abandon your end.

This interpretation of Kant on non-moral reasoning is controversial in at least one important respect. I have assumed that human wills can fail to live up to the basic standard of non-moral practical reason, just as they can fail to live up to the rational standards of morality. This is what most of us think, and it is implied in Kant's calling even the non-moral rational standards (hypothetical) *imperatives*. But some construe Kant's remarks about the analyticity of 'who wills the end wills the means' as a denial that anyone can will an end and fail to will the necessary means. This view fits with, and perhaps reinforces, an all-or-nothing view of the will in moral cases, according to which one cannot will contrary to rational moral standards.[9] In both cases, this all-or-nothing account says that one always wills what is rational by the standards in question, and so one's acts (or bodily movements) are either attributed to the agent's will, in which case they are rational, or they are seen as mere products of natural causes, in which case they are non-rational. *Irrational* willing becomes impossible.

The question whether one can (irrationally) fail to will the necessary means to one's ends is more complex than it may seem. Consider first the situation when one initially comes to will an end. What seems obvious, and may count as analytic, is that when one wills an end one intends to take *some* means to achieve it, even if one may not know what means will be necessary. But does one in willing an end, say to win an election, thereby intend (or will) to take *whatever* means prove to be necessary? Ends need not be willed so unrevisably. I may will to win the election, for example, thereby intending to take the necessary means unless those means prove unacceptable, in which case I intend to abandon my end. In effect, I will to take the necessary means or else revise my ends.

Now consider the common situation in which time lapses between an initial decision to pursue an end and the occasions for taking the means. One can know, I think, that certain means (e.g., lighter meals) are necessary to achieve a goal (e.g., to lose weight) and yet neither take the necessary means nor abandon the goal. This is the pattern, if any, which hypothetical imperatives would condemn as irrational willing: one wills something incompatible with the means known to be necessary to an end, thereby failing to will the means, but one also fails to take the only rational alternative, i.e., to reassess one's ends. It is arguable, of course, that this is impossible *if* the agent is fully and vividly focused upon his end and the immediate urgency of taking the means. To borrow Foot's example, if you intended to go to London tonight and you stand on the Oxford platform fully aware that the last train, your only means to London, is starting to pull away, then unless you step on that train you *have* in fact given up your end.[10] What follows, however, is just that the irrationalities falling under hypothetical reasoning always involve some failure of attention, careful reflection, or willingness to face up to one's options, and that when the necessary means are immediate, urgent, and obvious the failure may be impossible for anyone still rational enough to be an agent. But this concession does not deny my main point, which is that even Kant's hypothetical imperatives refer to a standard of rational choice which we can sometimes, by willing irrationally, fail to satisfy. When we fail, revealing that we are not perfectly rational, it is not that we do not will to act but rather move as mere products of natural forces; we will to act, but in this case 'reason' does not fully 'determine the will.' As Kant says, what is analytic is not simply that 'whoever wills the end, wills the (necessary) means' but that this is so 'so far as reason has decisive influence on his actions.'[11]

This means–end principle is in fact the only principle of rational choice that Kant explicitly acknowledges as analytic of rationality. One can easily imagine that Kant would have accepted certain other formal principles as analytic of means–ends reasoning: for example, Rawls's principle of inclusion and principle of greater likelihood. But it is significant that he did not recognize as analytic of rational choice any of the *substantive* or *maximizing* principles which philosophers have often accepted for non-moral practical reasoning. By 'substantive' principles I mean principles which declare certain ends, such as pleasure, as intrinsically worth pursuing or which specify certain particular sorts of acts, such as promise-keeping, as rationally required. Kant was well aware that previous rationalistic philosophers had simply declared their favorite moral principles to be rational without much argument, and, with his analytic/synthetic distinction in hand as a critical tool, he could see that a successful argument for the rationality of these principles could not be a simple inference from the familiar concept of rational choice. Similarly, he saw that there is no contradiction in supposing a rational agent might lack the particular ends of wealth, power, honor, and even pleasure. The point is not just that there are contexts in which a rational person might forego these ends; it is also that our disposition to pursue these ends is not a consequence of our having reason but rather of other aspects of our human nature. Even the universal human inclination to pleasure is not by its nature a reason to act; it becomes so when, with appropriate reflection, a rational agent chooses to include it in the system of ends he wills to pursue.[12] The same would be true, on Kant's view, of any natural altruistic disposition we may have to promote the pleasure of others.

It is significant, too, that Kant does not count as analytic of rationality any *maximizing* principle such as 'Maximize your expected utility over time' or 'Act in such a way that you maximally satisfy your current preferences (or the preferences you would have if fully informed).'[13] Such principles differ from Kant's Hypothetical Imperative in that they do not always leave an agent an option, whatever his preferences may be. Thus, if there are categorical moral imperatives, such maximizing principles could be in irreconcilable conflict with them: a categorical imperative might forbid X even though, given one's (informed) preferences, the maximizing principle demands X. Kant's Hypothetical Imperative, by contrast, can always be fully satisfied no matter what moral imperatives demand; for whenever it prescribes a means on the basis of one's end, it leaves the rational option of giving up the end.

Prudential hypothetical imperatives might seem to be an exception, for Kant says happiness is necessarily an end for all human beings. When morality conflicts with my happiness, how can I abandon my end of happiness? This raises an interesting problem, but I think it is more a problem in Kant's exposition than a deep inconsistency in his theory. The inclination to happiness may be irrepressible or, as Kant says, a 'natural necessity,'[14] but hypothetical imperatives refer to *ends* which we will and nothing becomes this except by choice of a rational agent.[15] Kant concedes at least that most people, most of the time, will happiness as a higher-order end, i.e., the goal of fulfilling all of their specific (desire-based) ends or of satisfying all their desires.[16] But since the set of all a person's desires, or desire-based ends, over time is an amorphous, vaguely conceived, and usually incoherent set, there is little that can be declared unequivocally both a means to happiness and inescapably necessary for happiness.[17] Even if there were, Kant clearly thought that when morality demands we can suspend, qualify, or abandon happiness as the end we will to pursue on the occasion. Thus, despite the universality of the inclination to happiness and its typical place in our rational deliberations, even the prudential imperatives to achieve happiness must be understood to leave the same option as all other hypothetical imperatives: take the means or (at least temporarily) abandon the end. Given the qualification, non-moral imperatives do not, strictly speaking, conflict with categorical imperatives: both can be satisfied.[18]

The point might be summarized by saying, darkly, that Kant's theory of non-moral practical reason 'makes room for freedom' even though it is not 'derived from freedom.' That is, the rational constraints on non-moral choice are not derived from the idea of a rational agent with freedom (autonomy) in the way moral constraints are supposed to be; but these non-moral rational constraints always leave us the rational option to do whatever is demanded by moral reasoning based on the idea of freedom.

2 Reasoning with autonomy: negative aspects of freedom

Kant held, of course, that the Hypothetical Imperative is not the only necessary principle of rational conduct, even though it is the only analytic one. This means that there is another sort of practical reasoning not captured by the pattern of argument we have been considering. Such reasoning is guided by principles which are acknowledged by every rational will with the property *autonomy* but which would be irrelevant to any 'will' without this property. Kant believed these further principles to be identical with the highest principles of morality, but this is a conclusion rather than a defining feature of rational autonomy.

In the *Groundwork* there are several ways Kant tries to show that common morality presupposes rational principles beyond hypothetical imperatives. The first, in chapter one, aims to show that ordinary judgments that certain acts are morally commendable are based on our attributing to the agent a motive, respect for moral law, which does not fit the hypothetical imperative pattern. Then, in chapter two, Kant argues that the concept of a moral duty is such that, if there are duties, then there must be principles which are rationally compelling even if following them fails to serve our ends. Reasoning with hypothetical imperatives, in the pattern we have considered, might often prescribe the sort of acts commonly regarded duties, but it obviously could not account for their being duties, i.e., rationally required independently of their serving our ends.[19]

Kant also argues, apart from moral assumptions, that the way we view ourselves in practical deliberation presupposes a capacity to reason independently of hypothetical imperatives. Even would-be moral skeptics, questioning whether there are really any duties, inevitably take themselves in deliberation to be capable of acting for reasons that inclinations together with the Hypothetical Imperative cannot provide.[20] A central feature of this self-concept is affirmed, Kant thinks, even when we make theoretical judgments, as in science; for here too we see ourselves as surveying and assessing reasons from a point of view where the question is not what do we want and what is needed to achieve some revisable personal goal.[21]

These arguments are open to all sorts of question, of course; but my present task is not to defend them but rather to draw out some main features of the idea of practical reason which the arguments claim to be so deeply embedded in our thought. I begin with some negative features.

(1) The first point is that immoral persons do not differ from the morally best persons in the standards of rational choice to which they are committed. They differ in what they do, and in the priorities represented in their deepest policies, but as human beings they both have wills with the property of autonomy, which implies an acknowledgment of the non-hypothetical standards of rationality with which we are now concerned.[22]

In this respect, I think, Kant's view is unlike that of some contemporary philosophers who also distinguish means–end reasoning from a richer conception ('the reasonable') which is at work in moral discussions. For the contemporary philosophers generally treat the commitment to the wider (more 'impartial') sort of reasoning as in a sense optional: a necessary part of thinking morally, perhaps, but not something one needs to be a fully consistent, informed rational agent. For example, in Rawls's terminology it is 'reasonable' to respect the principles of justice because it is (in a narrower sense) 'rational' for anyone who takes a certain impartial perspective to choose these principles for the basic structure of societies.[23] But Rawls admits that not everyone is committed to the (impartial) standards built into this idea of the 'reasonable.' One may ask, 'Why be reasonable?' or, in other words, 'Why is it rational for me to respect what rational persons *would* choose *if* impartial?' For the amoralist who rejects the moral perspective there may be no adequate answer. Kant's view, I think, is different, though of course it raises problems of its own. The wider conception of practical reason, i.e., rational autonomy, is thought to be an inescapable feature of rational agency, revealed in moral thinking but not an optional form of reasoning one takes on with a voluntary commitment to the moral point of view. Thus when Kant argues that an act is demanded by a principle that rational agents with autonomy would adopt, he considers one's rational options to be closed; for the perspective of rational autonomy is one, he thought, inherent in all rational human wills.[24] It is rational to do what rational agents with autonomy *would* prescribe because we are such agents and, as such, we *do* so prescribe to ourselves.

(2) The next feature of rational autonomy to consider is its alleged independence from natural causes. Something of this sort is entailed by Kant's identification of autonomy with negatively conceived freedom, together with the definition of the latter as a 'capacity to work independently of determination by alien causes.'[25] But the problem is to be clear about what sort of independence is in question. The point cannot be that the behavior we attribute to rational wills cannot be explained and predicted by causal laws in physical science or psychology; for Kant repeatedly insists that any observed phenomena, regarding human behavior or anything else, can in principle be comprehended under natural causal laws. Nor, I think, can his point be that we can equally well describe and explain human behavior from another metaphysical perspective compatible with the scientific one; for Kant repeats that the attribution of behavior to wills is warranted only for practical purposes and, in any case, it leaves us with unanswerable questions rather than any comprehensible account of how the will results in behavior.

The main point, instead, seems to be an idea about the task of practical deliberation, about what the deliberator is looking for. He is looking for reasons for choosing to act one way rather than another, which is not the same as looking for the causes, if any, which will have moved him to act when he does. In deliberation, one sees oneself as having options, some of which may be supported by better (practical) reasons than others. One cannot know prior to choosing what the causes are, if any, in terms of which one's choice can be explained or could have been predicted. But even if one knew all that is conceptually and empirically possible to know about oneself and the situation prior to choice, that still would not give the deliberator what he is looking for, namely, better reasons for choosing one option over the other.

We can imagine, perhaps, that one might learn on an occasion that he is so 'wired' that he will behave in a certain way no matter how he should deliberate, reflect on reasons, and 'choose'; but to imagine this is to imagine that, unless he forgets what he has learned, he has had to abandon the point of view of deliberation, for he no longer sees himself as having options. Causal determination does not, of course, imply that this is a common occurrence; for causal determinism does not imply that the phenomena corresponding to reflection on reason are causally inefficacious. And even supposing we could have evidence that this is a common, even universal, occurrence, the conclusion to draw would be that deliberation presupposes an illusion and becomes impossible once one is enlightened. However, shocking as this (fantastically implausible) conclusion would be, even this would not deny Kant's main point about practical reasoning which, once understood, seems hard to deny: that is, when one deliberates, one is engaged in the task of assessing the reasons for choosing among alternative outcomes one presumes will be influenced by one's reflection and choice, and whether one's reflection and choice are themselves causally determined, even whether the agent believes this as a metaphysical thesis, is irrelevant to his deliberative task.

A similar point, as Kant suggests, can be made about theoretical judgment in science: whether or not one's weighing of the evidence by rational standards is causally determined, even whether the scientist believes this, is irrelevant to a scientist's task of finding the conclusion best supported by the evidence.

(3) Practical reasoning with autonomy is, in some sense, independent of inclination; but in what sense? Sometimes Kant's expressions suggest a picture, or rather featureless idea, of a 'self' without desires, body, or even spatio-temporal location, and this mysterious 'self' is somehow giving abstract orders to a corrupt, embodied, lusty earth-bound being, and, oddly enough, I am both the mysterious giver and the embodied receiver of the orders. Kant also, of course, issues warnings against taking such a picture, or non-picture, too seriously or out of context; and I think the main force of his remarks about practical reasoning's being independent of inclination do not presuppose metaphysical (or metaphorical) ideas of this sort.

Part of the idea of independence from inclination is no doubt connected with the point of the previous section: that is, the point of view of a deliberator engaged in practical reasoning is one from which it is irrelevant whether or not scientific explanation of behavior proceeds by showing law-like connections between antecedent psychological states, such as inclinations, and consequent behavior. Just as the abstract thesis of causal determinism is irrelevant to the deliberator's task, so is the more specific psychological determinism that insists that there are always lawful correlations between behavior and prior observable psychological states. The deliberator asks whether having a certain inclination is a good reason for doing what he proposes, and this question is not resolved by believing or even knowing that some conjunction of psychological states, including that inclination, will correlate lawfully with his subsequent behavior. The deliberator sees himself as capable of squelching the inclination, no matter how urgent it feels, if there is sufficient reason to do so; but this is not a belief about *how* the resistance is to be explained, and it is not incompatible with any but the crudest psychological determinism (e.g., one which held that the most urgently felt desires determine behavior irrespective of reflection).

But the main point, I think, lies elsewhere, and is more interesting. The idea is that, for a rational agent with autonomy, the reasons for acting are not settled by knowing all one's current and future inclinations and how most effectively to satisfy them. There may be reasons for acting which do not correspond to one's felt inclinations, and there may be inclinations one has sufficient reason to suppress and not just for the sake of satisfying other inclinations. The point of view of the rational agent in deliberation, then, is that of one who presumes not only that he can act against, or without, inclination but also that he may have good reason to. He may grant, with Kant, that once he acts (even 'against inclination'), a scientist can in principle 'explain' his behavior by reference to his psychological states. But, as deliberator, he faced the different task of finding the best reasons for acting, and even the liveliest awareness of what he feels inclined to do would not settle this issue for him.

To say that the deliberator presumes that he can act 'against or without inclination' is perhaps misleading, in a way that makes the point seem less plausible than it is. If one acts against inclination, or in the absence of inclination, in the relevant sense, this need not mean that the best phenomenological explanation is that 'he did it though all the while he felt neither disposition to do so nor aversion to not doing so.' That would be puzzling, and would also run counter to what Kant says about the feeling of 'respect' for law.[26] The basic idea might be put this way: in acting for good reason but against or without inclination, one of course feels disposed to act as one does; but one does not acknowledge that there is good reason to act because one has such a disposition or because of any other inclination. Rather, when one acts against (or in the absence of) inclination, the felt disposition is seen as an acknowledgment of the reasons, not the basis for the reasons. When, for example, I forego the temptation to eat the piece of pie which someone else has been saving, I do feel averse to eating it but the reason I acknowledge is not that I have a feeling of aversion but that the pie belongs to someone else. I make sense of my aversion by reference to my judgment that my eating the pie would be unreasonable; and I do not justify the judgment that taking the pie is unreasonable by saying that the aversion felt stronger than the temptation.

Kant's position here runs counter to many familiar contemporary accounts of practical reason, but I suspect it is deeply rooted in common sense thinking. In the *Groundwork* the idea is pervasive, and in particular it is implicit in the argument that rational wills have negative freedom. This is said to be a capacity of rational agents to will independently of 'alien causes,' but the structure of the argument makes clear that the point is not merely the irrelevance of determinism but the capacity to will without the rationale being to satisfy inclination. In other words, it is not just that we treat our choices as not causally determined; it is that we treat the task of rational deliberation as not always settled by information about our inclinations.

3 Reasoning with autonomy: positive aspects of freedom

Two related features of the wider notion of practical reason are inherent in the claims (1) that a rational will cannot be 'lawless,' (2) that it has laws that are self-imposed but also rooted in its rational nature. Here interpretation is more difficult, and the view-point more controversial.

(1) The remark that the will cannot be lawless is made in the context of the argument to show that any negatively free rational will must have autonomy.[27] A negatively free will is conceived as one independent from causal determinism and from motivation by inclination, in the senses we have considered. The question then arises: how are we to understand attributions of behavior to a will, given that we have set aside both causal explanations and the rationale to satisfy inclinations? In saying that the agent willed the behavior, rather than merely that it occurred, we must have in mind some other sort of rationale we attribute to the agent. That is, the agent must be acting for reasons, even though the reason is not to satisfy inclinations. Suppose a particular reason is given, e.g., 'to keep my word' or 'to save a person's life.' If this really is a reason, there must be some general rational principle supporting the conclusion that one ought to keep one's word, or save a life, in the circumstances. When we cite the facts of the situation as 'reasons,' this is at best a partial statement of the rationale; we need also the principle of rationality according to which it follows that, given those facts, one has a reason.

The one general principle of practical reason we have considered so far, the Hypothetical Imperative, will not suffice here: for, by hypothesis, our agent's rationale is not to satisfy an inclination. The Hypothetical Imperative says, 'If you will an end for which your act is a necessary means, then you ought to do the act (or give up the end)'; but without inclination, or *some other sort of reason*, to will the end, the Hypothetical Imperative is inapplicable. There must be, then, some other sort of reason, independent of inclination and the Hypothetical Imperative, if (as we have supposed) rational wills can exercise the independence defined as negative freedom. And a full statement of that reason, or rationale, must include the principle of practical reason which justifies the conclusion about the particular case. Such a principle would be a 'law' in Kant's sense, i.e., a principle that any rational agent necessarily accepts (and, if fully rational, follows).

Note that the will is 'lawful,' on this account, not by virtue of being controlled by some mysterious noumenal 'causes' instead of natural causes. Rather, it is lawful in the sense that there are practical laws, or rational principles of conduct, to guide its choices. At least sometimes we can act from inclination or not; but when we choose not to, the choice is not thereby without reason. It is based on reasons of a different kind.

(2) Kant concludes from the above that, if they have negative freedom rational wills have *autonomy*.[28] This is said to be the property of 'being a law unto itself,' a phrase that suggests arbitrary, unconstrained choice, but one which must be understood along with Kant's repeated insistence that the laws come from one's 'rational nature.' The background, of course, in Kant's view that we, as human beings, have both a rational and a sensible nature and that, in some sense, the rational is more truly ourselves while the inclinations of sensibility are 'alien.'[29] This raises deep questions about personal identity which I set aside here; but we may be able nonetheless to discern some of the practical implications.

The metaphor of 'governing oneself,' by having one's reason 'legislate' laws to one's lower nature, is one that Kant obviously found captivating. Its roots, of course, can be traced back through a tradition to Plato. In Kant the picture appears in a bewildering variety of contexts: (a) the conscientious agent checking his maxims by trying to 'will' them as 'universal laws,'[30] (b) the 'legislator' in the 'kingdom of ends' making laws for himself (and other rational agents) as 'subjects,'[31] (c) the ideal 'social contract' underlying principles of the *Rechtslehre*,[32] and finally (d) the general idea of rational 'autonomy' as 'being a law unto oneself.'[33] Though related, these various uses of the metaphor need to be cashed out in somewhat different ways, and it is important to keep in mind that here our concern is with the last, most general use.

Because the law-giving in question is attributed to our 'rational nature,' the point is obviously not the 'existentialist' idea that individuals must simply choose, or make-up, what is to be a basic reason for them. Kant's view of the commands of a will with autonomy is no doubt modeled on traditional views of the commands of God, with the innovation that now the legislative will is attributed to each rational agent and not exclusively to an external being. But the model is more nearly Aquinas's God than Ockham's or Descartes': that is, it is a will that acknowledges what is rational and commands accordingly (with sanctions), rather than a 'voluntarist's' will that 'invents' the standards, making the non-rational rational by choice alone. Autonomy means identifying with rational constraints, not seeing them as imposed by others or as something we could give up without ceasing to be ourselves; but it does not mean we 'voluntarily' choose to commit ourselves to them in the way we might choose to accept the rules of a club, a church, or a private code.

The best clue to what Kant means by 'being a law unto oneself' is perhaps the list of moral theories which he declares to be based on the notion that the human will is heteronomous: perfectionism, divine command theories, hedonism, and moral sense theories.[34] In each case, Kant charges, something 'alien' to our rational wills is treated as the ground of moral obligation. In divine command theories, this is most obvious: we are under obligation because someone else, God, so commands. In hedonistic theories, of both egoistic and universalistic varieties, the basic principles are derived from common human dispositions but not from our rationality. The objection at this point is not that 'Always maximize pleasure (your own or everyone's)' is *incompatible* with morality or rationality; it is that the principle is not itself a (necessary) principle of rational choice and that discovery of a universal human inclination to follow it would not make it so. In discussing the Hypothetical Imperative, Kant has already implied that 'Maximize satisfaction of inclination' is not a principle of rationality; and so, even if it is a fact (as Epicurus and later utilitarians say) that all human beings are disposed to promote pleasure (their own or everyone's), this by itself would not show that it was rational to follow the hedonistic principles. Whether or not their conclusions are warranted, the arguments of hedonistic moral theories start from an unwarranted assumption: that we can determine what is rational to do by simple inference from generalizations about our non-rational dispositions.

The same objection, I take it, applies to any 'moral sense' theory which tries to derive the truth (and so, for Kant, the rational force) of moral judgments entirely from empirical facts about how human beings are disposed to feel when facing a moral problem. The objection, oddly enough, is one in which Hume would concur, for Hume agrees that moral judgments get neither truth nor *rational* force from moral sentiment.

The upshot is that, even in the moral sphere, Kant refuses to recognize as inherently rational any of the familiar substantive principles which philosophers labeled 'Kantian' sometimes offer to counteract egoistic reasoning. The fact that an act would cause another pleasure, or prevent him pain, is not by itself a reason for doing it. There are no objective 'intrinsic values' which rational agents necessarily aim to maximize; and, contrary to Nagel, the bare fact that I could prevent someone pain by warning him that there is a bee on his hamburger is not, without further argument, a reason to warn him.[35] Similarly, 'perfectionist' principles that urge the realization of various (non-rational) human capacities have no force unless willed by rational agents with autonomy.

There is one further feature of rational autonomy that is presupposed in Kant's arguments and so must be understood as part of the idea that its laws have their source in our common nature as rational beings. This is the notion that the standards, or ends, of rational autonomous wills are not relative to individuals in a certain sense. The sense, however, is not merely weak universalizability: that is, that a reason for one person is a reason for anyone exactly (or relevantly) like that person in exactly (or relevantly) similar circumstances. Nor is this the extreme impartialist thesis that rational agents count the *welfare* of each person as of equal weight in their deliberations as their own. The point, I think, is more limited than the latter and more substantial than the former: namely, there is something about our common rational nature, no matter who possesses it, that provides special reasons to all rational agents with autonomy. Thus principles which state the reasons for an agent need not be relativized to features of that individual agent, as in 'One has a reason to promote *one's own* pleasure (self-realization, knowledge, etc.).'[36]

The claim here is a strong and controversial one, imputing to all rational agents a limited rational concern that is not self-regarding; but it is important that the claim not be confused with the more familiar contemporary impartialism that gives equal prima facie weight to the (equally intense, etc.) desires or satisfactions of all persons. Like that more extreme impartialism, Kant holds that what is a reason for an agent is not always relativized to the agent, as in 'A has a reason to X because X does . . . for A, gets A . . ., or promotes A's. . . .' But the reasons in question are not, ultimately and without further argument, the fact that a pleasure will be promoted, a pain averted, civilization advanced, or any purported 'intrinsic value' other than what is inherently a concern to all rational agents as such.

4 Transition to morality: identifying the principles of rational autonomy

So far our account of rational autonomy may seem disappointingly abstract, negative, and 'formal,' though those familiar with the *Groundwork* (and Kant's other works) should not be surprised. The large question remains: how from these bare beginnings can one derive any substantive guidance in deciding what to do? The answer, if there is one, must lie in Kant's attempt to show that the various formulations of the Categorical Imperative express the sort of reasons, or guiding principles, that any rational agent with autonomy, as such, must acknowledge. Since I believe that Kant's attempt to prove this for his famous first formulation is a failure, resting on a deep confusion, I will conclude with some brief remarks on one of two other formulations that may be more promising.

One formula states that 'humanity,' or our rational nature, is an end in itself.[37] I take this to mean that rational agency itself is something of 'unconditional and incomparable worth,' which implies that each has a reason to preserve, develop, exercise, and 'honor' rational capacities in himself and others.[38] The *Metaphysics of Morals* is filled with examples of how Kant thought this principle yields practical guidelines, and the *Groundwork* offers some sketchy arguments for thinking that the principle is one to which any rational agent with autonomy is committed.

We might paraphrase one of these arguments as follows:[39] A value (or 'end') that any rational agent (with autonomy) would acknowledge, whatever his or her desires, is living as a rational agent. We recognize this first and most obviously in thinking of our own agency, but on reflection we see that what we value, by virtue of our rational nature rather than self-love, is the rational agency rather than the fact that it is our own. Because our particular ends are chosen by us, as rational agents, we count these particular ends as having at least some impersonal (though for Kant still 'relative') value, i.e., as worthy of consideration in others' deliberations as well as our own. This reflects an attitude, or point of view, which sees each rational agent as a source of value which other rational agents must take into account, not because of *what* is valued but because it is valued by a rational agent like ourselves. Moreover, in valuing rational agency in ourselves we attribute a special (impersonal) importance to our existence, development, and opportunities to pursue the system of ends we choose; we do not simply count these as important *to us* but see them as worthy of the concern of any rational agent. But in acknowledging this impersonal worth of rational agency in our own case, because of what it is and not because it is ours, we can see that we are committed to the worth of rational agency in others as well. Thus we cannot be indifferent to anything that affects the existence and development of other rational agents and their opportunities to pursue the system of ends they choose.

This argument does not imply that we value the happiness or the particular ends of others in *just the same way* we value our own; for even in valuing our own rational agency, as rational agents, we are not claiming that others should give equal regard to our happiness or our particular ends. Because we are rational agents, and not just because we want happiness or particular ends, we (supposedly) see our own rational agency as an 'end in itself,' i.e., as something worthy of respect and concern by all rational agents. But this valuing of rational agency in ourselves (where it first and most obviously invokes our respect) is not the same as valuing our happiness, or the satisfaction of our particular ends; it is the more limited attribution of an (impersonal) worth to our living as rational agents, and so primarily to our existence, rational development, and opportunities to exercise our rational agency. We do value our own happiness and particular projects, of course, but this is not the primary value we claim and acknowledge by virtue of being rational agents. Thus when we acknowledge, as we must, the same value of rational agency in others, what we grant as important *per se* is not their happiness or particular projects but their existence, development, and opportunity to live as rational agents. The happiness and projects of others get whatever importance they have to the rational agent derivatively: they are important in some cases because the agent happens to care for others but, even when this is absent, they are important because we cannot show respect for the rational agency of others without giving some weight to the projects they choose to pursue.

The contention that rational agents with autonomy necessarily value rational agency *per se* is a controversial one, of course; but at least it should not be confused with the even stronger claim that preserving and developing rational agency is a value to all rational agents no matter how rational agents are conceived. The argument sketched above presupposes we are addressing rational *agents with autonomy,* that is, rational agents which have *some* reasons, or rational commitments, not tied to inclinations or agent-relative concerns. To such agents

(assuming we all so conceive ourselves) Kant in effect argues by elimination: assume that there are such (impersonal) reasons for all rational
agents; we have seen that they are not the supposed 'intrinsic values' of
pleasure, etc.; so what else could they be but concern for rational agency
itself?

This can hardly convince anyone who professes to use narrower
means–end practical reasoning exclusively; nor, I think, is it meant to.
To convince those instrumentalists Kant needs to show that the point
of view of rational autonomy is, for all practical purposes, inescapable.
Kant has arguments to this effect in the *Groundwork*, though in the
second *Critique* he is content to rest the case on the unargued 'fact'
of moral consciousness. But, on either approach, the task of showing
that every deliberator must accept the point of view of rational
autonomy is distinct from the Kantian project which has been our
concern here: namely, to illuminate and draw the practical consequences from that rich but limited conception of rational autonomy
which Kant thought we all share.

To summarize: I have sketched some main features of Kant's theory
of practical reason, as I reconstruct it primarily from the *Groundwork*
but not, I think, as radically different from Kant's later ethical writings. My aim has not been to defend the theory, or even to establish
it as an interpretation; but I have made several main interpretive sugges-
tions. Among these are: (1) Non-moral practical reasoning is governed
by the Hypothetical Imperative, a principle which is analytic of ideal
rationality but is often violated. (2) The Hypothetical Imperative, as a
non-substantive and non-maximizing principle, is always compatible
with categorical moral principles, if there are any, and so non-moral
and moral reasoning do not conflict. (3) Kant argues that there is a
form of practical reasoning beyond hypothetical imperatives, and the
negative claim that this is independent of causes and inclinations does
not imply radical metaphysical views but rather expresses a widely held
view of what is relevant to practical deliberation. (4) Kant's positive
account of practical reasoning beyond hypothetical imperatives is again
not a metaphysical story about non-natural laws that explain (moral)
behavior but rather a claim about a special sort of practical reasons we
acknowledge. (5) These reasons are in a sense impersonal, or not relativized to the agent in the manner of familiar means–ends principles,
but they imply a more limited impersonal regard for others than many
contemporary theories of impartial reason.[40] (6) The rational standards
are 'self-imposed' but not in a sense that implies that we arbitrarily or
even 'voluntarily' commit ourselves to them. (7) One principle which
is supposed to express these special reasons is the formula that one

ought to treat humanity as an end in itself, and this conveys the idea that the existence of rational agency in anyone gives us special reasons which are not self-regarding but also not primarily concerned with the happiness of others.

To many this will not be a congenial theory, but it represents Kant's deep struggle to avoid what he regarded as two major temptations for theories of reason: first, treating reason as essentially self-regarding and, second, calling substantive values 'principles of reason' without reason.

Notes

1 *Groundwork of the Metaphysics of Morals*, tr. H.J. Paton (New York: Harper & Row), pp. 80–81. Hereafter this will be abbreviated 'G' and references to the Prussian Academy edition will follow in brackets, e.g., here [413–14].

2 See *Critique of Practical Reason* (hereafter 'CPrR'), tr. L.W. Beck (New York: Liberal Arts Press), 'The Concept of an Object of Pure Practical Reason,' pp. 59ff [58ff].

3 G 80 [412], 114 [446].

4 G 80 [412–13].

5 David Hume, *A Treatise of Human Nature*, ed. L.A. Selby-Bigge (Oxford: Clarendon Press), esp. pp. 458, 463.

6 G 80 [412], 95 [427].

7 This is especially clear in the primary context of practical reasoning, which is not third-person judgments but first-person deliberation in which the yet undecided agent tries to find the most rational option. In this context, practical reason searches for the best rationale, which is obviously different from trying to find an elusive inner something that will have moved one when one acts.

8 The ideas in this paragraph are spelled out more fully in my paper. 'The Hypothetical Imperative,' *The Philosophical Review*, vol. LXXXII, no. 4, 1973.

9 The clearest case of this is Robert Paul Wolff's commentary, *The Autonomy of Reason* (New York), 1975.

10 From a seminar at the University of California, Los Angeles, about 1975.

11 G 84–5 [417–18].

12 This point may be controversial and certainly needs more discussion, with specific reference to the texts; but I think it is the most plausible reconstruction of Kant's view into the contemporary terminology of 'reasons for action' (which is not Kant's). The idea is not, of course, that we view the choice to indulge a (harmless) pleasure or not with the same detached indifference as we might view the choice between two equally nourishing but tasteless foods; we care, and set our ends accordingly, thereby acquiring a reason (relative to the end). Also, especially when there is no reason not to indulge the pleasure, the agent's awareness of it will no doubt figure into the *explanation* ('reason why') the agent acted. But when the issue is what counts as a good reason in *deliberation*, for the agent who has not yet formed his ends, the alternative view (that inclination per se gives at

least prima facie reason to act) has implications I think Kant would not accept. For example, one who decides not to indulge an inclination (say, for pleasure) in the absence of reasons to the contrary would be thereby choosing irrationally, not merely in a strange manner hard to comprehend. And, more seriously, the *prima facie* force of many intense inclinations would have to be weighed against moral considerations to determine what is rational to do, and thus generating potential conflicts between moral and non-moral reasoning. Some specify that inclinations must be 'informed,' or capable of surviving appropriate reflection, in order for them to have *prima facie* rational force; but, unless the reflective process includes the Kantian 'setting oneself an end,' I doubt that Kant would count even reflection-surviving inclinations as necessarily providing the deliberator with normative reasons for acting.

To be sure, inclinations may explain why the agent sets the end, and the description of the end, or object of acting, may refer to the inclination (as in 'my end was to get pleasure'); but the choice of an end is not rationally required by an inclination, even in the absence of contrary inclinations. Oddly enough, despite the frequent claim that desires are reasons for Hume, I think that Hume would agree on the point: for, on Hume's view, desires motivate but do not generate requirements of reason. A consequence of my interpretation, incidentally, is that reason does not always dictate what we should do: for when moral principles are silent and one has not yet chosen one's ends, no rational requirement follows from a full understanding of one's inclinations. And even after one chooses one's ends, if moral principles remain irrelevant, one always has a rational option of revising or abandoning the ends.

13 For sophisticated theories of this type see, for example, Richard Brandt's 'The Concept of Rational Action' and John C. Harsanyi's 'Basic Moral Decisions and Alternative Concepts of Rationality' in *Social Theory and Practice*, vol. 9, nos. 2–3 (1983): 143–64, 231–44.

14 G 83 [415].

15 See *The Metaphysical Principles of Virtue: Part II of the Metaphysics of Morals*, tr. James Ellington (Indianapolis, IN: Bobbs-Merrill), hereafter abbreviated 'MM II', pp. 38–39 [381–82], 42 [384–85], 50 [392].

16 Kant works with different notions of 'happiness' at different points, but the dominant idea in the *Groundwork* is the idea of the satisfaction of all one's inclinations. See G 67 [399], 73 [405], 85 [418], MM II 45 [388], 149 [480], and *Critique of Pure Reason*, tr. Norman Kemp Smith (New York: St. Martin's Press), 632 [A800/B828].

17 G 85–86 [418–19].

18 This is not to deny, of course, that the pursuit of happiness often conflicts with morality and, even in the best persons, must be constrained by moral principles. The point is that, when it conflicts with morality, the pursuit of happiness is not prescribed by reason.

19 Another, more obscure, line of argument in ch. 2 consists of a series of illuminating reformulations of the principle initially identified as the 'supreme principle of morality,' a procedure which supposedly enables us to see that this principle is 'the principle of autonomy,' i.e., a constraint on rational willing independent of the concern to do what serves one's ends. See G 89–108 [421–41].

20 See G 114–18ff [446–51]. A reconstruction of this argument is attempted in my paper 'Kant's Argument for the Rationality of Moral Conduct,' *Pacific Philosophical Quarterly*, 1986.

21 I take this to be at least part of Kant's point in saying that even in theoretical judgments we see ourselves as members of an 'intelligible world.' G 116 [448], 118–19 [451–52].

22 This is discussed more fully in my paper previously mentioned (in PPQ).

23 John Rawls, 'Kantian Constructivism in Moral Theory: The Dewey Lectures 1980,' *Journal of Philosophy*, vol. LXXVII, no. 9 (1980): 515–72.

24 The point that all human beings are committed to the standards of rational autonomy is so deep and pervasive in Kant's thought that no one would overlook it if it were not for certain confusing matters of terminology. Unfortunately the word 'autonomy' is not always understood, even by Kant himself, in exactly the same sense. The primary use, for example in the central arguments of chs. 2 and 3 of the *Groundwork*, refers to a property we attribute to all rational wills, and this is said to be the same property, differently conceived, as negative freedom. It implies a capacity to deliberate and act independently, in some sense, from natural causes and from motivation by inclinations; and, crucially, it entails commitment to rational standards of conduct beyond the means–end standards underlying hypothetical imperatives. All wills with autonomy of this primary sort 'make universal laws' in the metaphorical sense of 'legislators' in the 'kingdom of ends'; but they are not all so perfectly conscientious that they act only on maxims which they, in another sense, 'can will as universal laws.' Unfortunately, the words 'autonomy' and especially 'autonomous' have come to be used more narrowly to refer to persons, motives, and acts that fully exemplify Kant's moral ideals or, in other words, to refer only to what fully lives up to the rational commitments we all have as agents with autonomy in the primary sense. There is some ambivalence in Kant's usage, I think, which perpetuates the problem. But the underlying points seem clear enough: the commitment to rational standards beyond means–ends reasoning is inherent in all rational wills, but only the morally best, if any, manifest, express, or live up to these standards consistently.

25 G 114 [446].

26 G 68 [400], CPrR 74ff [72ff].

27 G 114 [446], CPrR 28 [29].

28 Ibid.

29 G 125–26 [457–58].

30 G 89ff [421ff].

31 G 100ff [433ff].

32 *The Metaphysical Elements of Justice: Part I of the Metaphysics of Morals*, tr. John Ladd (Indianapolis, IN: Bobbs-Merrill), p. 80f [315–16].

33 G 108 [440], 114 [446–47].

34 G 110ff [443ff] CPrR 41f [39f].

35 See Thomas Nagel, *The Possibility of Altruism*.

36 Like the extreme impartialist position, this implies that what is important to one person (by virtue of rational autonomy) is important to any other (by virtue of his rational autonomy); but this thing of importance is not welfare or any 'intrinsic value' that exists independently of rational agency. And, crucially, this important common concern is not describable

in self-referential terms. Thus, for example, the basic principle of rational autonomy cannot even be 'Do what most enhances your own rational agency,' even though this cites a value that we have as rational agents rather than one (like pleasure or welfare) which we have as human beings with desires.

37 95ff [427ff].
38 The interpretation is developed in my 'Humanity as an End in Itself,' *Ethics*, 91, 1980.
39 See G 96 [428–29].
40 For example, Thomas Nagel's *The Possibility of Altruism*, Alan Gewirth's *Reason and Morality*, Kurt Baier's *The Moral Point of View*, R. M. Hare's *Moral Thinking*, though important qualifications need to be noted. Donagan, Darwall, and Rawls, I think, have more limited impartialist theories.

KANT'S ANALYSIS OF OBLIGATION: THE ARGUMENT OF *GROUNDWORK* I*

Christine Korsgaard

1 The normativity of morality

One of the debates of recent moral philosophy concerns the question whether moral judgments express 'internal' or 'external' reasons.[1] According to internalists, if someone knows or accepts a moral judgment then she must have a motive for acting on it. The motive is part of the content of the judgment: the reason why the action is right is a reason *for doing it*. According to externalists, this is not necessarily so: there could be a case in which I understand both that and why it is right for me to do something, and yet have no motive *for doing it*. Since most of us believe that an action's being right is a reason for doing it, internalism seems more plausible. It captures one element of our sense that moral judgments have *normative* force: they are *motivating*. But some philosophers believe that internalism, if correct, would also impose a restriction on moral reasons. If moral reasons are to motivate, they must spring from an agent's personal desires and commitments.[2] This is unappealing, for unless the desires and commitments that motivate moral conduct are universal and inescapable, it cannot be required of everyone. And this leaves out the other element of our sense that moral judgments have normative force: they are *binding*. Some internalists, however, have argued that the force of internalism cuts the other way. If moral reasons must motivate, and I show you that an action is morally right, I have *ipso facto* provided you with a motive for doing it. Moral reasons motivate *because* they are perceived as binding.[3] A good person, according to these internalists, does the right thing because it is the right thing, or acts from the motive of duty.

Many of the moves in the contemporary debate were anticipated in the debate between the Rationalists and the Sentimentalists of the eighteenth century. At the center of their dispute was the notion of *obligation*, a term they used primarily to refer to the *normativity* of duty. The term 'obligation' is a source of confusion, because 'an obligation' is sometimes used loosely as synonym for 'a duty,' a required action. But 'obligation' refers not so much to the action as to the *requiredness* of the action, to its normative pull. We say that we *feel* obliged, or are *under* an obligation, to express our sense that the claims of morality are claims *on us*. The idea that moral conduct is obligatory, like the idea that moral judgments express internal reasons, is intended to capture both elements of the normativity of morality: its power both to motivate and to bind. And the eighteenth century moralists, like contemporary internalists, ran into a difficulty when they tried to combine these two elements.

Rationalist moral philosophers criticized their opponents for not being able to explain how we are *bound* to do our duty. Samuel Clarke, for instance, levels this complaint against what he takes to be the view of Hobbes: that moral laws are the positive laws of a sovereign (possibly God) who has the power to enforce them. Either we are obliged to obey the sovereign, Clarke urges, in which case obligation is prior to positive law, or there is no real obligation at all.[4] According to later Rationalists, Sentimentalism is subject to the very same objection. The Sentimentalist Francis Hutcheson, for example, believes that God has provided us with a moral sense which causes us to approve benevolence and deem it virtuous. But Rationalists argue that providing us with a sense which endues certain motives with a moral quality is just a way for God to create morality by positive institution. Hutcheson admits as much, for he says that God could have given us a malice-approving moral sense had He so chosen. It is not because benevolence is obligatory in itself, but because God is benevolent, and approving benevolence is good for us, that God has caused us to approve it.[5] But the Rationalist Richard Price complains that this makes morality a kind of illusion. We may indeed have moral 'perceptions,' but unless what we perceive is a rightness that is really *in* the action, the action is not really right, and so not really obligatory, after all. Price says that moral sense theory implies 'That there being nothing intrinsically proper or improper, just or unjust; there is nothing *obligatory*. . . .'[6] The rightness of an action cannot be something extrinsic to it, projected onto it, like a secondary quality, by the operation of a sense. The action must be *intrinsically* obligatory if it is obligatory at all.

But Sentimentalists, in turn, criticized Rationalists for not being able to explain how we are *motivated* to do our duty. According to Rationalists, rightness is a real property of an action or of the relation of an action to its situation, discerned by reason. But the bare grasp of a rational truth seems to have no motivational power. Hume famously complains:

> ... men are often govern'd by their duties, and are deter'd from some actions by the opinion of injustice, and impell'd to others by that of obligation.
>
> Since morals, therefore, have an influence on the actions and affections, it follows, that they cannot be deriv'd from reason; and that because reason alone, as we have already prov'd, can never have any such influence.[7]

The problem was to find an account of obligation that combines the two elements of normativity: motivation and bindingness.

This problem was inherited by Kant. A form of Rationalism was the dominant ethical theory in Germany, and Kant was a Rationalist by training as well as by temperament. But he was also a great admirer of the British Sentimentalists.[8] As early as the so-called Prize Essay, Kant identifies obligation (*Verbindlichkeit*) as the 'primary concept' of ethics.[9] (PE 298/31)[10] There, he argues that the project of moral philosophy is to show how there can be obligations, understood as unconditional 'oughts' which both bind and motivate. It is easy to see how an action can be necessary to achieve a certain end, but for an unconditional 'ought' the end itself must also be necessary. (PE 298–299/31–32) At this point in his career Kant endorses the Wolffian ethical principles 'Do the most perfect possible by you' and 'Do not do that which would hinder the greatest possible perfection realisable through you' as the 'primary *formal ground* of all obligation.' (PE 299/32) But he levels against these principles a charge later to be levelled against his own view by Hegel: by themselves, they constitute an empty formalism, from which 'no particularly definite obligation flows.' (PE 299/33) The content of morality, Kant speculates, must be determined by the operation of unanalyzable feelings. He praises Hutcheson's idea of the moral sense as a possible source for this content. (PE 300/34) But the Prize Essay's discussion of ethics ends inconclusively. Kant says, '. . . it has still to be discovered in the first place whether the faculty of knowledge or feeling . . . exclusively decides the primary principles of practical philosophy.' (PE 300/34)

By Kant's critical period this uneasy alliance between Rationalism and Sentimentalism is over, and Rationalism has won the day. The problem of obligation, like any philosophical problem, must be solved in two stages. Since the concepts of morality are concepts of pure reason, we must start with a metaphysical account showing how pure reason generates these concepts and so what they (analytically) contain. But the claim that a concept of pure reason applies to the world is always synthetic. Kant cannot, like earlier Rationalists, simply insist that a rational moral order is intuited in the nature of things. Dogmatic metaphysics has no more place in ethics than in theoretical philosophy. So we must turn to a critical synthesis to show that the concepts of morality apply to that part of the world to which they purport to apply: to us. The first step, and the one I am concerned with in this paper, shows what obligation is, that is to say, what the concept of obligation contains. The second, or synthetical, step shows that the concept has application, that is, that we have obligations.[11]

In *Groundwork* II, Kant appears to think there is no difficulty about analyzing the concept of obligation. An obligation would be prescribed by a categorical imperative, and analyzing that idea leads us immediately to the Formula of Universal Law. Kant says:

> . . . we will first inquire whether *the mere concept* of a categorical imperative does not also furnish the formula containing the proposition which alone can be a categorical imperative. . . .
>
> . . . if I think of a categorical imperative, *I know immediately what it contains.* For since the imperative contains besides the law only the necessity that the maxim should accord with this law, while the law contains no condition to which it is restricted, there is nothing remaining in it except the universality of law as such to which the maxim of the action should conform. . . .
>
> There is, therefore, only one categorical imperative. It is: Act only according to that maxim by which you can at the same time will that it should become a universal law.
>
> (G 420–421/38–39; my emphases)

In fact, the analysis given in these cryptic passages is almost identical to the argument of *Groundwork* I.

In this paper my aim is to show how Kant's analysis of obligation, contained in the argument of *Groundwork* I, provides a solution to the problem of obligation that emerged from the controversy between Rationalism and Sentimentalism. In §2, I explain in more detail how the very concept of obligation generates a dilemma which is central to that controversy. The argument of *Groundwork* I, which I reconstruct in §3, shows the way out of this dilemma, and in so doing shows what sort of thing an obligation must be.

2 Hume's Dilemma

The argument of *Groundwork* I is an attempt to give what I shall call a 'motivational analysis' of the concept of a right action, in order to discover what that concept applies to, that is, which actions are right.[12] A motivational analysis is one that defines or identifies right actions in terms of the motives from which they are done by a morally good person.[13] The starting point of Kant's analysis is that a morally good action is one done from the motive of duty, or, we might say, a right action is one that is done by a morally good person *because it is right*. If the analysis works, Kant's achievement is to argue from this feature of right actions to a substantive moral principle which identifies which actions are right. In order to appreciate the importance of this achievement, we must consider it in light of an argument of Hume's which purports to show that exactly this cannot be done. This argument gives rise to what I shall call 'Hume's Dilemma.'

In opposition to the thesis that the sense of duty is the only moral motive, Hume argues that 'the first virtuous motive, which bestows a merit on any action, can never be a regard to the virtue of that action, but must be some other natural motive or principle.'[14] He points out that when we praise an action, and regard it as virtuous, we do so because we suppose that it has a virtuous motive. And:

> To suppose, that the mere regard to the virtue of the action, may be the first motive, which produc'd the action, and render'd it virtuous, is to reason in a circle. Before we can have such a regard, the action must be really virtuous; and the virtue must be deriv'd from some virtuous motive: And consequently the virtuous motive must be different from the regard to the virtue of the action. A virtuous motive is requisite to render an action virtuous. An action must be virtuous, before we can have a regard to its virtue. Some virtuous motive, therefore, must be antecedent to that regard.[15]

This argument can be recast in terms of rightness. Suppose that a right action is essentially, or by definition, one prompted by a morally good motive. To know which actions are right we must know which motives are good. But if the only good motive is the sense of duty, then we do seem to get the kind of circle Hume describes here. I want to do what is right and ask you what that is. You tell me: right actions are those done just because they are right. How can I derive any content from this? The objection may be taken to be a version of the 'empty formalism' objection, for the principle 'do the right thing because it is the right thing' appears to be an empty formalism. According to Hume, I need prior information about which acts are virtuous or right before I can do them with regard to their virtue or rightness. This shows the need for a moral sense, which will enable us to pick out the virtuous motives which make actions right. And the moral sense must approve motives other than the motive of duty, in order to get some content into the system. This leaves us with a dilemma. If we retain the thesis that it is motives that essentially make actions right, it apparently must be motives other than a regard for rightness itself. On the other hand, if we are to retain the thesis that the primary motive of virtuous action is the motive of duty, we must have some way of identifying or defining right actions which does not depend on their motives.

Sentimentalists opted for the motivational analysis, but at a cost. On Hume and Hutcheson's view, what renders actions virtuous is our approval of the natural affections which motivate them, and these are, accordingly, the 'first virtuous motives,' in Hume's phrase, to morally right action. This leads to two problems, one concerning the fact of obligation, and the other concerning the sense of obligation or motive of duty. I have already mentioned the problem concerning the fact of obligation. The action is supposed to be right because we approve its motive. But we might, had we been given a differently constituted moral sense, have approved a different motive and so a different action. So the action is not *necessarily* right. But then it is hard to see how it can be obligatory. An obligatory action is one that is binding – one that it is necessary to do. But if the action is not necessarily right, how can it be necessary to do? Contemporary internalists make a similar objection to externalism. If the moral motive is simply a natural affection such as benevolence, we can really have no obligations. For how can there be an obligation to have the motive which gives us obligations? And how can we be obliged to perform the actions, unless we are obliged to have the motive that produces them? If it is not necessary to have the motive, it is not really necessary to perform the actions.[16] Behind both objections is the idea that the rightness of an action cannot be extrinsically conferred. If it is *necessary* for us to have a benevolence-approving moral sense or benevolent motives, this must be because benevolent action is intrinsically obligatory. If benevolent action is not intrinsically obligatory, then neither an arbitrarily implanted moral sense nor dispensable natural affections can make it so.

As these arguments suggest, the idea that we are in fact obliged is naturally associated with the idea that we should act from the motive of obligation. To be obliged to the performance of an action is to believe that it is a right action and to find *in that fact* a kind of motivational necessity: the action is called for or demanded by the situation, and that is the motive for doing it. And this brings us to the second problem. If the 'first virtuous motives' are admirable natural motives, then the motive of obligation must play at best a secondary role.

Hutcheson, accordingly, dismisses most of what is said about obligation as 'confused' and 'obscure.'[17] When we say someone is morally obliged to an action we mean only that the moral sense approves the action: that there is *justifying* reason for it.[18] We are not talking about *exciting* or motivating reasons. The two parts of the normativity of morality, its power to bind, or justify, and its power to motivate, or excite, have separate sources. But, Hutcheson complains:

> Some farther perplex this subject by asserting, 'that the same reasons determining approbation ought also to excite to election.'[19]

Obviously he disagrees. A good action need not be motivated by the agent's approval of it. This does not mean that there are no actions to which we are motivated by moral approval. Hutcheson says:

> The prospect of the pleasure of self-approbation is indeed often a motive to choose one action rather than another; but this supposes the moral sense, or determination to approve, prior to the election.[20]

Hume's account of actions done from the motive of duty is similar:

> But may not the sense of morality or duty produce an action, without any other motive? I answer, It may: But this is no objection to the present doctrine. When any virtuous motive or principle is common in human nature, a person, who feels his heart devoid of that principle, may hate himself upon that account, and may perform the action without the motive, from a certain sense of duty, in order to acquire by practice, that virtuous principle, or at least, to disguise to himself, as much as possible, his want of it.[21]

In both accounts, the motive of obligation is reduced to a desire for self-approval. It is also reduced to a second-rate moral motive; action from spontaneous natural affection is more authentically virtuous.[22]

This is contrary to the widely-shared idea that obligation is central to moral experience, and that there are at least some actions which ought to be performed from the sense that they are obligatory. Now in our own century it has been argued that we should abandon these ideas about obligation. In her famous 1958 paper 'Modern Moral Philosophy,' Elizabeth Anscombe argued that the moral 'ought' and 'obligation' are specifically modern notions that classical philosophers like Aristotle did very well without. Anscombe claims that these ideas are naturally associated with a divine law conception of ethics, and, in the absence of that conception, lack sense.[23] Similar charges have been made more recently by Bernard Williams in the last chapter of his book *Ethics and the Limits of Philosophy*.[24] But Anscombe and, although to a lesser extent, also Williams, share an important assumption with their Sentimentalist predecessors, for both tend to think that the primary force of saying that I am obliged to do something is that I will be judged, punished, blamed, or will blame myself, if I do not.[25] This emphasis is characteristic of Sentimentalism, which constructs morality from the standpoint of the spectator or judge, taking the affections of approval and disapproval as the source of our most fundamental moral conceptions. For a Sentimentalist, the idea of obligation can only arise by turning disapproval against the self.[26] For a Rationalist, however, the focus on obligation comes from an agent-centered or deliberative perspective, not from that of the moral judge. The primary deliberative force of saying 'I am obliged to do this' is not 'I will blame myself if I do not' but 'my judgment that it is right impels me to do this.'[27] And this is at least related to an older thought, which *is* found in the classical philosophers. Aristotle's person of practical wisdom does the virtuous action for its own sake and *for the sake of the noble* (το καλόν).[28] He is moved to act by an ethical quality, a moral beauty and nobility, which he apprehends in the action. He does not merely act on some spontaneous natural affection which sideline judges applaud.[29] And this element of moral action – this feature of how it looks from the agent's point of view – essentially drops out of Sentimentalism.

This had a great deal to do, I believe, with keeping ethical Rationalism alive in the eighteenth century. On many points, Hutcheson and Hume's attacks on early Rationalism were effective, and later Rationalists, such as John Balguy and Richard Price, particularly admired Hutcheson.[30] But the idea of obligation and its connection to motivation was captured better by Clarke's ethical system than by either Sentimentalist or Hobbesian views. In describing right actions as 'fit to be done,' 'reasonable,' 'proportionate,' Clarke tries to capture the sense that right actions are called for or demanded by their situations, that they have a kind of rational necessity comparable to the necessity

of demonstrable truth.[31] He argues that 'the original *Obligation* of all
... is the eternal *Reasons* of Things'[32] and that the moral motive is
the sense of this obligation:

> For the Judgment and Conscience of a Man's own Mind,
> concerning the Reasonableness and Fitness of the thing, that
> his Actions should be conformed to such or such a Rule
> or Law; is the truest and formallest *Obligation*; even more
> properly and strictly so, than any opinion whatsoever of the
> Authority of the Giver of a Law, or any Regard he may have
> to its Sanction by Rewards and Punishments.[33]

Increasingly, as the eighteenth century progresses, we find philosophers
on both sides of the debate working to combine the best insights of
Sentimentalism with a more Rationalistic account of obligation.[34]

But Rationalism too has a cost, so long as Hume's argument is
accepted. For Hume's argument makes it appear that the idea that the
motive of duty is the primary motive to right action can be maintained
only at the expense of the idea that right actions are defined essentially in terms of good motives. Instead, the Rationalist must hold that
rightness is in the nature of the actions required. As Price puts it:

> ... all actions, undoubtedly, have a *nature*. That is, *some char-
> acter* certainly belongs to them, and somewhat there is to be
> *truly* affirmed of them. This may be, that some of them are
> right, others wrong. But if this is not allowed; if no actions
> are, *in themselves*, either right or wrong, ... it follows, that,
> in themselves, they are all indifferent.[35]

Since that is unacceptable, we must conclude that 'right and wrong
are real characters of *actions*.'[36] This, of course, removes any difficulty
about doing actions with regard to their rightness. If the rightness is
in the action, we can certainly do it for the sake of that rightness. But
now the Rationalist is saddled with the view that rightness is (to speak
anachronistically) a non-natural property, inherent in the actions, and
intuited by reason. In this way, Rationalism seems to entangle us in a
metaphysical moral realism, as well as an epistemological intuitionism,
which are both unpalatable. This will in particular be an objection for
Kant, since his project forbids the uncritical assumption that necessary
principles may be found, by rational intuition, to hold in the nature
of things. And, although the Rationalists rejected the empiricist theory
of reason from which it follows that reason cannot motivate, they had

no account of *how* we can be motivated by rational truths to put in its place. The Rationalists saw that obligation is only possible in one way: the perception of the bindingness of the right action must be what moves us. But instead of explaining how this is possible, they simply insisted that it is.

In England things got worse instead of better. In our own century, W.D. Ross defended intuitionism by an argument similar to Hume's. In the opening pages of *The Right and the Good*, Ross attacks the possibility of a motivational analysis of rightness. When we say that an act proceeds from a good motive, we are saying that it is morally good. So to say that rightness admits of a motivational analysis is to say that 'right' means 'morally good.'[37] But Ross says that he can show that this is wrong, or, as he startlingly puts it: 'that nothing that ought to be done is ever morally good.'[38] One of his arguments goes this way. Those who 'hold that our duty is to act from a certain motive' usually hold that the motive in question is the sense of duty. But:

> . . . if the sense of duty is to be my motive for doing a certain act, it must be the sense that it is my duty to do that act. If, therefore, we say 'it is my duty to do act *A* from the sense of duty', this means 'it is my duty to do act *A* from the sense that it is my duty to do act *A*'. And here the whole expression is in contradiction with a part of itself. The whole sentence says 'it is my duty to-do-act-*A*-from-the-sense-that-it-is-my-duty-to-do-act-*A*.' But the latter part of the sentence implies that what I think is that it is my duty to-do-act-*A* simply.[39]

Probably feeling that this is not perspicuous, Ross reiterates:

> Again, suppose that I say to you 'it is your duty to do act *A* from the sense of duty'; that means 'it is your duty to do act *A* from the sense that it is your duty to do act *A*.' Then I think that it is your duty to act from a certain motive, but I suggest that you should act under the supposition that it is your duty to do a certain thing, irrespective of motive, i.e. under a supposition which I must think false since it contradicts my own.
>
> The only conclusion that can be drawn is that our duty is to do certain things, not to do them from the sense of duty.[40]

This argument, like Hume's, turns on the idea that you cannot do your duty from the motive of duty until you know, independently, what your duty is. So far, like Hume's, it leaves it open that it could have been our duty to act from certain motives other than the motive of duty. But Ross has another argument which he thinks disallows any moral requirement on motives. This argument turns on the principle that 'ought implies can,' which Ross endorses. He says:

> It is not the case that I can by choice produce a certain motive (whether this be an ordinary desire or the sense of obligation) in myself at a moment's notice, still less that I can at a moment's notice make it effective in stimulating me to act.[41]

Therefore, Ross concludes, it cannot be the case that what I ought to do is act from certain motives.

Like earlier Rationalists, Ross concludes that rightness must simply be a property of certain actions. But Ross has a much more difficult time explaining the normative force of rightness than his predecessors. For Clarke, Price, and Balguy were all what we should now call internalists.[42] They believed that the perception of an action as right, or, what they took to be the same thing, obligatory, *is* a motive to do it. So the problem Ross notices in this last argument, that we cannot muster the sense of obligation at a moment's notice, does not arise for them. As Price says:

> When we are conscious that an action is *fit* to be done, or that it *ought* to be done, it is not conceivable that we can remain *uninfluenced*, or want a *motive* to action. It would be to little purpose to argue much with a person, who would deny this; or who would maintain that the *becomingness* or *reasonableness* of an action is no reason *for* doing it; and the *immorality* or *unreasonableness* of an action, no reason *against* doing it. An affection or inclination to rectitude cannot be separated from the view of it.[43]

Whereas Ross, following Prichard, is an externalist.[44] Like some internalists, Ross and Prichard think that a good person does the right thing 'because it is the right thing.' But Ross and Prichard think of the motive of duty as something like a desire that takes right action for its object, not as something that is involved in the very grasp of the fact that the action is right. So like Hutcheson, Ross in effect separates the justifying reason – the fact that the action is right – from the motivating reason – the desire to do what is right. And since this 'desire' might simply fail to be present, it cannot be our duty to act from it. All we can say is that acting from it is morally good. This means that for Ross, the fact that something is right only becomes a reason *for action*, in the sense of a motive, when the desire to do what is right happens to be on the scene to interest us in it. Furthermore, Ross denies that a right action need be in any way good. For, he argues, if someone does a right action from a bad or indifferent motive, that can at best be instrumentally good.[45] There is no guarantee that it will even be that, for 'right' neither means 'productive of good consequences' (since 'right' is unanalyzable) nor has it ever been shown to be coincident with that property.[46] So a right action is not necessarily instrumentally good, and according to Ross, it has no intrinsic value. What has value, says Ross, 'is the doing of the right act because it is right.'[47] But rightness by itself 'is not a form of value at all.'[48] By itself, then, rightness has no normative force. This makes it clear why Ross must be an externalist. Since rightness is not a value, the desire to do what is right is not a response to a value. Nor does it seem, therefore, to be an especially rational motive. Like the natural affections favored by Sentimentalists, it is merely a motive we happen to have. So rightness by itself neither motivates nor binds, nor are we bound to the desire to do what is right by any tie of reason or duty. Thus it turns out that, for Ross, the whole normative force of rightness springs from the supposed intrinsic value of acting from a certain motive, which we simply happen to have.

3 The Argument of *Groundwork* I

In the Preface to the *Groundwork*, Kant says that his method in the first part of the book will be 'to proceed analytically from common knowledge to the determination of its supreme principle.' (G 392/8) Specifically, *Groundwork* I seeks the principle behind 'common rational knowledge of morals.' (G 393/9) Because he is analyzing common knowledge, Kant starts from an idea which he expects the reader, once he recognizes it, to accept: that nothing is unconditionally valuable except a good will. Whenever we believe we have witnessed the exercise of such a will, we think we have seen an action that has a special kind of value: value that is independent of 'what it effects or accomplishes,' and so, unconditional. (G 394/10) In order to discover the principle of morality, or of unconditionally good action, we need to discover what principle a good will acts on.

The notion of duty includes that of a good will, since the notion of duty is the notion of a good will operating under 'certain subjective restrictions and hindrances.' (G 397/13) Therefore, Kant proposes to look at cases in which we should say that a person acted 'from duty' in order to discover the principle of action which characterizes a good will. He proceeds to distinguish three kinds of motivation. One may act from duty (do the right thing because it is the right thing), from direct inclination (perform an action because one enjoys it), or from indirect inclination (perform an action as a means to a further end). The first of Kant's four examples concerns a merchant who refrains from overcharging hapless customers because a good reputation helps business. This is an example of *indirect* inclination. We are unlikely to confuse such an action with an action from duty, Kant says,

> For it is easily decided whether an action in accordance with duty is performed from duty or for some selfish purpose. It is far more difficult to note this difference when the action is in accordance with duty and, in addition, the subject has a direct inclination to do it. (G 397/13)[49]

The other three examples are meant to illustrate this point: in each of them, we consider an action that one ought to do from duty, but that one may also be naturally inclined to do. For instance, Kant says, there are persons

> so sympathetically constituted that without any motive of vanity or selfishness they find an inner satisfaction in spreading joy, and rejoice in the contentment of others which they have made possible. (G 398/14)

Actions done on this basis are 'dutiful and amiable' and 'deserve praise and encouragement,' yet they do not evince the moral worth of the action done from duty. (G 398/14) To find the essence of duty and the good will, we must find the basis on which we distinguish these actions from those done from duty.

It is essential not to confuse the point of these examples with that of the honest merchant, who acts 'neither from duty nor from direct inclination, but only for a selfish purpose.' (G 397/14) According to a familiar but misguided reading of these passages, Kant holds a crudely hedonistic theory about all motives other than moral ones: he thinks that all actions except moral ones are done for the sake of one's own pleasure, and so are all equally selfish and without moral worth. So understood, Kant means to emphasize the *similarity* of actions done from direct inclination to those done from indirect inclination: their purpose, like the honest merchant's, is fundamentally selfish. But what

Kant clearly emphasizes here is the *difference* between direct and indirect inclination, and he says explicitly that the sympathetic person is 'without any motive of vanity or selfishness.' (G 398/14) He praises such actions as amiable and even 'dutiful' (*pflichtmäßig*), and he compares them to actions arising from the inclination to honor, which he elsewhere describes as a 'simulacrum' of morality. (IUH 26/21)[50] In fact, if we suppose that Kant holds a hedonistic theory of the *purpose* of all actions done from inclination, neither the distinction between direct and indirect inclination, nor (as I will show in a moment) the general argument of *Groundwork* I, makes much sense. Instead, Kant envisions the act of the sympathetic person as one done for its own sake. The pleasure a sympathetic person takes in helping is not an ulterior purpose, but is rather the reason why he makes *helping* his purpose.[51] Pleasure is not the purpose of his action, but the ground of the adoption of his purpose.

And the person who helps others from duty *also* does so for its own sake. The duty in question, as Kant makes clear elsewhere, is the duty to make the happiness of others one's *end*. (G 430/39; MPV 385/43; 388/46) It is because of this similarity of purpose that the sympathetic person's actions are characterized as 'dutiful' despite their lack of moral worth. We may say, going beyond Kant, that sympathy is a simulacrum of morality because it is an impulse inspired by the humanity in others, just as honor is a simulacrum of morality because it is a motive to obey certain strict laws of conduct for their own sake.[52] So the difference between the sympathetically helpful person and the dutifully helpful person does not rest in their purpose, but must lie elsewhere. This leads Kant to his 'second proposition,' namely, 'An action performed from duty does not have its moral worth in the purpose which is to be achieved through it but in the maxim by which it is determined.' (G 399/16)

To say that the worth of an action does not lie in its purpose, but in its maxim, is to say that its worth lies in the grounds on which the action along with its purpose has been chosen. Unfortunately, at this point in the argument Kant introduces the idea of a maxim with no preparation whatever – he simply says, in a footnote clumsily attached to its fifth usage, that a maxim is a 'subjective principle of volition.' (G 400n/17n) In fact, the idea of a maxim is essential to Kant's solution of the problem of obligation.

According to Kant it follows from the fact that a rational being acts 'under the idea of freedom' (G 448/66) that she acts for a reason or on a principle which she must regard as voluntarily adopted. The point here has to do with the way a rational being must think of her actions when she is engaged in deliberation and choice. When you make a choice, you do not view yourself as simply impelled into it by a desire or impulse. Instead, it is as if there were something over and above all of your desires, something that is *you*, and that decides which if any of your desires to gratify. You may of course *choose* to act on a desire, but that does not mean that you are impelled by it. It means you take this desire as a reason, or, in Kant's language, you make it your maxim to satisfy this desire. You may even choose to act on your strongest desire, but still that does not mean its strength is impelling you. It means that you are taking strength as a reason for choosing to satisfy one desire rather than another, making it your maxim to act on your strongest desire. Your maxim thus expresses what you take to be a reason for action; since reasons are derived from principles, or laws, it expresses your conception of a law.

Kant believes that all human action is purposive, and so that every maxim of action contains an end. (See G 427/45; 431/39; MV 381/38; MV 384–5/42; R 4/4) A maxim of action will therefore usually have the form 'I will do Action-A in order to achieve Purpose-P.' You will only act on that maxim if you also make it your maxim 'to achieve Purpose-P.' Since this maxim too must be adopted for a reason there are reasons for having purposes, which are again expressed in maxims. Although Kant does not emphasize this, it is perhaps easiest to think of maxims as hierarchically organized: 'I will do Action-A to achieve Purpose-P' is adopted on the basis of 'I will achieve Purpose-P' (plus a relevant hypothetical imperative); 'I will achieve Purpose-P' is in turn adopted on the basis of a further maxim that 'I will make it my purpose to have the things that I desire' or whatever it might be.

Therefore, when Kant says that the difference between the sympathetic person and the dutiful person rests in their maxims, the contrast he has in mind, is this: although the sympathetic person and the dutiful person both have the purpose of helping others, they have adopted this purpose on different grounds. The sympathetic person sees helping as something pleasant, and that is why he makes it his end. The morally worthy person sees helping as something called for, or necessary, and this is what motivates him to make it his end.[53]

A common complaint is that this suggests that a person who helps reluctantly and with a stiff upper lip is morally better than one who does so gladly and from spontaneous benevolence, and that this is both unintuitive and unattractive. This complaint, however, is based on a misunderstanding of Kant's point. There are three important things to remember. First, Kant makes it clear that the reason he contrasts cases of natural affection with cases where the motive of duty operates in the absence of natural affection is that the operation of the motive of duty is especially obvious in the latter kind of case. Despite the misunderstandings to which this strategy gives rise, the essential difference between the two people contrasted does not rest in whether the helping action is enjoyed. It rests in whether one helps only because of this enjoyment or because help is perceived as something it is necessary to give. Nothing prevents an action from being done from the motive of duty by someone in whom sympathy is also present. Actually, we must distinguish two cases here. There might be a person in whom sympathy serves as a supplementary or cooperating motive that provides needed support for the motive of duty. This person's motives are impure, in the sense developed in *Religion Within the Limits of Reason Alone*, and he would not, or not always, do the helping action when required if sympathy did not serve as a prop to duty. (R 24/29–30) This *does* decrease the person's moral worth. But another person in whom sympathy is present might be motivated entirely, or at least sufficiently, by the motive of duty, so that she would do the helping action even if sympathy were not present. This person has moral worth, yet her native sympathy will contribute to her enjoyment of the action.

However, a second point is even more important. Kant is talking here about the grounds on which a purpose is adopted and held. We must distinguish between the emotions, feelings, and desires which prompt us to *adopt* a purpose and those that *result from* the adoption of a purpose. Once you have adopted a purpose and become settled in its pursuit, certain emotions and feelings will naturally result. In particular, in ordinary circumstances the advancement or achievement of the purpose will make you happy, regardless of whether you adopted it originally from natural inclination or from duty. So a dutiful person, who after all really does value the happiness of others, will *therefore* take pleasure in making others happy.[54]

This is a point that Kant makes explicitly in his later ethical writings. For instance, in *The Metaphysical Principles of Virtue*, when Kant is explaining the duty of beneficence, he says:

> Beneficence is a duty. Whoever often exercises this and sees his beneficent purpose succeed comes at last really to love him whom he has benefited. When therefore it is said, 'Thou shalt love thy neighbor as thyself,' this does not mean you should directly (at first) love and through this love (subsequently) benefit him; but rather, 'Do good to your neighbor,' and this beneficence will produce in you the love of mankind (as a

readiness of inclination toward beneficence in general). (MV 402/61).

Of course you may wonder why then the dutiful person in Kant's *Groundwork* example does not enjoy the helping action. Kant suggests two scenarios. In one, the action is done by someone whose mind 'is clouded by a sorrow of his own which extinguished all sympathy with the lot of others.' (G 398/14) In the other, the person is 'by temperament cold and indifferent to the sufferings of others, perhaps because he is provided with special gifts of patience and fortitude.' (G 398/14–15) The conditions of these persons make them incapable of deriving enjoyment from their helping actions. These are cases in which the motive of duty shines, according to Kant, because the advancement of the happiness of others is so clearly conceived as necessary rather than merely pleasant. But neither case suggests that in ordinary conditions a dutiful person will not have the emotions normally consequent upon the adoption of a purpose, including enjoyment of its successful pursuit, and joy in its realization.

Once this is accepted, the intuition behind the common complaint should collapse, and this is the third important point. The complaint is based on the usual misreading of the examples, in which the person who acts from duty is envisioned as someone who does not really have the happiness of others as his end. This is simply a mistake. Duty is not a different purpose, but a different ground for the adoption of a purpose. So Kant's idea here is captured better by saying that the sympathetic person's motive is *shallower* than the morally worthy person's: both want to help, but there is available a *further* stretch of motivating thought about helping which the merely sympathetic person has not engaged in.[55] This further stretch of thought concerns the sort of world which this would be if no one helped – or better, if no one perceived the need for help as a *reason* to help, or a *claim* on help. Such a world would be unacceptable because we regard our own needs as reasons why *we* should be helped. (G 423/41; MV 453/117) Regarding my needs as normative for others, or, as Kant puts it, making myself an end for others, I must regard the needs of others as normative for me. (MV 393/52)[56] And this is to say that the needs of others are a law to me. So the morally worthy person helps because she believes that the needs of others make a claim on her and so that there is a normative demand, or a law, that she ought to help. This characterization of the point of the example brings us to Kant's third proposition, which is that 'Duty is the necessity of an action executed from respect for law.' (G 400/16)

Now at this point it is essential to remember that what Kant is doing is a *motivational analysis* of the notion of duty or rightness. Kant is analyzing the good will, characterized as one that does what is right because it is right, in order to discover the principle of unconditionally good action.[57] The assumption behind such an analysis is that *the reason why a good-willed person does an action, and the reason why the action is right, are the same.* The good-willed person does the right thing because it is the right thing, so if we can discover why the good-willed person does it, we will have *ipso facto* discovered why it is the right thing. What the analysis reveals is that the reason why the good-willed person does the action is not merely because it serves this or that purpose, but because it is necessary – that is, it is a law – to perform such an action or to have such a purpose. The maxim of the action, or the maxim of the purpose, has what I shall call a 'legal character': that is, it is normative, it has the capacity to express a demand made on us. Since the legal character of the maxim is what motivates the good-willed person, it is that, and nothing else, that makes the action or the purpose right. Kant's analysis identifies the rightness of the action *essentially* with the legal character of its maxim.

Now comes the critical step. It follows that the maxim must not get its legal character from anything outside of itself. For, if there were an outside source of legal character, then that source, rather than legal character itself, would be what makes the action right. Instead, the maxim's legal character must be intrinsic: it must have what I shall call a 'lawlike form.' This is why legal character, or *universality*, must be understood as lawlike form, that is, as a requirement of *universalizability*. Kant draws this conclusion this way:

> Since I have robbed the will of all impulses which could come to it from obedience to any law, nothing remains to serve as a principle of the will except universal conformity of its action to law as such. That is, I should never act in such a way that I could not also will that my maxim should be a universal law. Mere conformity to law as such (without assuming any particular law applicable to certain actions) serves as the principle of the will, and it must serve as such a principle if duty is not to be a vain delusion and chimerical concept. (G 402/18)

The point is a delicate one. You might suppose, at first, that the legal character by which the good-willed person is motivated could come from something other than lawlike form of the maxim. For instance, you might suppose that the action is prescribed by some law whose grounds are independent of everything Kant has said here, and that the maxim could be 'legal' in the sense that it conforms to this independent law. This is the possibility which Kant means to *block* in the above quotation when he adds the words 'without assuming any particular law applicable to certain actions,' and it is important to see why it is disallowed. Suppose that there were such a law, prescribing certain actions. I will call this the External Law. And suppose we say that the maxim gets its legal character not from its intrinsic lawlike form, but from the extrinsic fact that the action is prescribed by the External Law. Then we will have to ask why the External Law is a law before we have found the real reason why the action is right. That is to say, we will have to ask why the External Law is in force, why it is normative. Because obviously, the mere *grammatical* form of universality cannot make anything a law: a law must be normative. A law does not make a claim on me merely because it is addressed to me, or to some group that includes me. It must get its grip or hold on me, its capacity to bind me, from some intelligible source. But then the source of the External Law's normativity, rather than legal character of the maxim, will be what motivates the good-willed person. The reason why the External Law is in force, rather than the fact that the maxim has legal character, will be the good-willed person's motive, for it will be the real reason why the action is right. And this is contrary to Kant's analysis of the motive of duty.

An example will make this point clearer: Suppose that right actions were those commanded in laws laid down by God. According to Kant's analysis, the good-willed person does these actions because it is a law to do so. But why is it a law to do so? The answer is: because God so commands. Now, which of these two reasons is the reason why the good-willed person does the action, which is also the reason why the action is right? If the action is right because God commands it, it is not right because its maxim is intrinsically legal; and the reason why the good-willed person does it will not be grasp of its legal character, but response to divine command. This is contrary to Kant's analysis. The maxim of the action must be legal in itself, and this can only be because it has a lawlike form. The religious moralist may want to reply that the maxim's legal character, and the action's being divinely commanded, are the same thing. But its conformity to divine law can only make a maxim extrinsically, not intrinsically, legal. So the dilemma remains: If the person is moved by divine command, then legal character is not the motive, and the motive of duty is not at work. Since the legal character of a maxim and the divine commandedness of an action are not analytically the same thing, rightness must essentially lie in one of them or the other, and, according to the analysis, it is must be the legal character of the maxim. And so this must be its intrinsic lawlike *form*. This argument will apply to any attempt to derive the legal character of a maxim from anything other than its intrinsic lawlike form: only legal character and lawlike form are *analytically* or essentially the same thing.[58]

Now that last argument may make it clear why the legal character of a maxim cannot come from an External Law. But the conclusion – that it must therefore come from lawlike form, as specified by the universalizability test – may seem much less obvious. Why, then, does Kant conclude that a maxim has *intrinsic* legal character only if it has what the Universalizability test identifies as lawlike form?[59] To understand this, we must keep in mind two points. The first I have already noticed. In order to be a law, it is not enough that a principle be grammatically universal. It must also be normative for the person who is to follow it: there must be some intelligible reason why it binds *that person*. The second point concerns the way the universalizability requirement functions. The requirement tells us that we must act in such a way that we can at the same time will our maxims as universal laws. If a maxim passes this test, the action is right in the broad sense – it is all right, permissible, not wrong. It is only if a maxim fails the test that we get a duty – the duty of doing the opposite of what the failed maxim says, or, more precisely, of adopting the opposite of what the maxim says as law. So a maxim of *duty* is not merely one that you *can* will as universal law, but one that you *must* will as universal law. And this means that the maxim is a law to which your own will commits you. But a maxim to which your own will commits you is *normative for you*. And this, to return to the first point, is what a principle must be in order to be a law for you – it must be *normative for you*.

Again an example will clarify the point. I will take Kant's easiest example, that of the lying promise. (G 422/40) A man in financial difficulties considers getting ready money on the strength of a lying promise that he will repay. His maxim is 'I will make a lying promise, in order to get some ready money.' He asks himself whether he could will his maxim to be at the same time a universal law. This means that he imagines a world in which everyone who needs money makes a lying promise, and he imagines that, at the same time, he is part of this world, willing his maxim. His question is whether he can will this whole state of affairs. Now his maxim is derived from a hypothetical imperative: 'If you will to get some ready money, then make a lying promise.' This hypothetical imperative, in turn, is derived from the rational principle that whoever wills an end wills the necessary means, together with the 'causal' law that lying promises are a means to, or will cause, the possession of ready money. (G 417/34–35) However, in the world in which this maxim is universalized, this 'causal' law does not hold. For if everyone in want of ready cash tried to make a lying promise, Kant says, 'no one would believe what was promised to him but would only laugh at any such assertion as vain pretense.' (G 422/40) The man in the example cannot, at the same time, rationally will both acting on his maxim and a state of affairs which undermines the causal law from which the rationality of acting on his maxim is derived. A man who wills to use the institution of promising in pursuit of his end must will that the institution should work. And it does not work unless promises are generally made in good faith. So he *himself* is committed to willing the law that people should make their promises in good faith, so long as he wills this particular maxim. Therefore, he cannot rationally will to act on this maxim at the same time as he wills it as a law.[60]

The important thing to see here is that it is the man's own will that commits him to the law that promises should be made in good faith, if they are to be made at all. The argument is not that promising is generally a useful institution or that the rightness of keeping promises is written into the nature of things. The man is committed to the institution of promising by his own maxim because he wills to employ it as a means to his end. It is his own will, and nothing else, that makes it impossible for him to will the universality of lying promises. In this way the universalizability test shows us what principles our own maxims commit us to willing as laws. As Kant says, if the man does will the maxim, he cannot also be willing it as a law, but rather must be regarding himself as an exception. (G 424/42)[61]

Let me digress a moment. It is at this point in the argument that the objection Kant levelled against Wolff – the 'empty formalism' objection – enters the picture as an objection against Kant himself. According to the objection, the Formula of Universal Law lacks content, since there are no restrictions on what we *can* will as a universal law, and therefore no implications about what we *must* so will. Now I hope that the example that I have just given will suggest that this objection is mistaken, and that there are laws to which our own wills do commit us. But it is also important to see what is wrong with one proposal for solving the emptiness problem sometimes made by those who, like Hegel, approve Kant's account of moral motivation but think that the Formula of Universal Law is empty. This proposal is that some external law or normative consideration can be imported into the system to solve the supposed emptiness problem and give content to our duties.[62]

This was Kant's own solution in the Prize Essay, where the judgments of the moral sense were brought in to give content to the obligations of which the principle 'do that which is perfect' is the form. A variant of Kant's own argument in *Groundwork* I shows why this solution is disallowed. Either the action has its perfection in itself, or we are not doing it on account of its perfection, but on account of what gives it its perfection – in this case, the approval of the moral sense. The reason why the action is perfect, and the reason why a good person does it, must be exactly the same. The action's perfection cannot be extrinsically conferred by the moral sense, but must be intrinsic to the action itself. Content brought in from external normative sources violates Kant's analysis in the way we have seen.

We can now see a rather simpler way of making the argument against the External Law. Suppose, again, that the external Law is in force because it is the law of God's will. This is supposed to be what makes it normative. But how? God's will is only normative for me if it is the law of my own will to obey God's will. This is an old Hobbesian thought – that nothing can be a law for me unless I am bound to obey it, and nothing can bind me to obey it unless I have a motive for obeying it.[63] But Kant goes a step further than Hobbes. *Nothing* except my own will can make a law normative *for me*. Even the imposition of a sanction cannot bypass my will, for a reward or punishment only binds my will if I will to get the reward or avoid the punishment – that is, if I make it my maxim that my interest or preservation should be a law to me. Only those maxims shown to be necessary by the universalizability test – only those to which my own will commits me – are *intrinsically* normative. And this, as the Rationalists had argued all along, is what an obligation must be. Autonomy is the only possible source of intrinsic normativity, and so of obligation.

One result of this is that it shows that the British Rationalists to some extent mistook their target. They opposed Hobbesianism, moral sense theory, and divine command theory, all on the grounds, as they thought, that these make morality a matter of positive law. But Kant's analysis shows that positivity is not the problem. A law in the nature of things, if it is understood as a theoretical or metaphysical principle that is external to the will, gives rise to exactly the same problem that divine law does.[64] Laws in the nature of things can only make our maxims extrinsically, not intrinsically, normative. The problem with these theories is not that their laws are positive, but that their laws are not willed autonomously, and so are not intrinsically normative. But the Kantian laws of autonomy are positive laws: moral laws exist because *we* legislate them.

Another mistaken target, this time of British moral philosophy more generally, is the analyzability of moral concepts. Price and Hutcheson agree that moral ideas are fundamentally 'simple,' and can only be defined trivially by synonyms.[65] This idea is echoed in G.E. Moore's concern with the 'naturalistic fallacy': because 'pleasure' and 'good,' for instance, cannot be taken to mean the same thing, Moore concludes that 'good' is a simple idea.[66] Ross, following Moore, makes a similar claim about 'right.'[67] The truth in these arguments is this: claims about, say, pleasure, or what maximizes pleasure, are not intrinsically normative, the way claims about the right and the good are. The normativity of an ethical concept cannot be derived from any non-ethical concept, so no ethical concept can be completely analyzed in terms of a natural or factual one. All of these philosophers conclude that normative concepts are unanalyzable. As a result, they think that our understanding of the normative concept does not enable us to pick out its objects, and that we must therefore have recourse to a sense or to a faculty of intuition that functions like a sense.

But Kant's analysis does not reduce the normative concept to a non-normative one; instead, it reduces normative content to normative form. What the analysis yields is that right actions are those whose maxims have lawlike form, which is the form of normativity itself. Provided that the categorical imperative procedure can be made to work, Kant's analysis does enable us to pick out the objects of the concept; that is, it enables us to identify our duties. We discover the content of morality by seeing which maxims have normative forms.

But perhaps the most fundamental mistake of the British Moralists of both the eighteenth and twentieth centuries has been the acceptance of Hume's dilemma. For Hume's dilemma leaves us with an unfortunate choice. If the virtue of an action is conferred by its motive, then that motive cannot be the motive of obligation. The Rationalists found this objectionable, both because it seems as if at least some actions really ought to be done from the motive of obligation, and because the fact of obligation seems to be dependent on the possibility of the motive. The Rationalist saved obligation, but at the cost of locating morality in the metaphysical properties of actions, rather than in the motivational properties of people.

The argument of *Groundwork* I shows us we do not have to accept Hume's dilemma. For Kant shows that the premise of Hume's argument – that doing your duty from the motive of duty is an empty formalism – is false. An obligation, or an action done from the motive of duty, is one that the agent herself must will as a universal law. It is, in its very nature and essence, an action autonomously willed. To complete the argument, and show that obligations really exist, Kant needs only to show that human beings are capable of autonomous motivation: that is, that we can be motivated by those laws that we must will. If we are capable of giving laws to ourselves, then we have obligations.

Notes

* I would like to thank Charlotte Brown and Manley Thompson for their valuable assistance with this paper.

1 The contemporary debate began with W.D. Falk's '"Ought" and Motivation' (*Proceedings of the Aristotelian Society* 48 (1947–48): 492–510; rpt. in *Ought, Reasons and Morality: The Collected Papers of W.D. Falk* [Ithaca, NY: Cornell University Press, 1986]). Among other important discussions are William Frankena, 'Obligation and Motivation in Recent Moral Philosophy' (*Essays in Moral Philosophy*, ed. A.I. Melden [Seattle, WA: University of Washington Press, 1958] rpt. in *Perspectives on Morality: Essays of William K. Frankena*, ed. Kenneth E. Goodpaster)]; Part I of Thomas Nagel's *The Possibility of Altruism* (Oxford: Oxford University Press, 1970; later issued by Princeton University Press); Bernard Williams, 'Internal and External Reasons' (*Rational Action*, ed. Ross Harrison [Cambridge: Cambridge University Press, 1980], rpt. in Williams's *Moral Luck* [Cambridge: Cambridge University Press, 1981]; and Stephen Darwall, *Impartial Reason* (Ithaca, NY: Cornell University Press, 1983). I discuss the subject in 'Skepticism About Practical Reason' *The Journal of Philosophy* 83 (January, 1986): 5–25.

2 See for instance Frankena, 'Obligation and Motivation in Recent Moral Philosophy' (cited in n1, above) and Williams, 'Internal and External Reasons' (also cited above).

3 See for instance Nagel, *The Possibility of Altruism* (cited in n1, above) and my 'Skepticism About Practical Reason' (cited above).

4 Samuel Clarke, *A Discourse Concerning the Unalterable Obligations of Natural Religion and the Truth and Certainty of The Christian Revelation: The Boyle Lectures 1705* in *The Works of Samuel Clarke* (London: J. and P. Knapton: 1738; rpt. New York: Garland Publishing, 1978), pp. 609–10. Selections from the Boyle Lectures can be found in D.D. Raphael, ed. *The British Moralists 1650–1800* vol. I (Oxford: Oxford University Press, 1969), pp. 191–225; the passages cited at pp. 194–96. Hereinafter this work will be cited as 'Clarke' with page numbers from the Garland edition followed by those from the Raphael selections where available.

5 Francis Hutcheson, *Illustrations on the Moral Sense*, ed. Bernard Peach (Cambridge, MA: Harvard University Press, 1971), pp. 133–40. This work is the second part of *An Essay on the Nature and Conduct of the Passions and Affections. With Illustrations on the Moral Sense* (London: 1728). Hereinafter this work will be cited as 'Hutcheson's *Illustrations*.'

6 Richard Price, *A Review of the Principle Questions in Morals*, ed. D.D. Raphael (Oxford: Clarendon Press, 1948), p. 49. The *Review* was first published in London in 1758 under the title *A Review of the Principle Questions and Difficulties in Morals*. Raphael's edition is reprinted from the third edition of 1787. Selections from the *Review* can be found in D.D. Raphael, ed. *The British Moralists 1650–1800* vol. II (Oxford: Oxford University Press, 1969) pp. 131–98; the passage cited is at p. 147. Hereinafter this work will be cited as 'Price' with page numbers from Raphael's edition of the book followed by those from the selections in *British Moralists*.

7 David Hume, *A Treatise of Human Nature*, ed. L.A. Selby-Bigge and P.H. Nidditch (Oxford: Clarendon Press, 1978) p. 457. Hereinafter cited as 'Hume's *Treatise*.'

8 For discussion see Paul Schilpp, *Kant's Pre-Critical Ethics* (Chicago: Northwestern University Press, 1938: rpt. New York: Garland, 1977), ch. 3. Kant praises Hutcheson in the Prize Essay (see below), and in later works treats Hutcheson's view as representative of attempts to base morality on feeling. In his Introduction to Adam Smith's *Theory of Moral Sentiments* (Oxford: Oxford University Press, 1976; rpt. Indianapolis, IN: Liberty Classics, 1982), D.D. Raphael describes a letter of 1771 from Markus Herz to Kant in which Herz refers to Smith as 'your favorite.' (31)

9 'So-called' because it was written for a prize offered in 1763 by the Berlin Academy. Kant did not actually win the prize, which went to Moses Mendelssohn. See Lewis White Beck, *Early German Philosophy: Kant and His Predecessors* (Cambridge, MA: Harvard University Press, 1969) pp. 441–42.

10 All references to Kant's own works are inserted into the text. The following abbreviations are used:

PE   *Enquiry concerning the clarity of the principles of natural theology and ethics.* ('Prize Essay,' 1763) The first page number is that of the Prussian Academy Edition (*Kants gesammelte Schriften. Preussische Akademie der Wissenschaften*: Berlin, 1900–1942) vol. II; the second is that of the translation by G.B. Kerferd and D.E. Walford in *Kant: Selected Pre-Critical Writings and Correspondence with Beck*. (Manchester: Manchester University Press and New York: Barnes & Noble, 1968).

IUH   'Idea for a Universal History from a Cosmopolitan Point of View.' (1784) Prussian Academy vol. VIII; trans. Lewis White Beck in *Kant On History*, ed. Lewis White Beck. (Indianapolis, IN: Bobbs-Merrill Library of Liberal Arts, 1963).

C1   *Critique of Pure Reason.* (1st ed. 1781, 2nd ed. 1787) Page numbers of the A and B editions are followed in parentheses by those of the translation by Norman Kemp Smith. (New York: Macmillan, St. Martin's Press, 1965).

G   *Foundations of the Metaphysics of Morals.* (1785) Prussian Academy vol. IV; trans. Lewis White Beck. (Indianapolis, IN: Bobbs-Merrill Library of Liberal Arts, 1959).

C2   *Critique of Practical Reason.* (1788) Prussian Academy vol. V; trans. Lewis White Beck. (Indianapolis, IN: Bobbs-Merrill Library of Liberal Arts, 1956).

R   *Religion Within the Limits of Reason Alone*. (1793) Prussian Academy vol. VI; trans. Theodore M. Greene and Hoyt H. Hudson. (La Salle, IL: Open Court, 1934. rpt. New York, Harper Torchbooks, 1960).

MJ   *The Metaphysical Elements of Justice*. Part I of *The Metaphysics of Morals*. (1797) Prussian Academy Edition vol. VI; trans. John Ladd. (Indianapolis, IN: Bobbs-Merrill Library of Liberal Arts, 1965).

MV   *The Metaphysical Principles of Virtue*. Part II of *The Metaphysics of Morals*. (1797) Prussian Academy vol. VI; trans. James Ellington in *Immanuel Kant: Ethical Philosophy*. (Indianapolis, IN: Hackett, 1983).

11 The two steps described correspond approximately to the metaphysical and transcendental deductions of the categories in the *Critique of Pure Reason*; although the relation between a metaphysical deduction of an *a priori* concept and its analysis is not perfectly clear. In any case the analysis of the concept of obligation, with which I am concerned here, will show that it is logically possible – that the idea contains no contradiction – while the synthesis will show how it is really possible, how it can apply to us. For the distinction between logical and real possibility, see C1 A243–244/ B301–02 (pp. 262–63) and A596n/B624n (p. 593n). The account of real possibility in these passages is given in terms of the possibility of experience and therefore does not apply to ethical concepts, but there must be an analogue of it for ethical concepts if dogmatic rationalism in ethics is to be avoided.

12 For the most part, I will use 'right' and 'obligatory' to denote any action that is morally called for. The term 'right' may be used more broadly, to include permissible actions, and Kant's analysis also explicates this notion, but my focus will be on required actions. Both 'right' and 'obligatory' can also be used more specifically, to refer to actions called for by so-called perfect duties, or still more specifically to actions called for by justice. Some philosophers, for example Hume and Bernard Williams, believe that 'right' and 'obligatory' should only be used for one of these latter two classes of actions, and at various points would find in this view grounds for objecting to the argument of this paper. I do not try to deal with the issue, but I do try to notice the points where it comes up. See nn14, 22, and 24.

13 Rightness is strictly speaking a property of acts, and any given act can be done from a variety of motives, good, bad, or indifferent. But right acts can be defined or identified in terms of motives even if they are not always done from those motives; they can be defined as the ones a person with good motives would do, or ones that good motives would prompt. The strategy is thought to be characteristic of virtue-centered ethical theories, but as I will show it is also Kant's.

14 Hume's *Treatise*: 478. This argument occurs at the beginning of the section in which justice is identified as an artificial virtue, and it is important to point out that its conclusion in a certain way only applies to the natural virtues. The 'first motive' to justice turns out to be self-interest (492;495), but this is neither an especially virtuous motive (492) nor is it the motive usually at work in agents performing just actions. Particular acts of Justice taken separately are not necessarily in our interest. (497) We approve of justice because sympathy makes us approve whatever is in the collective interest (499–500); we perform just actions, or restrain ourselves from

unjust ones, because we approve of justice: that is, because justice is virtuous, and we value our own characters. (500–01; see also the *Enquiry Concerning the Principles of Morals*, ed. L. A. Selby-Bigge and P. H. Nidditch [Oxford; Clarendon Press, 1975] pp. 282–83). This is one sense in which justice is an 'artificial' virtue. This point becomes important later in the argument; see n22.

15 Hume's *Treatise*, p. 478.

16 See for instance Nagel, *The Possibility of Altruism* (cited in n1, above) pp. 4–5.

17 Hutcheson's *Illustrations*, p. 130.

18 Ibid., pp. 121, 130.

19 ibid., p. 139.

20 Ibid., p. 140. See also Hutcheson's *Inquiry Concerning the Original of Our Ideas of Virtue or Moral Good* (London: 1725) in D.D. Raphael, ed. *The British Moralists 1650–1800* vol. I (Oxford: Oxford University Press, 1969) p. 293.

21 Hume's *Treatise* p. 479.

22 However, as I point out in n14, the motive of obligation *is* the usual motive at work in the case of *just* actions (and, when we are tempted, abstentions), and this is an important point in Hume's favor. Our belief that obligation should be the motive of just actions is much firmer than our belief that it should be the motive of those actions springing from what Hume would call the natural virtues, which we may regard as meritorious rather than required. (See n12.) It should be observed that in the passage in which he complains that Rationalists cannot account for morality's power to motivate us, which I have quoted on p. 125, Hume is careful about this: he speaks specifically about just actions. Thus Hume could argue, against the point I am making here, that his system favors the operation of the motive of duty in exactly those cases in which we feel most sure that it should operate.

23 *Philosophy* 33 (1938); rpt. in *Ethics, Religion, and Politics: Collected Philosophical Papers of G.E.M. Anscombe, Volume III* (Minneapolis, MN: University of Minnesota Press, 1981) pp. 26–42.

24 (Cambridge, MA: Harvard University Press, 1985). Williams wants us to recognize that obligations 'form just one type of ethical consideration.' (p. 196) Some actions are not obligatory but more or less than obligatory: admirable, or heroic, or simply what a person of good character would do. (p. 179) Williams's view is similar to Hume's view that the motive of obligation is appropriate for one kind of moral consideration (that of justice) but not all. (See nn12, 14, 22.) Williams regards attempts to treat all ethical claims as forms of obligation (by means of such devices as Ross's *prima facie* obligations, or imperfect duties, or general duties, or duties to oneself) as fundamentally misguided. (pp. 178–92) The point of such attempts, I believe, is not merely to impose an artificial orderliness on the moral terrain, nor to license blaming people who ignore certain ethical claims, but to explain how these claims have normative force for the agents who act on them. Williams does see that this is part of the motive for the idea of general or imperfect or *prima facie* obligations, but thinks that it is an error to suppose that all practical necessity, or normative force, springs from obligations. (p. 196) Even if he is right,

some account of the normative force of these claims is needed, as he would agree. See n27.

25 Anscombe says that the terms 'should' and 'ought' have now acquired a special so-called 'moral' sense – i.e., a sense in which they imply some absolute verdict (like one of guilty/not guilty on a man) on what is described in the 'ought' sentences. (cited in n22, p. 29, see also p. 32) Williams says: '. . . once I am under the obligation, there is no escaping it, and the fact that a given agent would prefer not to be in this system [the morality system] or bound by its rules will not excuse him; nor will blaming him be based on a misunderstanding. *Blame is the characteristic reaction of the morality system.*' (n24, above, p. 177; my emphasis) This seems to me wrong; the morality system Williams describes in the text is distinctly Rationalistic, but the emphasis on blame, and on the general ideas of merit and demerit, is more characteristic of Sentimentalist theories, for reasons I mention in the text. Kant notices the ways the duties of respect *restrict* our practices of blaming: he says that 'the reproach of vice . . . must never burst out in complete contempt or deny the wrongdoer all moral worth, because on that hypothesis he could never be improved either – and this is incompatible with the idea of man, who as . . . a moral being can never lose all predisposition to good.' (MV 463/128–129). I discuss this attitude to blame in 'Morality as Freedom,' forthcoming in *Kant's Practical Philosophy Reconsidered: Proceedings of the Seventh Jerusalem Philosophical Encounter*, forthcoming from Kluwer Academic Publishers.

26 This is most explicit in the theory of Adam Smith, who has more to say about moral motivation than Hume or Hutcheson, and who gives a more positive account of the role of the motive of duty. Smith says: 'When our passive feelings are almost always so sordid and selfish, how comes it that our active principles should often be so generous and so noble? . . . It is not the soft power of humanity, it is not that feeble spark of benevolence which Nature has lighted up in the human heart, that is thus capable of counteracting the strongest impulses of self-love. It is a stronger power, a more forcible motive, which exerts itself upon such occasions. It is reason, principle, conscience, the inhabitant of the breast, *the man within, the great judge and arbiter of our conduct.*' (*The Theory of Moral Sentiments, loc. cit.* p. 137; my emphasis) The 'man within,' Smith's impartial spectator, develops by a process of internalization that begins with our judgment of the conduct of others. Sympathizing with others who in a similar way judge us turns our attention to our own conduct, and by this process we are led to the idea of an internal spectator whose judgment is the motive of duty. (*loc. cit.* 109–78)

27 To be fair, Williams also discusses this side of the idea of obligation, in the chapter cited and in 'Practical Necessity' (*The Philosophical Frontiers of Christian Theology: Essays presented to D. M. MacKinnon*, ed. Brian Hebblewaite and Steward Sutherland [Cambridge; Cambridge University Press, 1982] rpt. in Williams's *Moral Luck* [Cambridge: Cambridge University Press, 1981]).

28 See for instance *Nicomachean Ethics* III.7 1115b11–14; III.12 1119b15; IV.1 1120a23; X.9 1179b30; and X.9 1180a6–8.

29 I discuss this in my 'Aristotle on Function and Virtue' [*History of Philosophy Quarterly* 3 (July, 1986): 259–79, see especially 269–72]. The point is

related to the fact that '. . . it is not merely the state in accordance with the right rule, but the state that implies the *presence* of the right rule, that is virtue.' (*Nicomachean Ethics* VI. 13 1144b27. trans. David Ross, revised by J. L. Ackrill and J.O. Urmson [Oxford: Oxford University Press, 1980] p. 157.) There *is* a sense in which Aristotle's virtuous person acts *from* the right rule, although it is not the same sense that the Rationalists had in mind.

30 Both Price's *Review* and John Balguy's *The Foundation of Moral Goodness: Or a Further Inquiry into the Original of our Idea of Virtue* (London, 1728; rpt. New York: Garland, 1976; hereinafter cited as 'Balguy') were written directly in response to Hutcheson's theory.

31 Clarke, pp. 596–97; 608–12/192–99.

32 Ibid., pp. 614/202.

33 Ibid., pp. 614/202. These passages are quoted with approval by Price (118) and Frankena (*loc. cit.*, p. 59).

34 On the one side, Price incorporated Hutcheson's idea of a moral sense into his Rationalist theory. (See Price, pp. 57–68/148–52). On the other side, Adam Smith developed an account of the genesis the motive of duty, and gave it a prominent role, in a Sentimentalist context. (See n26, above.) And Joseph Butler, while aspiring like the Sentimentalists to explain morality in terms of human nature, argued that conscience is intrinsically authoritative and no sanction is needed for obeying it. See Joseph Butler, *Five Sermons Preached at the Rolls Chapel*, ed. Stephen Darwall (Indianapolis, IN: Hackett, 1983; hereinafter cited as *Butler*), pp. 11, 43.

35 Price, pp. 47–48, 146–47.

36 Price, pp. 15, 133.

37 W.D. Ross, *The Right and the Good* (Oxford: Clarendon Press, 1930, p. 3. Hereinafter referred to as 'Ross.') I have already mentioned that a motivational analysis does not require this: 'right act' can mean an act that a person with a certain sort of motive would do, without any implication that every such act is done from that motive and so is morally good. (See n13, above.) But this does not affect Ross's argument and so is not to the point here. Notice that Hume's use of the term 'virtuous' in the original statement of the dilemma does carry both the implication of 'right' and of 'morally good'.

38 Ross, p. 4.

39 Ibid., p. 5.

40 Ibid., pp. 5–6.

41 Ibid., p. 5.

42 See the quotation from Clarke on p. 129 and the one from Price below, p. 131.
Balguy says 'What is the Reason exciting a Man to the Choice of a Virtuous Action? I answer, his very Approbation of it. . . .' Balguy, p. 45; see also pp. 56, 61.

43 Price, pp. 186–87, 194.

44 See H.A. Prichard, 'Duty and Interest' in his *Duty and Interest* (Oxford: Clarendon Press, 1928; rpt. in *Readings in Ethical Theory*, ed. Wilfrid Sellars and John Hospers (Englewood Cliffs, NJ: Prentice-Hall, 1970). Falk's paper ' "Ought" and Motivation,' which introduced the internalism/externalism distinction, is addressed to Prichard and Ross on just this point.

45 Ross, pp. 132–33.

46 Ibid., pp. 7–11 and 34–39.

47 Ibid., p. 122n.

48 Ibid., p. 122.

49 Kant must mean that there is room for conceptual confusion in the case of direct inclination. If you perform a dutiful act that is also, for some people, pleasant in itself, we cannot tell whether you acted from duty or only from pleasure. But no one gives correct change just for the pleasure of it, so here we know that the action was either from duty or self-interest. But there is surely no way to tell about an actual honest action that happens to be in someone's interest that she *did it* from interest rather than duty.

50 In the passage cited Kant sounds negative about honor; he says that 'The ideal of morality belongs to culture; its use for some simulacrum of morality in the love of honor and outward decorum constitutes mere civilization' and that 'Everything good that is not based on a morally good disposition . . . is nothing but pretense and glittering misery.' But in another passage Kant speaks more leniently of honor. He is discussing the question whether the government has the right to punish two kinds of murderers: young officers who kill in duels, and unmarried mothers who kill their children to avoid disgrace. Rather surprisingly, Kant thinks there is reason to doubt whether these murderers may be punished, for he says that honor 'is no delusion in these cases' and that 'legislation itself . . . is responsible for the fact that incentives of honor among the people do not accord (subjectively) with the standards that are (objectively) appropriate to their purpose.' (MJ 336–37/106–07). Kant is generally characterized as believing that duty and inclination are the only two kinds of motivation, but both of these passages suggest that he regards honor as something in between – a sort of proto-moral motive that precedes the genuine motive of duty in the education of the human species. I speculate that Kant means that the motive of honor approximates the motive of moral autonomy insofar as the person governed by it follows, for its own sake, a strict law of conduct which represents an ideal of character. Yet motives of honor fall short of the full-fledged moral motive because the laws of honor are not derived from autonomy itself. See n52, below.

51 See Andrews Reath, 'Hedonism and Heteronomy,' forthcoming.

52 Kant calls the sympathetic person a '*Menschenfreundes*' (G 398): a friend to humanity. And Sentimentalist moral philosophers thought of sympathy as a response we have to human beings as such (not just to those to whom we are particularly attached) in virtue of the universal human characteristics which make them similar to ourselves. Thus sympathy makes an end of humanity and so serves as a simulacrum of the Formula of Humanity just as honor serves as a simulacrum of the Formula of Universal Law.

53 After Butler wrote his famous Sermon XI on the consistency of benevolence with self-love, it was not uncommon for eighteenth-century philosophers to treat the principle of self-love as providing a method of choosing among various ends, all of which are valued for their own sakes. Butler argued that the pleasure we get from satisfying a desire presupposes, rather than explains, the desire: it is because we have the desire that we enjoy achieving its object. (*Butler*, pp. 46–54) The principle of self-love selects among things, all of

which we desire for their own sakes, on the basis of how much pleasure we will get from achieving them. Kant apparently did not read Butler, but Butler's picture of the operation of self-love was adopted both by Hume in the *Enquiry Concerning the Principles of Morals* (ed. L.A. Selby-Bigge and P.H. Nidditch [Oxford; Clarendon Press, 1975], pp. 281–82; 301–02), and to some extent by Hutcheson in *Illustrations Upon the Moral Sense*. Kant uses the principle of self-love in this sense – as one way of choosing among things we desire for their own sakes – but sets the principle of duty up as rival to it – as another way of choosing our purposes.

54 It may seem as if I am guilty of a commonplace error in making these remarks: confusing pleasure with satisfaction or gratification. Once I've made up my mind to do or achieve something, I am of course gratified to see it done. But that point applies even to actions undertaken for the most purely instrumental reasons, actions that are only means to other ends. The point I am making here is a different one, having to do with what it *means* to say that you have made something your purpose. My claim is that if you really succeed in making something your purpose, and so value it as an end, you will come to take pleasure in its successful pursuit. I explain this further in 'Morality as Freedom.' (*loc. cit.*)

55 The same point is made by other Rationalists. Price distinguishes rational from instinctive benevolence, and, like Kant, claims that instinctive benevolence is lovable but falls short of virtue. (Price, pp. 190–91, 196–97) Balguy makes a similar comparison. (Balguy, pp. 59–60) Ross says 'The conscientious attitude is one which *involves* the thought either of good or of pleasure for some one else, but it is *a more reflective attitude* than that in which we aim directly at the production of some good or some pleasure for another, since . . . we stop to think whether in all the circumstances the bringing of that good or pleasure into existence is what is really incumbent upon us. . . .' (Ross, pp. 162–63; my emphasis)

56 Nagel employs a similar argument in *The Possibility of Altruism* (cited in n1, above), pp. 82–84.

57 I say this in spite of the fact that in the third section of the *Groundwork*, Kant says that the principle that 'an absolutely good will is one whose maxim can always include itself as a universal law' is synthetic because 'by analysis of the concept of an absolutely good will that property of the maxim cannot be found.' (G 447/65) I believe that this is a misstatement, or at least a poor way of putting the point. What is synthetic is that the moral law holds *for us* – that we are capable of having absolutely good wills. The statement that a good will is one whose maxim is universalizable is synthetic only if 'good' is being used in a fully normative sense – to signify a demand on us.

58 I formulated an earlier version of this argument in a comment on David Cummiskey's paper 'Kant's Refutation of Consequentialism' at the American Philosophical Association meetings in April 1988, and I would like to thank Cummiskey for prompting me to do so.

59 Perhaps it is worth saying a word about what it means to claim that a maxim has a 'form.' The 'form' of a thing is ordinarily thought to rest in the relations among its parts, and the parts of a maxim of action (to take the simplest case) are the action to be performed and the purpose to be realized. The plausibility of Kant's thought that the rightness of a particular action

rests in the form of its maxim can be seen intuitively by considering the following triples of maxims:

A) I will knock Alex down, in order to remove him from the path of an oncoming bullet.

B) I will knock Alex down, in order to relieve my temper.

C) I will punch a punching bag, in order to relieve my temper.

Or:

A) I will avoid visiting my grandmother in the hospital, in order to avoid a contagion to which I am especially susceptible.

B) I will avoid visiting my grandmother in the hospital, in order to spare myself unpleasantness.

C) I will avoid watching prime-time television, in order to spare myself unpleasantness.

In each set, maxims A and B concern the same act or omission, yet adopting maxim A is permissible or even good, while B is wrong. But this is not simply because of the purpose in maxim B, for maxim C contains the same purpose, yet it, once again, is permissible. What is wrong with the action whose maxim is B, then, does not rest either in the action that is performed or in the purpose for which it is performed, but in the relation between the two. And the relation between the two parts of the maxim is its form.

60 I explain my views about how the Formula of Universal Law should be applied more fully in 'Kant's Formula of Universal Law,' *Pacific Philosophical Quarterly* 66 (1985): 24–47.

61 It is essential to keep in mind that these considerations by themselves do not show why the action is irrational. All that this argument shows is why the maxim cannot be willed as a law – not why a rational being must only will maxims that can be willed as laws. For that part of the argument we need to take the further step described in the conclusion of this paper.

62 For instance, after praising and affirming Kant's conception of the autonomy of the will Hegel says '. . . still to adhere to the exclusively moral position, without making the transition to the conception of ethics, is to reduce this gain to an empty formalism . . . of course, material may be brought in from the outside and particular duties may be arrived at accordingly. . . .' *The Philosophy of Right*, trans. T.M. Knox (Oxford: Oxford University Press, 1952), pp. 89–90. I owe the reference to Daniel Brudney.

63 See especially *Leviathan*, Part I, ch. 14.

64 This may be especially hard to see, because the arguments that British Rationalists use to show that moral laws are indeed laws of reason are similar to those that Kant uses to show that moral laws are laws we must rationally will. Strictly speaking, Rationalists should not give arguments *for* moral laws, since they think these laws are self-evident. But Clarke, in particular, tries to impress this self-evidence upon his audience by appeal to arguments from the 'Golden Rule,' and arguments from this principle are similar to those from the categorical imperative. For instance, Clarke says that if we were not corrupt, 'It would be as impossible that a Man, contrary to the eternal Reason of things, should desire to gain some

small profit to Himself, by doing violence and damage to his Neighbor; as that he should be willing to be deprived of necessaries himself, to satisfy the unreasonable Covetousness or Ambition of another.' (Clarke, pp. 619–20/208)

65 Price, p. 41/141; Hutcheson, *Inquiry Concerning the Original of Our Ideas of Virtue or Moral Good* (cited in n20, above), p. 305.

66 G.E. Moore, *Principia Ethica* (Cambridge: Cambridge University Press, 1903), pp. 5–17.

67 Ross, pp. 7–12.

CONSISTENCY IN ACTION

Onora O'Neill

1 Universality tests in autonomous and in heteronomous ethics

Many recent discussions of universality tests, particularly those in English, are concerned either with what everybody wants done or with what somebody (usually the agent: sometimes an anonymous moral spectator) wants done either by or to everybody. This is true of the universality tests proposed in Singer's Generalization Argument, in Hare's Universal Prescriptivism and generally of various formulations of Golden Rules as well as of Rule Utilitarianism. Since universality tests of these sorts all make moral acceptability in some way contingent upon what is *wanted* (or, more circumspectly expressed, upon what is preferred or found acceptable or promises the maximal utility) they all form part of moral theories which are *heteronomous*, in Kant's sense of that term. Such theories construe moral acceptability as contingent upon the natural phenomena of desire and inclination, rather than on any intrinsic or formal features of the agent or his intentions. If we rely on any of these proposed criteria of moral acceptability, there will be no types of act which would not be rendered morally acceptable by some change or changes in human desires.

By contrast Kant's proposed universality test, the Categorical Imperative, contains no reference either to what everybody wants done or to what somebody wants done either by or to everybody. Kant's first formulation of the Categorical Imperative, the so-called Formula of Universal Law, runs

Act only on that maxim through which you can at the same time will that it should become a universal law.[1]

154

We are invited here to consider that we *can* will or intend, what it is *possible* or *consistent* for us to 'will as a universal law' (not what we *would* will or *would* find acceptable or *would want* as a universal law). Since the principle contains no reference to what everybody or anybody wants, nor to anything which lies beyond the agent's own capacity to will, it is part of a moral theory for agents who, in Kant's sense of the term, act *autonomously*. The principle asserts that such agents need only to impose a certain sort of consistency on their actions if they are to avoid doing what is morally unacceptable. It proposes an uncompromisingly rationalist foundation for ethics.

Nevertheless, Kant interpretation, particularly in English, is rich in heteronomous readings of the Formula of Universal Law and in allegations that (despite claims to the contrary) it is impossible to derive non-trivial, action-guiding applications of the Categorical Imperative without introducing heteronomous considerations.[2] Textual objections apart (and they would be overwhelming objections), such heteronomous readings of Kant's ethics discard what is most distinctive and challenging in his ethical theory. These are the features of his theory on which I intend to concentrate. I want to challenge the view that Kantian ethics, and non-heteronomous ethical theories in general, must be seen as either trivially empty or relying covertly on heteronomous considerations in order to derive substantive conclusions. To do so I shall try to articulate what seem to me to be the more important features of a universality test for agents who, in a certain sense of the term, act autonomously, that is without being determined solely by their natural desires and inclinations.[3]

I shall take Kant's Formula of Universal Law as the canonical case of such a universality test, and shall argue that it is neither trivially formalistic nor requires supplementing with heteronomous considerations if it is to be action guiding. However, my main concern here is not to explicate Kant's discussion of his universality test, nor to assess the difficulty or adequacy of his various moves.[4] I shall say nothing about his vindication of the Categorical Imperative, nor about his powerful critique of heteronomy in ethics, nor about his conception of human freedom. By setting aside these and other more strictly textual preoccupations I hope to open the way for a discussion of some features of universality tests for autonomous agents which have an interest which goes far beyond a concern with reading Kant accurately. I hope to show that Kant's formula, taken in conjunction with a plausible set of requirements for rational intending, yields strong and interesting ethical conclusions which do not depend on what either everybody or anybody wants, and so that reason can indeed be practical.

Over the last twenty years considerable light has been shed on the underlying structure of heteronomous ethical theories (as well as on other, particularly economic and political, decisions) by drawing on studies of the formal aspects of decision making under various conditions which have been articulated in various models of rational choice. In such discussions it is generally taken for granted that rational choosing is in some way or other contingent upon a set of desires or preferences.[5] I shall suggest that a similar concentration on certain requirements of rationality which are not contingent upon desires or preferences can help to provide a clearer picture of the underlying structure and strength of an ethical theory for autonomous beings.

The sequence of argument is straightforward. Section 2 provides an explication of Kant's Formula of Universal Law and of some of the ways in which this affects the character of an ethic for autonomous beings. Section 3 discusses some ways in which intentional action can fall into inconsistency even when the question of universalizing is not raised. Sections 4, 5 and 6 show how requirements for rational intending can be conjoined with Kant's universality test to yield determinate ethical conclusions.

2 Maxims and moral categories

The test which Kant's Formula of Universal Law proposes for the moral acceptability of acts can be divided into two aspects. In the first place it enjoins us to *act on a maxim*; secondly it restricts us to action on those maxims *through which we can will at the same time that it should be a universal law*. It is only the latter clause which introduces a universality test. However, for an understanding of the nature of this test it is essential in the first place to understand what Kant means by 'acting on a maxim'. For, contrary to appearances, this is not a trivial part of his criterion of morally acceptable action. Because a universality test for autonomous beings does not look at what is wanted, nor at the results of action, but merely demands that certain standards of consistency be observed in autonomously chosen action, it has to work with a conception of action which has the sort of formal structure which can meet (or fail to meet) standards of consistency. It is only those acts which embody or express syntactically structured principles or descriptions which can be thought of as candidates either for consistency or for inconsistency. Mere reflexes or reactions, for example, cannot be thought of as consistent or inconsistent: nor can acts be considered merely instrumentally as means for producing certain outcomes. In requiring action on a maxim Kant is already insisting that whatever is morally assessable should have a certain formal structure.

A maxim, Kant tells us, is 'a subjective principle of action'; it is 'the principle on which the subject acts'.[6] A maxim is therefore the principle of action of a particular agent at a particular time; but it need not be 'subjective' in the sense that it seeks to fulfil that particular agent's desires. In speaking of maxims as subjective principles Kant is not adopting any sort of heteronomous standard, but means to propose a standard against which the principles agents propose to act on, of whatever sort, may be tested. The Categorical Imperative provides a way of testing the moral acceptability of what we autonomously propose to do. It does not aim to generate plans of action for those who have none.

While maxims are the principles of action of particular agents at particular times, one and the same principle might be adopted as a maxim by many agents at various times or by a given agent on numerous occasions. It is a corollary of Kant's conception of human freedom that we can adopt or discard maxims, including those maxims which refer to our desires.

On the other hand acting on a maxim does not require explicit or conscious or complete formulation of that maxim. Even routine or thoughtless or indecisive action is action on *some* maxim. However, not all of the principles of action that a particular agent might exemplify at a given time would count as the agent's maxim. For principles of action need only incorporate *some* true description of an agent and *some* true description of his act and situation, whether these descriptions are vacuous and vague or brimming with detail. But an agent's maxim in a given act must incorporate just those descriptions of the agent, the act and the situation upon which the doing of the act depends.

An agent's maxim in a given act cannot, then, be equated simply with his intentions. For an agent's intentions in doing a given act may refer to incidental aspects of the particular act and situation. For example, in making a new visitor feel welcome I may offer and make him or her some coffee. In doing so there will be innumerable aspects of my action which are intentional – the choice of mug, the addition of milk, the stirring; and there will also be numerous aspects of action which are 'below the level of intention – the gesture with which I hand the cup, the precise number of stirs and so on. But the various specific intentions with which I orchestrate the offer and preparation of coffee are all ancillary to an underlying intention. *Maxims are those underlying intentions by which we guide and control our more specific intentions.* In this particular example, had I lacked coffee I could have made my visitor welcome in other ways: the specific intention of offering and making coffee was subordinate to the maxim of making a visitor welcome. Had I had a quite different maxim – perhaps to make my visitor unwelcome – I would not in that context have acted on just those specific intentions. In another context, e.g. in a society where an offer of coffee would be understood as we would understand an offer of hemlock, the same or similar specific intentions might have implemented a maxim of making unwelcome.

The fact that maxims are underlying or fundamental intentions has important implications.[7] It means in the first place that it may not be easy to tell on which maxim a given act was done. For example, a person who helps somebody else in a public place may have the underlying intention of being helpful – or alternatively the underlying intention of fostering a certain sort of good reputation. Since the helpful act might equally well be done in furtherance of either underlying intention, there may be some doubt as to the agent's maxim. Merely asking an agent what his underlying maxim is in such a situation may not settle the issue. The agent might himself be unsure. Both he and others can work out that if he would have done the action even if nobody had come to know of it, then his underlying intention would not have been to seek a certain sort of reputation. But he may after all be genuinely uncertain what his act would have been had he been faced with the possibility of helping, isolated from any effects on his reputation. Isolation tests can settle such issues[8] – if we know their outcome; but since most such tests refer to counterfactual situations we often don't know that outcome with any great certainty. Further, isolation tests provide only a *negative* test of what an agent's maxim is not. Even the person who has used such a test to show that his maxim is not to acquire a reputation may still be unsure whether his maxim was just to be helpful. He may perhaps wonder whether his underlying intention was not to preserve a certain sort of self image or to bolster his own sense of worth. Kant remarks on the opacity of the human heart and the difficulty of self-knowledge; he laments that for all we know there never has been a truly loyal friend.[9] And he does not view these as dispellable difficulties. Rather these limits to human self-knowledge constitute the fundamental context of human action. Kant holds that we can know what it would be to try to act on a maxim of a certain sort, but can never be sure that what we do does not reflect further maxims which we disavow. However, the underlying intentions which guide our more specific intentions are not in principle undiscoverable. Even when not consciously formulated they can often be inferred with some assurance, if not certainty, as the principles and policies which our more specific intentions express and implement.

On a certain view of the purpose of a universality test the fact that the maxim of a given action is neither observable nor always reliably inferable would be a most serious objection. For it would appear to render the outcome of any application of a universality test of dubious moral importance – since we might mistakenly have applied the test to a principle other than the agent's maxim. Further, even if the maxim had been correctly formulated, whether by the agent or by others, the maxim itself might reflect mistaken beliefs or self-deception in the agent, or the agent's act might fail to live up to his maxim. How then could any test applied to the agent's maxim be expected to classify acts into moral categories such as the right and the forbidden? For these categories apply to the outward and observable aspects of action. It is after all common enough for us to think of acts which are at least outwardly right (perhaps even obligatory) as nevertheless reflecting dubious intentions (I aim to kill an innocent, but mistakenly incapacitate the tiger who is about to maul him), and of acts whose intentions are impeccable as issuing tragically in wrong action (I aim for the tiger but despatch the innocent).

The answer Kant gives to this problem is plain. It is that rightness and wrongness and the other 'categories of right' standardly used in appraisal of outward features of action are *not* the fundamental forms of moral acceptability and unacceptability which he takes the Categorical Imperative to be able to discriminate.[10] Since the locus of application of Kant's universality test (and perhaps of any non-heteronomous universality test) is agents' fundamental intentions, the moral distinction which it can draw is in the first place an intentional moral distinction, namely that between acts which have and those which lack moral worth. In an application of the Categorical Imperative to an agent's maxim we ask whether the underlying intention with which the agent acts or proposes to act – the intention which guides and controls his other more specific intentions – is consistently universalizable; if it is, according to Kant, we at least know that the action will not be morally unworthy, and will not be a violation of duty.

The fact that Kant is primarily concerned with judgments of moral worth is easily forgotten, perhaps because he speaks of the Categorical Imperative as a test of *duty*, while we often tend to think of duty as confined to the *outward* aspects of action. It is quite usual for us to think of principled action as combining both duty and moral worthiness, which we regard as separate matters (e.g. showing scrupulous respect for others) or alternatively as revealing a moral worthiness which goes beyond all duty (e.g. gratuitous kindness which we think of as supererogatory). Correspondingly it is quite usual for us to think of unprincipled action as in any case morally unworthy but still, in some cases, within the bounds of duty (e.g. the case of a would-be poisoner who mistakenly administers a life-saving drug). This is quite foreign to Kant's way of thinking, which sees the *central* case of duty as that of action which has moral worth, and regards as *derivative* that which accords merely in external respects with morally worthy action. On Kant's view the would-be poisoner who inadvertently saves life has violated a duty by acting in a morally unworthy way.

By taking an agent's fundamental or underlying intention as the point of application of his universality test Kant avoids one of the difficulties most frequently raised about universality tests, namely that it seems easy enough to formulate *some* principle of action for any act, indeed possibly one that incorporates one of the agent's intentions, which can meet the criterion of any universality tests, whatever the act. Notoriously some Nazi war criminals claimed that they were only 'doing their job' or only 'obeying orders' – which are after all not apparently morally unworthy activities. The disingenuousness of the claim that such acts were not morally unworthy lies in the fact that these Nazis were not only doing this, and indeed that in many cases their specific intentions were ancillary to more fundamental intentions which might indeed have revealed moral unworthiness in the agent. (Such fundamental intentions might range from 'I'll do whatever I'm told to so long as it doesn't endanger me' to a fundamental maxim of genocide.) The fact that we can formulate *some* universalizable surface intention for any action by selecting among the agent's various surface intentions is no embarrassment to a universality test which is intended to apply to agents' maxims, and offers a solution to the problem of relevant descriptions.

It is equally irrelevant to a universality test that applies to maxims that we may be able to find some non-universalizable intentions among the more specific intentions with which an agent implements and fills out any maxim. If in welcoming my visitor with a cup of coffee I intentionally select a particular cup, my specific intention clearly cannot be universally acted on. The very particularity of the world means that there will always be aspects of action, including intentional aspects, which could not be universally adopted or intended. Kant's universality test, however, as we shall see, construes moral worth as contingent not on the universalizability or otherwise of an agent's specific intentions but on the universalizability of an agent's fundamental or underlying intention.[11]

For Kant, then, the Categorical Imperative provides a criterion in the first place for duties to act on underlying intentions which are morally worthy. It is only as a second and derivative part of his ethical theory that he proposes that the Categorical Imperative also provides a test of the outward wrongness and rightness of acts of specific sorts. He proposes in the *Groundwork* that acts which accord in outward respects with acts done on morally worthy maxims of action should be seen as being 'in conformity with' or 'in accord with' duty. The claim that we can provide a *general* account of which specific actions conform to the outward expressions of morally worthy maxims is highly controversial. We have already noted that there are many ways in which ancillary intentions may be devised in undertaking action on a given maxim, and there may be no single specific intention which is indispensable in all circumstances for action on a given maxim. Hence it is not generally clear what outward conformity conforms to. Kant appears to accept that the notion of outward conformity to duty is empty in many cases of duties of virtue, which are not sufficiently determinate for any particular more specific intentions to be singled out as required. He speaks of such duties as being 'of wide requirement'. But he also speaks of duties of narrow or strict requirement, and includes among these duties of justice and certain duties of respect to ourselves and to others.[12] Hence he takes it that there could in principle be a merely outward conformity to these strict or 'perfect' duties. Whether this claim is justified depends on the success of his demonstration that the underlying maxims of justice and respect have determinate specific implications for all possible human conditions. If they do not, then there will be no wholly general account of the requirements of justice and respect for all possible situations. It is then at any rate not obvious that we can derive a standard for the outward rightness of acts from a standard for the moral worth of underlying intentions. This is a major problem which I intend to set on one side in order to explore the implications of a universality test which applies to underlying intentions and so aims, at least primarily, at a test of the moral worth rather than the outward rightness of actions.

The fact that Kant's universality test focuses on maxims, and so on the moral worth of action, implies that it is a test which agents must seek to apply to their own proposals for action. This is not, however, because an agent is in a wholly privileged epistemological position with respect to his own underlying intentions. No doubt others may often have some difficulty even in discerning all of an agent's surface intentions, and may be quite unsure about his underlying intention. But Kant does not regard the agent's vantage point as affording infallible insight into his own intentions – self-consciousness is not transparent – and would not deny that on occasion others might arrive at a more accurate appreciation of an agent's underlying intention than the agent could himself reach.

The reason why a universality test in an autonomous ethical theory is primarily one for the use of agents rather than of moral spectators is rather that it is only an agent who can adopt, modify or discard maxims. While a test of the outward moral status of acts might be of most use and importance to third parties (legislators, judges, educators – those of us who pass judgment on others), because it may be possible or indeed necessary to prevent or deter or praise or punish in order to elicit or foster outward action of a certain sort, it is difficult if not impossible for outward regulation or pressure to change an agent's underlying intention. Surface conformity can be exacted; intentional conformity is more elusive.[13] Precisely because we are considering what a universality test for autonomous beings must be like, we must recognize that the test is one which we can propose to but not impose upon moral agents.

3 Inconsistency without universalizing

This account of acting on a maxim shows at least how action can be construed in a way which makes consistency and inconsistency possible, and provides some grounds for thinking that a focus on maxims may avoid some of the difficulties which have arisen in attempts to apply universality tests unrestrictedly to principles of action of all sorts. This opens the way for showing how action on a non-universalizable maxim is inconsistent and for considering whether such inconsistency constitutes a criterion of moral unworthiness. Before dealing with these topics it will be useful to run over some of the many ways in which action on a maxim may reveal inconsistency even when universalizing is not brought into the picture.

It is, of course, true that any act which is done is possible, taken in itself. But it does not follow that the intentions which are enacted are mutually consistent. There are two sorts of possibilities here: in the first place there may be an internal inconsistency within an agent's maxim; in the second place there may be contradictions between the various specific intentions an agent adopts in pursuit of his maxim, or between some of these specific intentions and the agent's maxim. These two sorts of contradiction correspond closely to the two types of contradiction which Kant thinks may arise when attempts to universalize maxims fail, and which he characterizes as involving respectively 'contradictions in conception' and 'contradictions in the will'.[14] Since I am also interested in charting the inconsistencies which can arise independently of attempts to universalize, as well as in those which arise when universalizing fails, I shall use the rather similar labels 'conceptual inconsistency' and 'volitional inconsistency' to distinguish these two types of incoherence in action. A consideration of the different types of incoherence which maxims may display even when the question of universalizability is not raised provides a useful guide to the types of incoherence which non-universalizable maxims display.

A maxim of action may in the first place be incoherent simply because it expresses an impossible aspiration. An agent's maxim might be said to involve a conceptual inconsistency if his underlying intention was, for example, both to be successful and to be unworldly, or alternatively to be both popular and reclusive, or both to care for others and always to put his own advantage first, or both to be open and frank with everybody and to be a loyal friend or associate, or both to keep his distance from others and to have intimate personal relationships. Agents whose underlying maxims incorporate such conceptual inconsistencies do not, of course, succeed in doing impossible acts; rather the pattern of their action appears to pull in opposite directions and to be in various ways self-defeating. At its extreme we may regard such underlying incoherence in a person's maxim, and consequent fragmentation of his action, as tragic or pathological (and perhaps both), since there is no way in which he or she can successfully enact the underlying intention. In other cases we may think of the pattern of action which results from underlying conceptual incoherence as showing no more than ambivalence or presenting conflicting signals to others, who are consequently at a loss as to what they should expect to do, finding themselves in a 'double bind'.

However, not all cases of disjointed action constitute evidence of an internally inconsistent maxim. For it may well be that somebody adopts some accommodation of the potentially inconsistent aspects of his underlying intention. For example, somebody may adopt the maxim of being competitive and successful in public and professional life but disregarding such considerations in private life; or of being obedient and deferential to superiors but overbearing and exacting with all others. Provided such persons can keep the two spheres of action separated, their underlying intention can be internally consistent. Hence one cannot infer an inconsistency in someone's underlying intentions merely from the fact that he or she exhibits tendencies in opposing directions. For these tendencies may reflect a coherent underlying intention to respond or act differently in different types of context or with different groups of people. A non-universalized maxim embodies a conceptual contradiction only if it *aims* at achieving mutually incompatible objectives and so cannot under any circumstances be acted on with success.

A focus on maxims which embody contradictions in conception pays no attention to the fact that maxims are not merely principles which we can conceive (or entertain, or even wish) but principles which we *will* or intend, that is to say principles which we adopt as *principles of action*. Conceptual contradictions can be identified even in principles of action which are never adopted or acted upon. But a second and rather different type of incoherence is exhibited in some attempts to will maxims whose realization can be quite coherently envisaged. Willing, after all, is not just a matter of wishing that something were the case, but involves committing oneself to doing something to bring that situation about when opportunity is there and recognized. Kant expressed this point by insisting that rationality requires that whoever wills some end wills the necessary means in so far as these are available.

> Who wills the end wills (so far as reason has decisive influence on his actions) also the means which are indispensably necessary and in his power. So far as willing is concerned, this proposition is analytic: for in my willing of an object as an effect there is already conceived the causality of myself as a working cause – that is, the use of means; and from the concept of willing an end the imperative merely extracts the concept of actions necessary to this end.[15]

This amounts to saying that to will some end without willing whatever means are indispensable for that end, insofar as they are available, is, even when the end itself involves no conceptual inconsistency, to involve oneself in a volitional inconsistency. It is to embrace at least one specific intention which, far from being guided by the underlying intention, is inconsistent with that intention.

Kant, however, explicitly formulates only *one* of the principles which must be observed by an agent who is not to fall into volitional inconsistency. The 'Principle of Hypothetical Imperatives', as expressed in the passage just quoted, requires that agents intend any indispensable means for whatever they fundamentally intend. Conformity with this requirement of coherent intending would be quite compatible with intending no means to whatever is fundamentally intended whenever there is no specific act which is indispensable for action on the underlying intention. Further reflection on the idea of intending the means suggests that there is a *family* of Principles of Rational Intending, of which the Principle of Hypothetical Imperatives is just one, though perhaps the most important one. The following list of further Principles of Rational Intending which coherent intending (as opposed to mere wishing or contemplating) apparently requires agents to observe may not be complete, but is sufficient to generate a variety of interesting conclusions.

First, it is a requirement of rationality to intend not merely all *indispensable* or *necessary* means to that which is fundamentally intended but also to intend some *sufficient* means to what is fundamentally intended. If it were not, I could coherently intend to eat an adequate diet, yet not intend to eat food of any specific sort on the grounds that no specific sort of food is indispensable in an adequate diet.

Secondly, it is a requirement of rationality not merely to intend all necessary and some sufficient means to what is fundamentally intended, but to seek to make such means available when they are not. If it were not, I could coherently claim to intend to help bring about a social revolution but do absolutely nothing, on the grounds that there is no revolutionary situation at present, so settling for rhetoric and gesture rather than politics. But if I do this, I at most wish for, and do not intend to help to bring about, a social revolution.

Thirdly, it is a requirement of rationality to intend not merely all necessary and some sufficient means to whatever is fundamentally intended but to intend all necessary and some sufficient *components* of whatever is fundamentally intended. If it were not, I could coherently claim to intend to be kind to someone to whom, despite opportunity, I show no kindness in word, gesture or deed, merely because acting kindly is not the sort of thing which requires us to take means to an end but the sort of thing which requires that we act in some of the ways that are *constitutive* of kindness.[16]

Fourthly, it is a requirement of rationality that the various specific intentions we actually adopt in acting on a given maxim in a certain context be mutually consistent. If it were not, I could coherently claim to be generous to all my friends by giving to each the exclusive use of all my possessions.

Fifthly, it is a requirement of rationality that the foreseeable results of the specific intentions adopted in acting on a given underlying intention be consistent with the underlying intention. If it were not, I could coherently claim to be concerned for the well-being of a child for whom I refuse an evidently life-saving operation, on the grounds that my specific intention – perhaps to shield the child from the hurt and trauma of the operation – is itself aimed at the child's well-being. But where such shielding foreseeably has the further consequence of endangering the child's life, it is clearly an intention which undercuts the very maxim which supposedly guides it.

There may well be yet further principles which fully coherent sets of intentions must observe, and possibly some of the principles listed above need elaboration or qualification. The point, however, is to reveal that once we see action as issuing from a complex web of intentions, many of which are guided by and ancillary to certain more fundamental intentions under particular conditions, intending coherently and avoiding volitional inconsistency becomes a demanding and complex affair.

Reflection on the various Principles of Rational Intending reveals a great deal about the connections between surface and underlying intentions to which a rational being must aspire. Underlying intentions to a considerable extent express the larger and longer term goals, policies and aspirations of a life. But if these goals, policies and aspirations are willed (and not merely wished for) they must be connected with some set of surface intentions which express commitment to acts that, in the actual context in which the agent finds himself, provide either the means to or some components of the underlying intention, or at least take the agent in the direction of being able to form such intentions, without at any point committing the agent to acts whose performance would undercut his underlying intention. Wherever such coherence is absent we find an example of intending which, despite the conceptual coherence of the agent's maxim, is volitionally incoherent. In some cases we may think the deficiency cognitive – the agent fails despite available information to appreciate what he needs to do if he is indeed to act on his maxim (he may be stupid or thoughtless or calculate poorly). In other cases we might think of the deficiency as primarily volitional: the agent fails to intend what is needed if he is to will his maxim and not merely to wish for it to be realized. Each of these types of failure in rationality subdivides into many different sorts of cases. It follows that there are very many different ways in which an agent whose intentions are not to be volitionally inconsistent may have to consider his intentions.

Perhaps the most difficult of the various requirements of coherent willing is the last, the demand that the agent not adopt specific intentions which in a given context may undercut his own maxim. There are many cases in which agents can reach relatively clear specific intentions about how they will implement or instance their maxim, yet the act selected, though indeed selected as a means to or component of their underlying intention, backfires. It is fairly common for agents to adopt surface intentions which, when enacted, foreseeably will produce results which defeat the agent's own deeper intentions. Defensive measures generate counterattack; attempts to do something particularly well result in botched performances; decisive success in battle is revealed as Pyrrhic victory. It is perhaps unclear how long a view of the likely results of his own action an agent must take for us not to think action which leads to results which are not compatible with his underlying intention is irrational. But at the least the standard and foreseeable results of his action should not undercut the underlying intention if we are to think of an agent as acting rationally. Somebody who claims to intend no harm to others, and specifically merely intends to share a friendly evening's drinking and to drive others home afterwards, but who then decides on serious drinking and so cannot safely drive, cannot plausibly claim to intend merely the exuberant drinking and bonhomie and not the foreseeable drunkenness and inability to drive safely. Given standard information, such a set of intentions is volitionally incoherent. For it is a normal and foreseeable result of exuberant drinking that the drinker is incapable of driving safely. One who intends the drinking also (given normal intelligence and experience) intends the drunkenness; hence cannot coherently also intend to drive others home if his underlying intention is to harm nobody.[17]

This brief consideration of various ways in which agents' intentions may fail to be consistent shows that achieving consistency in action is a difficult matter even if we do not introduce any universality test. Intentions may be either conceptually or volitionally incoherent. The demand that the acts we do reflect conceptually and volitionally coherent sets of intentions therefore constitutes a powerful constraint on all practical reasoning. This provides some reason for thinking that when these demands for consistency are extended in the way in which the second aspect of Kant's Formula of Universal Law requires we should expect to see patterns of reasoning which, far from being ineffective or trivial, generate powerful and interesting results.

4 Inconsistency in universalizing

The intuitive idea behind the thought that a universality test can provide a criterion of moral acceptability may be expressed quite simply as the thought that if we are to act as morally worthy beings we should not single ourselves out for special consideration or treatment. Hence whatever we propose for ourselves should be possible (note: not desired or wanted – but at least *possible*) for all others. Kant expresses this commonplace thought (it is, of course, not his argument for the Categorical Imperative) by suggesting that what goes wrong when we adopt a non-universalizable maxim is that we treat ourselves as special:

> . . .whenever we transgress a duty, we find that we in fact do not will that our maxim should become a universal law – since this is impossible for us – but rather that its opposite should remain a law universally: we only take the liberty of making an *exception* to it for ourselves (or even just for this once) . . .[18]

It is evident from this understanding of the Formula of Universal Law that the notion of a community of other autonomous agents is already implicit in the Formula of Universal Law. It is not the case that Kant only introduces that notion into his ethics with the Formula of the Kingdom of Ends, which would imply that the various formulations of the Categorical Imperative could not be in any way equivalent. To universalize is from the start to consider whether what one proposes for oneself *could* be done by others. This seems to many too meagre a foundation for ethics but not in itself an implausible constraint on any adequate ethical theory.

Clearly enough whatever cannot be consistently intended even for oneself also cannot be consistently intended for all others. The types of cases shown conceptually or volitionally inconsistent by the methods discussed in the previous section are *a fortiori* non-universalizable. This raises the interesting question of whether one should think of certain types of cognitive and volitional failure as themselves morally unworthy. However, I shall leave this question aside in order to focus on the types of failure in consistent intending which are *peculiar* to the adoption of non-universalizable intentions.

I shall therefore assume from now on that we are considering cases of maxims which are in themselves not conceptually incoherent, and of sets of underlying and surface intentions which are not themselves volitionally inconsistent. The task is to pinpoint the ways in which inconsistency emerges in some attempts to universalize such internally consistent intentions. The second part of Kant's Formula of Universal Law enjoins action only on maxims which the agent can at the same time will as a universal law. He suggests that we can imagine this hypothetical willing by working out what it would be like 'if the maxim of your action were to become through your will a universal law of nature'.[19] To universalize his maxim an agent must satisfy himself that he can both adopt the maxim and simultaneously will that others do so. In determining whether he can do so he may find that he is defeated by either of the two types of contradiction which, as we have already seen, can afflict action even when universalizing is not under consideration. Kant's own account of these two types of incoherence, either of which defeats universalizability, is as follows:

We must *be able to will* that a maxim of our action should become a universal law – that is the general canon for all moral judgement of action. Some actions are so constituted that their maxim cannot even be *conceived* as a universal law of nature without contradiction, let alone be *willed* as what *ought* to become one. In the case of others we do not find this inner impossibility, but it is still impossible to *will* that their maxim should be raised to the universality of a law of nature, because such a will would contradict itself.[20]

Kant also asserts that those maxims which when universalized lead to conceptual contradiction are the ones which strict or perfect duty requires us to avoid, while those which when universalized are conceptually coherent but not coherently willable are opposed only to wider or imperfect duties.[21] Since we probably lack both rigorous criteria and firm intuitions of the boundaries between perfect and imperfect duties it is hard to evaluate this claim. However it is remarkably easy to display contradictions which arise in attempts to universalize maxims which we might think of as clear cases of violations of duties of justice and self-respect which Kant groups together as perfect duties; and it is also easy to show how contradictions emerge in attempts to universalize maxims which appear to exemplify clear violations of duties of beneficence and self development, which Kant groups together as imperfect duties. By running through a largish number of such examples I hope to show how groundless is the belief that universality tests need supplementing with heteronomous considerations if they are to be action guiding.

5 Contradictions in conception

Maxims which may lead to contradictions in conception when we attempt to universalize them often do not contain any conceptual contradiction if we merely adopt the maxim. For example, there is no contradiction involved in adopting the maxim of becoming a slave. But this maxim has as its universalized counterpart – the maxim we must attempt to 'will as a universal law' – the maxim of everybody becoming a slave.[22] But if everybody became a slave there would be nobody with property rights, hence no slave holders, hence nobody could become a slave.[23] Consider alternatively a maxim of becoming a slave holder. Its universalized counterpart would be the maxim that everybody become a slave holder. But if everybody became a slave holder then everybody would have some property rights, hence nobody could be a slave, hence there could be no slave holders. Action on either of the non-universalizable maxims of becoming a slave or becoming a slave holder would reveal moral unworthiness: it could be undertaken only by one who makes of himself a special case.

Contradictions in conception can also be shown to arise in attempts to universalize maxims of deception and coercion. The maxim of coercing whoever will not comply with my will has as its universalized counterpart the maxim that everybody will coerce others when they do not comply with his will: but this requires that each party coerce others, including those who are coercing him, hence that each party both complies with others' will (being coerced) and simultaneously does not comply with others but rather (as coercer) exacts their compliance. A maxim of coercion cannot coherently be universalized and reveals moral unworthiness. By contrast, a maxim of autonomous coordination can be consistently universalized. A maxim of deceiving others as convenient has as its universalized counterpart the maxim that everyone will deceive others as convenient. But if everyone were to deceive others as convenient then there would be no such thing as trust or reliance on others' acts of communication, hence nobody could be deceived, hence nobody could deceive others as convenient.

An argument of the same type can be applied to the maxim which is perhaps the most fundamental for a universality test for autonomous action, namely the maxim of abrogating autonomy. One whose maxim it is to defer to the judgment and decisions of others – to choose heteronomy[24] – adopts a maxim whose universalized counterpart is that everyone defer to the judgments and decisions of others. But if everyone defers to the judgments and decisions of others, then there are no autonomous decisions to provide the starting point for deferring in judgment, hence it cannot be the case that everybody defers in judgment. Decisions can never be reached when everyone merely affirms 'I agree'. A maxim of 'elective heteronomy' cannot consistently be universalized.

Interpreters of Kant have traditionally made heavier weather of the contradiction in conception test than these short arguments suggest is necessary. There have perhaps been two reasons for this. One is clearly that Kant's own examples of applications of the Categorical Imperative are more complex and convoluted than these short arguments suggest.[25] But while detailed analysis of these examples is necessary for an evaluation of Kant's theory, it is clarifying to see whether a contradiction in conception test works when liberated from the need to accommodate Kant's particular discussion of examples.

But a second reason why the contradiction in conception test has seemed problematic to many of Kant's commentators is perhaps of greater importance for present concerns. It is that while many would grant that we can detect contradictions in attempts to universalize maxims simply of slave-holding or coercing or deceiving or deference, they would point out that no contradiction emerges if we seek to universalize more circumspect maxims such as 'I will hold slaves if I am in a position of sufficient power' or 'I will deceive when it suits me and I can probably get away with it' or 'I will defer in judgment to those I either admire or fear'. Still less do contradictions emerge when we aim to universalize highly specific intentions of deception or deference such as 'I will steal from Woolworths when I can get away with it' or 'I will do whatever my Parish Priest tells me to do'.

However the force of this objection to the claim that the contradiction in conception test can have significant moral implications is undercut when we remember that this is a test which applies to agents' maxims, that is to their underlying or fundamental intentions and that as a corollary it is a test of moral worth. For what will be decisive is what an agent's fundamental intention in doing a given act really is. What counts is whether the expression of falsehood expresses a fundamental attempt to deceive, or whether agreement with another (in itself innocent enough) expresses a fundamental refusal to judge or think for oneself. For an agent cannot truthfully claim that his underlying intent was of a very specific sort unless the organization of his other, less fundamental, intentions reveals that his intention really was subject to those restrictions. Precisely because the Categorical Imperative formulates a universality test which applies to *maxims*, and not just to any intention, it is not rebutted by the fact that relatively specific intentions often can be universalized without conceptual contradiction. Conversely, further evidence for the interpretation of the notion of a maxim presented in Section 2 is that it leads to an account of the Categorical Imperative which is neither powerless nor counterintuitive. However, for the same reason (that it applies to maxims and not to intentions of all sorts) the Categorical Imperative can most plausibly be construed as a test of moral worth rather than of outward rightness, and must always be applied with awareness that we lack certainty about what an agent's maxim is in a given case. This is a relatively slight difficulty when we are assessing our own proposed maxims of action, since we at least can do no better than to probe and test the maxim on which we propose to act (but even here we have no guarantee against self-deception). And it means that we will always remain to some extent unsure about our assessment of others' acts. Kant after all insists that we do not even know whether there *ever* has been a truly morally worthy act. But that is something we do not need to know in order to try to do such acts. Self-deception may cloud our knowledge of our own maxims; but we are not powerless in self-guidance.

6 Contradictions in the will

Just as there are maxims which display no conceptual incoherence until attempts are made to universalize them, so there are maxims which exhibit no conceptual incoherence even when universalized, but which are shown to be volitionally inconsistent when attempts are made to universalize them. Such maxims cannot be 'willed as a universal law'; attempts to do so fail in one way or another to meet the standards of rationality specified by the group of principles which I have termed Principles of Rational Intending. For to will a maxim is, after all, not just to conceive the realization of an underlying intention; that requires no more than speculation or wishing. Willing requires also the adoption of more specific intentions which are guided by and chosen (in the light of the agent's beliefs) to realize the underlying intention, or, if that is impossible, as appropriate moves towards a situation in which such specific intentions might be adopted. Whoever wills a maxim also adopts more specific intentions as means to or constituents of realizing his underlying intention, and is also committed to the foreseeable results of acting on these more specific intentions. Since intending a maxim commits the agent to such a variety of other intentions there are various different patterns of argument which reveal that certain maxims cannot be willed as a universal law without contradiction.

Clearly the most comprehensive way in which a maxim may fail to be willable as a universal law is if its universal counterpart is inconsistent with the specific intentions which would be necessary for its own realization. Universalizing such a maxim would violate the Principle of Hypothetical Imperatives. The point is well illustrated by a Kantian example.[26] If I seek to will a maxim of non-beneficence as a universal law, my underlying intention is to help no others when they need it and its universalized counterpart is that nobody help others when they need it. But if everybody denies help to others when they need it, then those who need help will not be helped, and in particular I will not myself be helped when I need it. But if I am committed to the standards of rational willing which comprise the various Principles of Rational Intending, then I am committed to willing some means to any end to which I am committed, and this must include willing that if I am in need of help and therefore not able to achieve my ends without help I be given some appropriate help. In trying to universalize a maxim of non-beneficence I find myself committed simultaneously to willing that I not be helped when I need it and that I be helped when I need it. This contradiction, however, differs from the conceptual contradictions which emerge in attempts to universalize maxims such as those considered in the last section. A world of non-benevolent persons is conceivable without contradiction. Arguments which reveal contradictions in the will depend crucially upon the role of the various Principles of Rational Intending – in this case on the Principle of Hypothetical Imperatives – in constraining the choice of specific intentions to a set which will implement all underlying intentions. It is only because *intending* a maxim of non-benevolence as a universal law requires commitment to that very absence of help when needed, to which all rational intending requires assent, that non-benevolence cannot coherently be universalized.

A second Kantian example,[27] which provides an argument to volitional incoherence, is a maxim of neglecting to develop any talents. A world of beings who develop no talents contains no conceptual incoherence. The maxim of an individual who decides to develop no talents, while imprudent, reveals no volitional inconsistency. For it is always *possible* that he finds that others fend for him and so that there will be means available for at least some autonomous action on his part. (It is not a fundamental requirement of practical reason that there should be means available to any project he adopts, but only that he should not have ruled out all autonomous action.) However, an attempt to universalize a maxim of neglecting talents commits one to a world in which no talents have been developed, and so to a situation in which necessary means are lacking not just for some but for any sort of autonomous action. Any autonomous agent who fails to will the development, in himself or others, of whatever minimal range of talents is required and sufficient for *some* autonomous action is committed to internally inconsistent sets of intentions. He intends both that autonomous action be possible and that it be undercut by neglect to develop even a minimal range of talents which would leave some possibility of autonomous action. This argument shows nothing about the development of talents which may be required or sufficient for any *specific* projects, but only points to the inconsistency of failing to foster such talents as are needed and sufficient for autonomous action of some sort or other. It is an argument which invokes not only the Principle of Hypothetical Imperatives but the requirement that rational beings intend some set of means sufficient for the realization of their underlying intention.

These two examples of arguments which reveal volitional inconsistencies show only that it is morally unworthy to adopt maxims either of systematic non-benevolence or of systematic neglect of talents. The duties which they ground are relatively indeterminate duties of virtue. The first of these arguments does not specify whom it is morally worthy to help, to what extent, in what ways or at what cost, but only that it would be morally unworthy to adopt an underlying intention of non-benevolence. Similarly the second argument does not establish which talents it would be morally worthy to develop, in whom, to what extent or at what cost, but only that it would be morally unworthy to adopt an underlying intention of making no effort to develop any talents. The person who adopts a maxim either of non-benevolence or of non-development of talents cannot coherently universalize his maxim. He or she must either make an exception of himself, and intend, unworthily, to be a free-rider on others' benevolence and talents, or will be committed to some specific intentions which are inconsistent with those required for action on his own maxim.

Another example of a maxim which cannot consistently be willed as a universal law is the maxim of refusing to accept help when it is needed. The universalized counterpart of this underlying intention would be the intention that everyone refuse to accept help when it is needed. But autonomous beings cannot consistently commit themselves to intending that everyone forgo a means which, if ever they are in need of help, will be indispensable for them to act autonomously at all.

A further example of a non-universalizable maxim is provided by a maxim of ingratitude, whose universalized counterpart is that nobody show or express gratitude for favours received. In a world of autonomous but non-self-sufficient beings a universal maxim of ingratitude would require the systematic neglect of an important means for ensuring that help is forthcoming for those who need help if they are to realize their intentions. Hence in such a world nobody could coherently claim to will that those in need of help be helped. Yet we have already seen that failure to will that those in need of help be helped is volitionally inconsistent. Hence, willing a maxim of ingratitude also involves a commitment to a set of intentions not all of which can be consistently universalized. The volitional inconsistency which overtakes would-be universalizers of this maxim arises in two stages: the trouble with ingratitude is that, practised universally, it undercuts benevolence; the trouble with non-benevolence is that it cannot be universally practised by beings who (being autonomous) have at least some underlying maxims, yet (lacking self-sufficiency) cannot guarantee that their own resources will provide means sufficient for at least some autonomous project.

The hinge of all these arguments is that human beings (since they are autonomous adopters of maxims) have at least some maxims or projects, which (since they are not self-sufficient) they cannot always realize unaided, and so must (since they are rational) intend to draw on the assistance of others, and so must (if they universalize) intend to develop and foster a world which will lend to all the support of others' benevolence and talents. Such arguments can reveal the volitional inconsistencies involved in trying to universalize maxims of entirely neglecting the social virtues – benevolence, beneficence, solidarity, gratitude, sociability and the like – for beings who are autonomous yet not always able to achieve what they intend unaided. It follows from this that the social virtues are very differently construed in autonomous and in heteronomous ethics. An ethical theory for autonomous agents sees the social virtues as morally required, not because they are desired or liked but because they are necessary requirements for autonomous action in a being who is not self-sufficient. The content of the social virtues in an autonomous framework cannot be spelt out in terms of the provision of determinate goods or service or the meeting of certain set needs or the satisfaction of a determinate set of desires. Rather the content of these virtues will always depend on the various underlying maxims and projects, both individual and collaborative, to which autonomous agents commit themselves. What will constitute beneficence or kindness or care for others will depend in great part on how others intend to express their autonomy, and to collaborate in exercising their autonomy, in a given context.

7 Contradictions in the will and further results

The patterns of argument which can be used to show underlying anti-social intentions morally worthy make use of various Principles of Rational Intending in addition to the Principle of Hypothetical Imperatives. In particular they draw on the requirements that rational agents intend not merely necessary but sufficient means to or components of their underlying intentions, and that they also intend whatever means are indirectly required and sufficient to make possible the adoption of such specific intentions. However, the particular features of the fifth Principle of Rational Intending – the Principle of Intending the Further Results – have not yet been displayed. Attempts to evade this Principle of Rational Intending lead to a peculiar sort of volitional inconsistency.

Good examples of arguments which rely on this principle can be developed by considering cases of maxims which, when universalized, produce what are frequently referred to as 'unintended consequences'.

For example, I can adopt the underlying intention of improving my economic well-being, and the specific intention of doing so by competing effectively with others. The maxim of my action can be consistently universalized: there is no conceptual contradiction in intending everyone's economic position to improve. The specific intention of adopting competitive strategies is not inconsistent with the maxim to which it is ancillary; nor is universal action on competitive strategies inconsistent with universal economic advance (that indeed is what the invisible hand is often presumed to achieve). But if an agent intends his own economic advance to be achieved solely by competitive strategies, this nexus of intentions cannot consistently be willed as universal law, because the further results of universal competitive activity, by itself, are inconsistent with universal economic advance. If everyone seeks to advance by these (and no other) methods, the result will not put everybody ahead economically. A maxim of economic progress combined with the specific intention of achieving progress merely by competitive strategies cannot be universalized, any more than the intention of looking over the heads of a crowd can be universally achieved by everyone in the crowd standing on tiptoes.[28] On the other hand, a maxim of seeking economic advance by means of increased production can be consistently universalized. It is merely the particular specific intention of advancing economically by competitive strategies alone that leads to volitional inconsistency when universalized. Competitive means are inherently effective only for some: competitions must have losers as well as winners. Hence, while it can be consistent to seek individual economic advance solely by competitive methods, this strategy cannot consistently be universalized. Once we consider what it would be to intend the consequences of universal competition – the usually *unintended* consequences – we can see that there is an inconsistency not between universal competitive activity and universal economic progress, but between the *further results of intending only universal competitive activity and universal economic progress*. Economic progress and competitive activity might each of them consistently be universal; indeed it is possible for them to coexist within a certain society. (Capitalist economies do experience periods of general economic growth.) Nevertheless there is a volitional inconsistency in seeking to achieve universal economic growth *solely by way of* universal adoption of competitive strategies.

This argument does not show that either the intention to advance economically or the intention to act competitively cannot be universalized, but only that the composite intention of pursuing economic advance solely by competitive tactics cannot be universalized. It does not suggest that either competition or economic progress is morally unworthy, but only that an attempt to achieve economic progress solely by competitive methods and without aiming at any productive contribution is not universalizable and so morally unworthy.

Similarly there is no inconsistency in an intention to engage in competitive activities of other sorts (e.g. games and sports). But if such competition is ancillary to an underlying intention to win, then the overall intention is not universalizable. Competitive games must have losers. If winning is not the overriding aim in such activities, if they are played for their own sake, the activity is consistently universalizable. But to play competitively with the fundamental intention of winning is to adopt an intention which makes of one's own case a necessary exception.

8 Conclusions

The interest of an autonomous universality test is that it aims to ground an ethical theory on notions of consistency and rationality rather than upon considerations of desire and preference. Kant's universality test meets many of the conditions which any such universality test must meet. In particular it focuses on features of action which are appropriate candidates for assessments of coherence and incoherence, namely the maxims or fundamental intentions which autonomous agents may adopt and the web of more specific ancillary intentions which they must adopt in a given context if their commitment to a maxim is genuine. While Kant alludes specifically to conceptual inconsistencies and to those volitional inconsistencies which are attributable to non-observance of the Principle of Hypothetical Imperatives in attempts to universalize intentions, there is in addition a larger variety of types of volitional inconsistency which agents who seek to subject their maxims to a universality test (and so not to make an exception of their own case) must avoid. A universality test applied to autonomously chosen maxims and their ancillary, more specific, intentions can be action-guiding in many ways without invoking any heteronomous considerations.

However, precisely because it applies to autonomously chosen intentions, a universality test of this sort cannot generally provide a test of the rightness or wrongness of the specific outward aspects of action. It is, at least primarily, and perhaps solely, a test of the inner moral worth of acts. It tells us what we ought to avoid if we are not to use our autonomy in ways which we can know are in principle not possible for all others. Such a test is primarily of use to agents in guiding their own moral deliberations, and can only be used most tentatively in assessing the moral worth of others' action, where we are often sure only about specific outward aspects of action and not about the maxim. This point will not be of great importance if we do not think it important whether an ethical theory enables us to pass judgment on the moral worth of others' acts. But specific outward aspects of others' action are unavoidably of public concern. The considerations discussed here do not reveal whether or not these can be judged right or wrong by Kant's theory. Kant no doubt thought that it was possible to derive specific principles of justice from the Formula of Universal Law; but the success of this derivation and of his grounding of *Rechtslehre* is beyond the scope of this inquiry.

The universality test discussed here is, above all, a test of the mutual consistency of (sets of) intentions and universalized intentions. It operates by showing some sets of proposed intentions mutually inconsistent. It does not thereby generally single out action on any one set of specific intentions as morally required. On the contrary, the ways in which maxims can be enacted or realized by means of acts done on specific intentions must vary with situation, tradition and culture. The specific acts by which we can show or fail to show loyalty to a friend or respect to another or autonomy in our dealings with the world will always reflect specific ways of living and thinking and particular situations and relationships. What reason can provide is a way of discovering whether we are choosing to act in ways (however culturally specific) which we do not in principle preclude for others. The 'formal' character of the Categorical Imperative does not entail either that it has no substantive ethical implications or that it can select a unique code of conduct as morally worthy for all times and places. Rather than presenting a dismal choice between triviality and implausible rigorism, a universality test for autonomous action can provide a rational foundation for ethics and maintain a serious respect for the diversity of content of distinct ethical practices and traditions.

Notes

1 I. Kant, *Grundlegung zur Metaphysik der Sitten*, tr. H.J. Paton as *The Moral Law*, Hutchinson, London, 1953 (hereafter *Grundlegung*), p. 421 (Prussian Academy pagination).

2 Heteronomous readings of Kant's ethics include Schopenhauer's in *On the Basis of Morality*, tr. E.F.J. Payne, Bobbs Merrill, Indianapolis, 1965, Section 7, but are most common in introductory works in ethics. Recent examples include William K. Frankena, *Ethics*, Prentice Hall, New Jersey, 1963, p. 25; Gilbert Harman, *The Nature of Morality*, Oxford University Press, New York, 1977, p. 73 and D.D. Raphael, *Moral Philosophy*, Oxford University Press, Oxford, 1981, p. 76. Allegations that Kant, despite his

intentions, must invoke heteronomous considerations if he is to reach substantive ethical considerations can notoriously be found in J.S. Mill, 'Utilitarianism', in *Utilitarianism, Liberty and Representative Government*, J.M. Dent & Sons, London, 1968, p. 4, but are now more common in the secondary literature on Kantian ethics. Examples include C.D. Broad, *Five Types of Ethical Theory*, Littlefield Adams and Co., New Jersey, 1965, p. 130 and (with respect to imperfect duties) M. Singer, *Generalization in Ethics*, Alfred Knopf, New York, 1961, p. 262.

3 In Kant's terminology such action is *spontaneous* (not determined by alien causes, negatively free) and it is a further claim that it is also *Kantianly autonomous* (determined by pure practical reason). The argument here will not hinge on this strong and distinctive conception of human autonomy, but only on the weaker and more common conception of autonomy as independence from determination by outside forces including desires.

4 I have done so in O.O'Neill (O. Nell), *Acting on Principle*, Columbia University Press, New York, 1975. The account I offer here reflects some changes in my understanding of Kant's notion of a maxim. For this I am particularly indebted to Otfried Höffe, 'Kants kategorischer Imperativ als Kriterium des Sittlichen', *Zeitschrift für Philosophische Forschung*, 31, 1977, pp. 354–84.

5 Even a very wide-ranging and reflective recent discussion of rational choice theory such as Jon Elster's in *Ulysses and the Sirens*, Cambridge University Press, Cambridge, 1979, does not discuss any non-heteronomous conceptions of rational choosing.

6 *Grundlegung*, p. 421, n.; see also p. 401, n. 1; as well as I. Kant, *The Metaphysics of Morals*, of which Part II, the *Tugendlehre* appears as *The Doctrine of Virtue*, tr. M.J. Gregor, Harper and Row, New York, 1964 (hereafter *Metaphysic of Morals*), p. 225 (Prussian Academy pagination).

7 However, the claim that maxims are underlying or fundamental intentions should not be collapsed into the claim, which Kant makes in the *Religion*, that for any agent at a given time there is one fundamental maxim which underlies all his other maxims. I shall not here consider whether there are fundamental maxims in this sense. But see I. Kant, *Religion within the Limits of Reason Alone*, tr. T. Greene and H. Hudson, Harper and Row, New York, 1960, p. 16ff.

8 This is presumably why Kant often argues from isolation tests. E.g. *Grundlegung*, pp. 398–9 and 407.

9 See, for example, *Metaphysic of Morals*, pp. 440 and 445–6; *Grundlegung*, pp. 407–8 and *Religion*, p. 16.

10 See *Grundlegung*, 397–8 ('. . . the concept of *duty*, which includes that of a good will'). The persistence of the view that Kant is primarily concerned with a criterion of right action perhaps reflects a modern conception that duty *must* be a matter of externals more than it reflects the Kantian texts. See also *Acting on Principle*, Ch. 4 and O. O'Neill, 'Kant After Virtue', *Inquiry*, 26, 1983, pp. 387–406.

11 The points mentioned in this and in the preceding paragraph suggest why a focus on maxims may make it possible to bypass a variety of problems which are said to plague universality tests when applied to principles which are 'too general' or 'too specific'; these problems include those of invertibility, reiterability, moral indeterminacy, and those of the generation either of no results or of trivial or of counter intuitive results.

12 Kant then does not see all acts which are specific, strict requirements of
duty as matters of justice. There are also strict or perfect requirements for
some duties of virtue, such as refraining from suicide, mockery or detrac-
tion which he views as indispensable means to the rather indeterminate
maxims that we act on when we act on a maxim of virtue. See *Metaphysic
of Morals*, pp. 421ff. and 463ff. and *Acting on Principle*, pp. 52–8.

13 Cf. *Metaphysic of Morals*, pp. 380–81.

14 *Grundlegung*, p. 424 and cf. Sections 5 and 6 below.

15 *Grundlegung*, p. 417.

16 Kant's discussions of duties of virtue suggest that he would in any case
count the necessary constituents or components of some end – and not
merely the instrumentally necessary means to that end – as among the
means to that end.

17 The fifth requirement of Rational Intending clearly deals with the very
nexus of intentions on which discussions of the Doctrine of Double Effect
focus. That doctrine claims that agents are not responsible for harm which
foreseeably results from action undertaken with morally worthy intentions,
provided that the harm is not disproportionate, is regretted and would
have been avoided had there been a less harm producing set of specific
intentions which would have served the same maxim in that situation. (The
surgeon foresees but regrets the pain unavoidably inflicted during life-saving
procedures, and so is not to be held responsible for inflicting this pain.)
While the Doctrine of Double Effect holds that agents are not to be held
responsible for such results, it allows that agents do, if 'obliquely' rather
than 'directly', intend the results. It is therefore quite compatible with the
Doctrine of Double Effect to insist that an agent whose oblique intention
foreseeably undercuts the fundamental intention for the sake of which what
is directly intended is done acts irrationally. For where the fundamental
intention is undercut the foreseeable results of specific intentions were not
proportionate; rather they defeat the very intention to which they are
supposedly ancillary.

18 *Grundlegung*, p. 424.

19 This is the so-called Formula of the Law of Nature, cf. *Grundlegung*, p.
421, as well as p. 436, 'Maxims must be chosen as if they had to hold as
universal laws of nature' and *Metaphysic of Morals*, p. 225, 'Act according
to a maxim which can at the same time be valid as a universal law.' In this
discussion I shall leave aside all consideration of the relationships between
different formulations of the Categorical Imperative and in particular of
the differences between versions which are formulated quite generally 'for
rational beings as such' and those versions which are restricted to the human
condition ('typics'). These topics have been extensively discussed in the
secondary literature including in H.J. Paton, *op. cit.*; John Kemp, *The
Philosophy of Kant*, Oxford University; R.P. Wolff, *The Autonomy of Reason*,
Harper and Row, New York, 1973, Ch. 2; Bruce Aune, *Kant's Theory of
Morals*, Princeton University Press, Princeton, New Jersey, Chs. II to IV.

20 *Grundlegung*, p. 424.

21 *Ibid.*, as well as *Metaphysic of Morals*, Introduction, esp. p. 389.

22 For further discussion of the notion of the universalized counterpart of a
maxim cf. *Acting on Principle*, pp. 61–3.

23 For an application of the Formula of Universal Law to the example of

slavery see also Leslie Mulholland, 'Kant: On Willing Maxims to Become Laws of Nature', *Dialogue*, 17, 1978.

24 To see why Kant thinks that the abrogation of autonomy would be the most fundamental of moral failings see I. Kant, 'An Answer to the Question "What is Enlightenment?"', tr. H.B. Nisbet, in Hans Reiss, ed., *Kant's Political Writings*, Cambridge University Press, Cambridge, 1970 as well as Barry Clarke's discussion of 'elective heteronomy' in 'Beyond the Banality of Evil', *British Journal of Political Science*, 10, 1980, pp. 17–39.

25 Cf. the various works of commentary listed under note 17 above as well as Jonathan Harrison, 'Kant's Examples of the First Formulation of the Categorical Imperative' and J. Kemp, 'Kant's Examples of the Categorical Imperative', both in R.P. Wolff, ed., *Kant: Foundations of the Metaphysics of Morals*, Bobbs Merrill, Indianapolis, 1969.

26 Cf. *Metaphysic of Morals*, pp. 447–64 for Kant's discussion of the various virtues of love and sociability.

27 Cf. *Metaphysic of Morals*, pp. 443–7 for Kant's discussion of the duty to seek to develop talents (duty to seek one's own perfection). It is important to remember that 'talents' here are not to be understood as any particularly unusual human accomplishments, but rather as any human powers which (unlike natural gifts) we may choose either to cultivate or to neglect. The morally significant talents are powers such as those of self-mastery and self-knowledge.

28 Cf. F. Hirsch, *Social Limits to Growth*, Harvard University Press, Cambridge, Mass., 1976.

MORALITY AND FREEDOM: KANT'S RECIPROCITY THESIS

Henry E. Allison

At the end of the second part of the *Groundwork* Kant reflects that he has so far shown only that the autonomy of the will ('the property the will has of being a law to itself')[1] is the supreme principle of morality in the sense of being the ultimate presupposition of morality as it is commonly understood.[2] The articulation of this principle marks the culmination of an analytic or regressive argument, the aim of which is to uncover and present with philosophical precision the basic assumptions and principles of the ordinary, pre-philosophical conception of morality. Although Kant hardly minimizes this result, he also displays an awareness of the fact that, of itself, it leaves unanswered the crucial question of validation. Accordingly, he sets himself the task in the third part of the *Groundwork* of answering the moral skeptic by showing that morality is not a 'chimerical Idea,' a mere 'phantom of the brain.'[3] In Kantian terms, this requires that he provide a transcendental deduction of morality.

Unfortunately, not only has Kant's effort to accomplish this important goal been severely criticized by even his most sympathetic critics, but the purely exegetical question of what kind of argument, if any, the text supplies, has been the topic of an on-going dispute. In fact, there seems to be no agreement as to whether the deduction is of the moral law, the categorical imperative, freedom, all three; or even whether there is properly a deduction at all.[4] Furthermore, the uncertainty about the *Groundwork* has given rise to additional questions about its relationship to the *Critique of Practical Reason*. The problem here is that while in the *Groundwork* Kant at least seems to have attempted a transcendental deduction of the moral law and/or the categorical imperative on the basis of the necessity of presupposing the

Idea of freedom, in the *Critique of Practical Reason* he explicitly denies the possibility of any such deduction and claims instead that the moral law as a 'fact of reason' can serve as the basis for a deduction of freedom.[5] This suggests a significant reversal in Kant's thought regarding the justification of morality; although even here the existence of such a reversal has been denied both by those who see no real deduction of the moral law in the *Groundwork* and by those who claim to find a deduction in the *Critique of Practical Reason* as well as in the *Groundwork*.[6]

Undoubtedly, most of the confusion can be traced to Kant's own confusing and sloppy formulations of both his problematic and his argument, especially in *Groundwork* III. Nevertheless, I do believe that part of the blame can be attributed to a failure on the part of Kant's critics to give proper attention to a thesis which is at least relatively clear, and which looms large in both the *Groundwork* and the *Critique of Practical Reason*. This is the claim that freedom of the will and the moral law are reciprocal concepts. Kant affirms this explicitly in both works; correlatively, he also insists in both works that, although the moral law (or, better, the bindingness of the moral law for all rational agents) expresses a synthetic *a priori* proposition, it would be analytic if freedom of the will were presupposed.[7] For convenience sake I shall henceforth refer to this as the 'Reciprocity Thesis.' Its significance stems from the fact that it entails that freedom of the will is not only a necessary but also a sufficient condition of the moral law.[8] Clearly, this thesis underlies Kant's attempt in the *Groundwork* to argue from freedom (or at least from the necessity of the presupposition of freedom) to the moral law, and in the *Critique of Practical Reason* from the moral law (as a putative 'fact of reason') to the reality of freedom.

The goal of this paper is to provide a defense of this thesis, which lies at the very heart of Kant's moral philosophy. The defense will begin with an examination of the Kantian texts; but since his 'official' arguments for the thesis are obviously inadequate, it will be necessary to go considerably beyond Kant's explicit statements on the topic. Thus, the proposed defense is also a reconstruction of Kant's argument, albeit one based largely on material which Kant himself has provided. Since the Reciprocity Thesis is only the first step in the Kantian justification of morality, a defense of this thesis will not amount to a complete defense of the Kantian 'deduction.' It is, however, a necessary first stage in such a project. Moreover, I hope to show that the recognition of the cogency and systematic role of the thesis is itself enough to obviate some of the standard objections to Kant's procedure. I also hope to show that, properly construed, the Reciprocity

Thesis is not open to the devastating criticism which is frequently raised against it: namely, that it entails that no free action can be morally wrong.

I

The best known and most perplexing of Kant's formulations of the Reciprocity Thesis is at the beginning of *Groundwork* III. After defining will [*Wille*] as a 'kind of causality belonging to living beings so far as they are rational,' and freedom (negatively construed) as 'the property this causality has of being able to work independently of determination by alien causes,' Kant offers his positive conception of freedom, which presumably 'springs' from this negative one:

> The concept of causality carries with it that of *laws* (*Gesetze*) in accordance with which, because of something we call a cause, something else – namely, its effect – must be posited (*gesetzt*). Hence freedom of will, although it is not the property of conforming to laws of nature, is not for this reason lawless: it must rather be a causality conforming to immutable laws though of a special kind; for otherwise a free will would be self-contradictory. Natural necessity, as we have seen, is a heteronomy of efficient causes; for every effect is possible only in conformity with the law that something else determines the efficient cause to causal action. What else then can be freedom of will be but autonomy – that is, the property which will has of being a law to itself? The proposition 'Will is in all its actions a law to itself' expresses, however, only the principle of acting on no maxim other than one which can have for its object itself and at the same time a universal law. This is precisely the formula of the categorical imperative and the principle of morality. Thus a free will and a will under moral laws are one and the same.[9]

Kant also argues for the same thesis in §6 of the *Critique of Practical Reason*. After contending on the basis of an analysis of the concept of a practical law 1), that such a law must be formal in the sense that it could only impose the formal condition of lawfulness on the maxims of a rational agent §4 and that only a will that is free in the transcendental sense could have its 'determining ground' in such a law §5; he then §6 poses the problem: 'Granted that a will is free, find the law which alone is competent to determine it necessarily' [*welches ihn allein nothwendig zur bestimmen tauglich ist*]. The proposed solution exploits the dichotomy between the form (lawfulness or universality) and the matter (desired object or end) of a practical principle developed in §§2–4. Kant claims that since 1) a free will (by definition) must be independent of all 'empirical conditions,' which includes the 'material' element of practical principles; and that 2) a free will must nonetheless be 'determinable' (presumably according to some law); that 3) 'the legislative form, insofar as it is contained in the maxim, is the only thing which can constitute a determining ground of the [free] will.' On this basis Kant concludes at the very beginning of the Remark following the analysis that 'freedom and unconditional practical law reciprocally imply each other.'[10]

The argument at this point is completely hypothetical, and consequently does not involve any claims concerning the reality of either freedom or an unconditional practical law. Nevertheless, given the identification §7 of an unconditional practical law with the moral law ('So act that the maxim of your will could always hold at the same time as a principle establishing universal law'),[11] it is but a short step to the conclusion that 'It [the moral law] would be analytic if freedom of the will were presupposed.' Admittedly, this last claim is somewhat strange. How, one might ask, could the presupposition of freedom convert a synthetic proposition into one that is analytic? The most reasonable reading, I take it, is that analyticity is to be attributed to the hypothetical, 'If freedom then the moral law,' and to its reciprocal. Kant clarifies his position near the end of the *Analytic of Pure Practical Reason* when he remarks:

> if [*per impossibile*] we saw the possibility of freedom of an efficient cause, we would see not only the possibility but also the necessity of the moral law as the supreme practical law of rational beings, to whom freedom of the causality of their will is ascribed. This is because the two concepts are so inextricably bound together that practical freedom could be defined through the will's independence of everything except the moral law.[12]

Kant does not explicitly argue for the Reciprocity Thesis in *Religion within the Limits of Reason Alone*. Nevertheless, in the course of denying that the source of moral evil can be located either in man's sensuous nature or in his 'morally legislative reason' [*Wille*], he does suggest that to affirm the latter is equivalent to saying that 'reason could destroy the authority of the very law which is its own, or deny the obligation arising therefrom.' This, however, he claims is impossible because:

> To conceive of oneself as a freely acting being and yet as exempt from the law which is appropriate [*angemessen*] to such a being (the moral law) would be tantamount to conceiving a cause operating without any laws whatsoever (for determination according to natural laws is excluded by the fact of freedom); this is a self-contradiction.[13]

The argument in the *Groundwork*, in particular, appears to be vitiated by a gross equivocation regarding the concept of law. As even Paton, the most sympathetic of Kant interpreters notes, it is hardly legitimate to jump (as Kant there seems to do) from the notion of a causal law, which is a law connecting causes and effects, to a 'law of freedom,' which, by definition, would be a law for decision itself, not one which connects decisions (as causes) with their effects in the phenomenal world.[14] Leaving this aside, however, it is possible to specify a common core of argumentation that is contained, implicitly at least, in all of the texts. The argument takes roughly the following form: 1) As a 'kind of causality' the will must, in some sense, be law-governed or, in the language of the Second Critique, 'determinable' according to some law (a lawless will is an absurdity). 2) As free, it cannot be governed by laws of nature. 3) It must, therefore, be governed by laws of a different sort; that is, self-imposed ones. 4) The moral law is the required self-imposed law.

Although a compatibilist would certainly object to steps 2 and 3, the major difficulties which we need consider concern steps 1 and 4. Clearly, if a free will (in a non-compatibilist sense) is to be law-governed or 'determinable,' it can only be through self-imposed laws. In that minimal sense, then, the positive concept of freedom (autonomy) can be derived analytically from the negative concept (independence). However, apart from the already noted equivocation regarding the concept of law, Kant does not seem to offer any argument in support of the claim that a free will must be law-governed or 'determinable' at all. On the contrary, the account in the Second Critique suggests that this essential question is simply begged.

At first glance at least, step 4 appears to be equally problematic; for even if we assume that a free will must be governed or determinable by a self-imposed law, it does not seem at all obvious that only the moral law, as defined by Kant, can do the job. In fact, considering only the *Groundwork* account, it once again seems that Kant has begged the main question by means of his prior characterization of the principle of autonomy as the 'supreme principle of morality.' This characterization makes it all too easy for Kant to slide from the claim that a free will is autonomous in the sense that it is determinable only by self-imposed laws to the claim that the law which it spontaneously yet necessarily imposes upon itself is the moral law.[15]

With regard to the latter problem, it is crucial to note that Kant holds that the moral law is the only conceivable candidate for a practical law. Consequently, for Kant at least, the claims that a free will is necessarily subject to a practical law (step 1) and that it is necessarily subject to the moral law (step 4) are equivalent. According to Kant's implicit definition, a practical law is an objectively and unconditionally valid practical principle. To claim that a practical principle is *objectively* valid is to claim that it holds for all rational agents, whether or not they in fact adhere to it, that is, whether or not it holds subjectively (as a maxim). In the case of imperfectly rational beings such as ourselves, such a principle takes the form of an imperative (which is likewise objectively valid). The imperative is hypothetical if its objectivity is a function of certain ends or desires; it is categorical if this is not the case. An objectively valid practical principle is also *unconditionally* valid just in case it holds independently of any ends or desires. The imperative issuing from such a principle is always categorical, whatever its grammatical form.[16]

Given this conception, Kant claims 1) that such a law must be 'formal,' since it abstracts from all ends or desires (which constitute the 'matter' of a principle), and 2) that, as such, it can require only that rational agents select their maxims on the basis of their suitability as universal laws. This is, of course, precisely what the moral law or, better, the categorical imperative requires. Although much more work would be needed to make this line of argument fully convincing, I do find it a plausible unpacking of the implications of Kant's definitions. In any event, for the purposes of this paper, I propose to accept this claim. Thus, its goal will have been achieved if, in Kant's words, it can be shown that 'freedom and unconditional practical law reciprocally imply each other.'

II

Kant's claim that the notion of a lawless will involves an absurdity places him squarely within the metaphysical tradition that rejects the conception of a 'liberty of indifference.' This rejection is a constant in Kant's thought; it can be found in his earliest significant discussion of freedom, where he defends the Leibnizian view.[17] It resurfaces, however, in the 'critical period' in connection with a very different, radically un-Leibnizian, conception of the will and its freedom.

The gist of this new conception of the will is indicated in the famous statement in the *Groundwork* that 'Everything in nature works in accordance with laws. Only a rational being has the power to act in accordance with his *Idea* of laws – in accordance with principles – and only so has he a will.'[18] Kant then goes on to define the will as practical reason on the grounds that reason is required to derive actions from laws.[19] Somewhat later he defines 'will' [*Wille*] as a 'kind of causality belonging to rational beings so far as they are rational.'[20] Rationality, construed as the capacity to form general principles, together with the power to act on the basis of these principles, thereby producing changes in the phenomenal world (if only in the psychological state of the agent) are, therefore, the defining characteristics of 'will' as Kant construes it in the *Groundwork*. Only a being with both of these capacities can be said to have a will. Such a being is also one for whom reason is practical.

If one is to understand Kant's thought at this point, it is crucial to realize that 'rationality' is here construed in a very broad sense. Since all that is required is the capacity to form and act upon general principles, an agent is 'rational' in the relevant sense even when the principles he adopts as rules for action are morally pernicious, imprudent, or even self-defeating, that is, 'irrational' in the usual sense. Kant's technical term for the 'principle' or 'Idea of law' on the basis of which rational agents supposedly act is 'maxim'. Consequently, it is appropriate to begin our examination of Kant's claim that a lawless will is an absurdity with a brief consideration of his account of maxims. This consideration must, of necessity, be superficial. It will concentrate solely on the presumed role of maxims in human action, thereby ignoring many of the complexities and ambiguities of Kant's account, as well as the interesting questions regarding the specification of maxims.

As is all too frequently the case, in his characterization of maxims Kant succeeds in being technical without being precise. For present purposes, however, it suffices to describe a maxim as a subjective practical principle, that is, a general rule or policy on which a rational agent actually acts in a given situation and tends to act in relevantly similar situations.[21] Expressed algebraically, maxims have the form: 'To do A if B.' As subjective, maxims are closely connected with the 'interests' of an agent, which are themselves never the simple result of mere impulse or sensuous desire, but always involve some conception of an end. It is only because I consciously choose to pursue certain ends or, equivalently, have certain interests, that I adopt certain policies of action, designed to realize these ends. A maxim thus has a purposive component built into it; although this component need not be made explicit in the formulation.[22] Moreover, this is true even when the interest is 'pure,' that is, not based on any sensuous desire for the object, as is supposedly the case in action for the sake of the moral law.

Although there can be no quarrel with the claim that people often act on the basis of consciously adopted maxims, it is also frequently thought that the emphasis Kant places on maxims in his account of human action makes human behavior appear much more rule-governed than it actually is.[23] This is particularly true if maxims are construed as relatively fixed policies of life or *Lebensregeln*, which specify the most fundamental choices of an individual, and which, as such, are contrasted with mere precepts or 'rules of thumb.'[24] So construed, maxims certainly provide ready candidates for moral evaluation, and it is to maxims in this sense that Kant appeals in his well known attempts to illustrate the application of the categorical imperative. The problem is simply that many, if not most, human actions cannot be plausibly regarded as the result of an explicit reflection on rules of this sort; but this neither exempts them from moral evaluation (we are justly condemned for our 'impulsive' acts), nor reduces them to mere bits of behavior, not worthy of being termed 'actions.'

There are, I think, two possible responses to this fairly obvious line of objection, both of which have a basis in the Kantian texts. The first involves a certain broadening of the notion of a maxim, making it roughly equivalent to an intention.[25] On this interpretation, the claim that an agent acted on the basis of a maxim does not entail either that he acted on the basis of a principle to which he has been committed for any determinate length of time or that he explicitly 'subsumed' his action under this principle, in the manner of someone who goes through all of the steps of an Aristotelian practical syllogism. It entails only that he acted with conscious intent, that there is a specifiable reason for the action. To formulate the maxim is to describe this intent and to give the reason. Here it will be helpful to follow Onora Nell, who, appealing to Kant's later formulation in the *Metaphysics of Morals* (which presupposes the *Wille-Willkür* distinction), characterizes a maxim as a 'determination of the power of choice' [*Willkür*]. As she correctly points out in her comment on this characterization, 'To say that an agent's power of choice is determined is simply to say that he intends to do a specific sort of act or pursue a specific end in some situation. If an agent has a maxim "To do A if B", then he intends to do A if B.'[26] All that needs to be added at this point is that the converse of the last claim likewise holds. If an agent really intends to do A if B, then he has a maxim 'To do A if B,' whether or not he is explicitly aware of it.

By construing maxims in this way it is possible to ascribe them to many actions which are performed 'on the spur of the moment,' without reflection or the explicit adoption of a settled policy. To borrow an example from Onora Nell: A person can suddenly decide to have an extra cup of coffee one morning without any deliberation and without the adoption of a specific policy regarding the amount of coffee to be consumed each morning. Certainly, we cannot claim plausibly that such an action involves a maxim in the sense of a *Lebensregel* (or even a 'rule of thumb'). Nevertheless, we can connect it with a maxim in the broad sense insofar as we can attribute an intention to the agent, for example, to get warm or to combat the effects of a sleepless night. Moreover, as Nell notes, even if the agent himself does not reflectively formulate this maxim or intention, it can still (in principle) be discovered by determining what changes in the circumstances would have led him to decline the extra cup.[27]

This line of interpretation suggests that a Kantian maxim is very close, if not equivalent, to the 'plan as it were' that J.L. Austin claims to be an essential ingredient in an intentional action. According to Austin, for an agent to act intentionally, which he is careful to distinguish from acting deliberately or purposefully, he must have a conscious idea of what he is doing, and this requires having, at least in some minimal sense, a plan of action.[28] To have such a plan, for example, 'Do A if B,' is precisely what it means to 'know what one is doing,' while the latter is a necessary condition of an intentional action. Following Austin, it can, therefore, be claimed that for any description under which an action is intentional, it must be possible to assign some 'plan as it were' to the agent. But the same can be said, *mutatis mutandis*, of maxims broadly construed. Moreover, since the notion of a will without any intentions is manifestly absurd, it follows that the notion of a will without maxims (a 'lawless will') is likewise absurd.

Although there are good reasons for interpreting maxims in this way (How else can one square the fact that people are deemed morally responsible for their so-called 'impulsive' acts with Kant's insistence that morality is concerned with the maxims of action?), it is not necessary to insist upon it here. Even if we assume that by 'maxims' is meant something like *Lebensregeln*, which would preclude any straightforward identification of intentional action with action based on a maxim, it can still be maintained that an agent capable of intentional action at all, that is, one with the capacity for rational choice (in the broad sense of 'rational') cannot be totally without maxims. The point here is simply that an agent completely bereft of maxims (in the sense of *Lebensregeln*) would also be without any self-chosen goals or interests, and this means that he would have no basis for rational choice. Consequently, his 'actions' would have to be regarded either as random happenings (which is absurd) or as direct responses to stimuli, explicable in neuro-physiological terms. In short, his 'actions' would, like other natural occurrences, be 'in accordance with laws,' not, as in the case of rational agents, 'in accordance with the Idea of laws.'

III

The preceding analysis may help to explain and give plausibility to Kant's claim that rational agents act in accordance with the 'Idea of laws,' but it obviously does not suffice to establish the thesis that a free will (the will of a rational agent) must be law-governed in any but a trivial sense of 'law'. In fact, we have seen that Kant defines maxims as subjective practical principles and explicitly contrasts them with objective practical principles or laws. Thus, given Kant's own defini-tions, there can be no immediate transition from being maxim-governed to being subject to an 'unconditional practical law.' We are still in need of an argument to bridge this gap.

The argument that comes immediately to mind at this point is a familiar one, and so is the objection to it. I do not believe that it is Kant's own argument (although it is frequently taken to be such), but I do think that it can be construed as an essential first step in an extended Kantian argument. I also think that when it is viewed merely as a first step in an extended argument rather than as a complete argu-ment in its own right, the standard objection loses its force.

In the endeavor to sketch this argument or, more accurately, argu-ment-segment, it will be helpful to return to the analysis of maxims in terms of intentions. This analysis strongly suggests that to stipulate an agent's maxim in performing a certain action is to give the agent's 'reason' for that action, at least in one important sense of that noto-riously elusive notion. (To state my intention *in* X-ing – the 'plan as it were' that I have 'in mind' is to give my reason *for* X-ing.) More specifically, it is to give the kind of reason in terms of which an action can be justified (or criticized) as opposed to being explained or even excused.

Such justification (or criticism) certainly includes, but is not limited to, the moral variety. A given action could be praised as morally appro-priate or as prudent or, correlatively, condemned as immoral or as foolish. These are obviously quite different kinds of evaluations, but the key point is that in all cases they are based upon assumptions regarding the agent's intention to act in a certain way in a given set of circumstances. Moreover, in both the moral and prudential contexts the justification takes a similar form: namely, showing that the reason (in the sense of intention) for acting in a certain way is a 'good reason.' Naturally, the same can be said, *mutatis mutandis*, regarding the criticism of actions, whether this be on moral or on prudential grounds.

The next step is to note that in claiming that one's reason for acting in a certain way is a 'good' in the sense of justifying reason, one is, implicitly, at least, assuming its appropriateness for all rational beings. The intuition behind this is simply that if reason R justifies my X-ing in circumstances C, then it must also justify the X-ing of any other agent in such circumstances. As Marcus Singer, paraphrasing Sidgewick, remarks, 'A reason in one case is a reason in all cases – or else it is not a reason at all.'[29] To be sure, there is a perfectly legitimate sense in which I might claim that something is 'right for me' and not for others; but this must be construed as an elliptical way of stating that there is something peculiar about my circumstances (which can include, among other things, my desires and capacities). Thus, I might claim that a course of action, say going to the race track to relax, is justifiable for me because of my superior ability as a handicapper, great wealth, or luck, etc., while it is not justifiable for others who lack these attributes. What I may not do is to claim that the possession of these attributes justifies my action but not that of other similarly inclined and endowed agents. In roughly this way, then, the universalizability of one's intention, maxim or plan of action, seems to be presupposed as a condition of the possibility of justifying one's action, even when this justification does not take an explicitly moral form.

Finally, a rational agent cannot simply refuse to play the justification game, that is, refuse to concern himself with the question of whether the reasons for his actions are 'good' reasons, at least in a non-moral sense of 'good.' This is, of course, not to say that such an agent always acts on the basis of good and sufficient reasons or that, in retrospect, he must always believe himself to have done so. The point is rather the familiar one that an agent for whom the whole question of justification is irrelevant, who never weighs the reason for his action, who acts without at least believing at the time that his reasons are 'good' reasons, would not be regarded as rational. But since, as we have just seen, to regard one's reason for acting in a certain way as 'good' is to assume its legitimacy for all rational beings in similar circumstances, it would seem, so the argument goes, that a rational agent cannot reject the universalizability test without, at the same time, denying his rationality. This, in turn, means that the universalizability test functions as the ultimate standard governing one's choice of maxims or, equivalently, that it has the status of a practical law. This line of argument is too familiar to require further elaboration, and so, too, is the objection to it. The problem is simply that one cannot move from the claim that every rational agent must regard his principles of action as universalizable in the sense that he be willing to acknowledge that it would be reasonable for every other agent in the relevantly similar circumstances[30] to adopt the same principles, or even that such agents ought to adopt them (where the 'ought' is the ought of rationality), to the desired conclusion that the agent ought to be able to will (as a universal law) that every rational agent act on the basis of the principle in question. The rational egoist might very well be willing to admit that the maxims on which he acts in pursuit of his own perceived self-interest are also those on which every other rational agent ought to act (and would act, if sufficiently enlightened). It hardly follows from this, however, that the rational egoist is committed (on pain of self-contradiction) to will that all other rational agents behave likewise.[31]

While there can be little question about the cogency of this line of objection, considered as a response to the project of somehow deducing morality, conceived in Kantian terms, from the concept of rationality, there are serious questions about its relevance to Kant's own procedure. The reason that this is generally thought to provide a decisive criticism of Kant can no doubt be attributed to Kant's misleading claim that, since moral laws hold for rational beings as such, they ought to be derived from the 'general concept of a rational being as such.'[32] This is intended, however, to preclude any appeal to anthropology, that is, to empirical knowledge of human nature, and not to suggest that the reality of moral obligation can be deduced from the 'mere concept' of a rational being. In fact, not only does Kant himself not attempt to deduce the moral law from this concept, he explicitly rejects the possibility of doing so. We must keep in mind that the starting point of Kant's analysis is not the concept of a rational being *simpliciter*, it is rather the concept of a rational being possessing a free will (in the transcendental sense). This is because Kant realized that, for all that we can learn from its 'mere concept,' practical reason might involve nothing more than the capacity to determine the best possible means for the satisfaction of one's desires. Certainly many distinguished philosophers have thought as much; and there is nothing self-contradictory or otherwise absurd in the claim. Indeed, as Kant himself remarks in a highly significant but strangely neglected note in *Religion within the Limits of Reason Alone*:

> For from the fact that a being has reason it by no means follows that this reason, by the mere representing of the fitness of its maxims to be laid down as universal laws, is thereby rendered capable of determining the will unconditionally, so as to be 'practical' of itself; at least, not so far as we can see. The most rational mortal being in the world might still stand in need of certain incentives, originating in objects of desire, to determine his choice. He might, indeed, bestow the most rational reflection on all that concerns not only the greatest sum of these incentives in him but also the means of attaining the end thereby determined, without ever suspecting the possibility of such a thing as the absolutely imperative moral law which proclaims that it is itself an incentive and, indeed, the highest.[33]

The conclusion to be drawn from this is that the problem with the argument 'from rationality' sketched above is not that it is totally wrongheaded, but merely that it is incomplete.[34] Let us see, then, if we can meet with more success in the endeavor to establish the Reciprocity Thesis if we focus explicitly on the transcendental freedom as well as the rationality of the agent. As a first step in this process we shall take a brief look at the relevant aspects of Kant's account of freedom.

IV

Central to Kant's conception of freedom is the contrast between practical and transcendental freedom. For present purposes, practical freedom (*freie Willkür, arbitrium liberum*) can be equated with the previously considered capacity of a rational agent to act on the basis of maxims, that is, in light of the 'idea' or 'representation' of a law. This involves the capacity to act independently of, and even contrary to, any particular desire. Instead of responding automatically to the strongest desire (the mark of a pathologically necessitated *Willkür* or *arbitrium brutum*), a practically free agent can weigh and evaluate his desires, give priority to some and suppress others. Only *qua* conceptually determined, for example, taken up or 'incorporated into a maxim,' does a desire constitute a reason for acting. This does not rule out the possibility of what we normally regard as impulsive behavior, for example, an action out of anger. The point is only that in such cases the agent must be thought to give into the emotion, to let it move him to action.[35]

Transcendental freedom, by contrast, is usually defined as absolute spontaneity or as complete independence from any determination by antecedent conditions.[36] This creates the impression that the difference between practical and transcendental freedom is between a modest conception, presumably one that a compatibilist might accept, and a radical conception, requiring indeterminism together with all of its well known difficulties. After all, independence from 'pathological necessitation' is hardly equivalent to independence from all causal determination; and if practical freedom involves only the former, then it is far from obvious that it requires indeterminism. Nevertheless, Kant seems to maintain that it does. At least he claims in the *Critique of Pure Reason* that 'the practical concept of freedom is based on this *transcendental* Idea,' (A533/B561) and even that 'The denial of transcendental freedom must, therefore, involve the elimination of all practical freedom' (A534/B562).

Largely as a result of passages such as these, Kant is frequently deemed guilty of an illicit slide from a respectable conception of practical freedom (pathological independence) to a disreputable or, at best, highly problematic transcendental conception. It is sometimes further claimed that the latter conception brings with it no discernible advantages and many significant disadvantages for Kant's moral philosophy.[37] Consequently, it is not surprising to find recent efforts to reinterpret Kant's whole theory of freedom in explicitly compatibilist terms.[38]

Although the question of whether Kant's First Critique conception of practical freedom requires indeterminism is quite complex, with texts pointing in both directions, I am inclined to think that it does. I cannot, however, argue the point here.[39] Similarly, I do not intend to discuss either the general issue of indeterminism or the plausibility of the Kantian version. Since we are concerned here only with the implications of transcendental freedom for Kant's moral philosophy, we can set aside these larger issues. For present purposes, the key point is that, even assuming that both practical and transcendental freedom require indeterminism, there remains a significant difference between them. Moreover, this difference is crucial for Kant's moral philosophy.

This becomes clear if we distinguish between independence from determination by any particular desire or inclination and independence from determination by desire or inclination *überhaupt*. Practical freedom involves the first and transcendental freedom the second. Given this distinction, it follows that an agent would be free in the practical (but not in the transcendental) sense if the agent's choices were ultimately governed by some fundamental drive or natural impulse, for example, self-preservation or maximization of pleasure, which can be acted upon in any number of ways but which cannot be contravened. Such an agent would be practically free, possibly even in an incompatibilist sense, because the drive or impulse serves to limit the agent's options rather than to necessitate a given choice.[40] At the same time, however, the agent's choice would be ineluctably heteronomous; since it would be limited to the determination of the best means for the attainment of some end implanted in us by nature. Obviously, such a conception of agency is incompatible with the central tenets of Kant's mature moral philosophy.[41]

The situation with respect to transcendental freedom is quite different. According to this conception, the ground of the selection of a maxim can never be located in an impulse, instinct, or anything 'natural'; rather, it must always be sought in a higher order maxim and, therefore, in an act of freedom.[42] Consequently, even if one posits a natural drive such as self-preservation, it remains the case that a transcendentally free agent is, *ex hypothesi*, capable of selecting maxims that run directly counter to its dictates. Moreover, since the choices of a transcendentally free agent, including those based on desire or inclination, are grounded in a 'law' (maxim) which is self-imposed, such an agent would be autonomous in a morally neutral sense. Finally, it should be clear that only an agent that is free in this sense is capable of acting out of 'respect for the law,' and therefore of acting autonomously in the specifically moral sense on which Kant insists.

V

We are finally in a position to consider the implications of the presupposition of transcendental freedom for the problem of justification. The basic point is simply that without this presupposition, that is, assuming merely practical freedom, a maxim based on self-interest, happiness, or some such putatively ultimate yet non-moral end or motivational ground could be justified by an appeal to 'human nature' or some given determinant of behavior. (The details are irrelevant to the argument.) With it, however, this familiar move is blocked. If self-preservation, self-interest, or happiness is the principle of my behavior, if it dictates my maxims, it is I (not nature in me) that gives it this authority. At least this is the case under the presupposition that I am free in the transcendental sense. Moreover (and this is an essential premise of the entire argument), the justification requirement is still in place. In fact, the presupposition of transcendental freedom not only blocks certain kinds of justification, it also extends this requirement to first principles or fundamental maxims. Since such maxims, like all others are, *ex hypothesi*, freely adopted, it must be possible to offer reasons in support of their adoption. Correlatively, since such principles or maxims are first or fundamental in the sense that they provide the ultimate grounds for the justification of lower order maxims, they obviously cannot be justified by deducing them from some higher order principle.[43]

How, then, is the rational egoist to deal with this problem? To be sure, the proponent of such a position can continue to assert that it would be reasonable (if not desirable for the egoist) for every rational agent to act according to that principle and, therefore, that it passes the universalizability test in the sense in which the rational egoist acknowledges it. The real question, however, is whether this claim can be justified, given the presupposition of transcendental freedom. Obviously, the claim that it is somehow in one's best interests to act according to the dictates of rational egoism is question begging at best. (At worst it may be simply false.) But the presupposition of transcendental freedom rules out what seems to be the only alternative strategy for justification, namely, the appeal to some given determinant or ultimate fact about human nature, which somehow of itself justifies the adoption of a maxim. Presumably, the same would hold, *mutatis mutandis*, for any other 'heteronomous' principle.[44]

Admittedly, the most that this line of reasoning can show is that rational egoism and similar familiar doctrines cannot be rationally justified, at least not if they are combined with the presupposition of transcendental freedom. This is not a trivial result; but it is hardly equivalent to the claim that a rational and transcendentally free agent is constrained to acknowledge the validity (as the ultimate norm) of an unconditional practical law. Consequently, even assuming that the moral law, as defined by Kant, is the only conceivable candidate for a practical law, we cannot claim to have established that such an agent is necessarily subject to that law.

Nevertheless, we are finally in possession of the materials needed for such an argument. Although Kant himself never formulated it explicitly, I believe that it is implicit in all of his major writings in moral philosophy. The argument I have in mind is from the assumption of rational and transcendentally free agency to the conditions of the possibility of the justification of the maxims (including the fundamental maxims) of such agents. It proceeds in two stages: the first contends that conformity with an unconditional practical law is a sufficient condition for the justification of these maxims; the second contends that it is also a necessary condition.

The first point I take to be relatively unproblematic. What stronger justification could there be for one's adoption of a maxim than its conformity to an unconditionally valid practical law? If a rule of action is 'right' for all rational agents whatever their interests or desires, then, clearly, it is 'right' for me. Again, if my reason for X-ing is that it is dictated by such a law (in Kant's deontic terms, that it is my duty), then I have all the justification I would conceivably need for X-ing. This is not to deny that there may be grave difficulties determining exactly what such a law requires in a given instance (what my duty is), and, therefore, that Kant's moral philosophy may run into severe difficulties in this regard. The present point is only that *if* a maxim can be shown to meet this requirement then that maxim has been fully justified.

Obviously, the main difficulties concern the claim that this requirement is a necessary condition for justification. In dealing with this issue, it will be helpful to begin with the consideration of a familiar yet misguided criticism of Kant's moral theory. Couched in terms of the present discussion, the claim is that the requirement (at least as here construed) is too strong. If, so the argument goes, the only legitimate reason for adopting a maxim were its conformity to a practical law binding upon all rational agents, regardless of their interests or desires, then it would seem that no maxim to pursue one's interests or desires could ever be justified. But this is patently absurd. Thus, even if it be granted that conformity to a practical law is a sufficient condition for the justification of one's maxims, it is certainly not also a necessary condition. To claim otherwise is to commit oneself to the doctrine that only actions performed 'for the sake of duty' are justifiable; and this is to conflate justifiability with moral worth.

Although there is undoubtedly a strand in Kant's moral philosophy that suggests this line of interpretation and criticism, it does not reflect his considered opinion. What this reading neglects is the centrality for Kant of the distinction between the permissible and the obligatory.[45] Not surprisingly, then, it also fails to recognize that the moral law is intended as a criterion of the former as well as of the latter.[46] This is, of course, a large topic in its own right. Indeed, it calls to mind all of the familiar difficulties concerning Kant's distinctions between positive and negative, imperfect and perfect duties. I introduce it here only because it indicates that, rather than ruling out as illegitimate all desire or interest based maxims, the notion of conformity to a practical law is intended by Kant as a criterion for determining which maxims of this (or any) sort are permissible. Moreover, since it seems clear that no maxim could be regarded as justified if it were not at least shown to be permissible, it follows that establishing this claim is equivalent to showing that conformity to a practical law functions as a necessary condition for the justification of maxims.

Permissibility, like other deontic notions, has both a specifically moral and a morally neutral sense. In the former case it encompasses whatever is not contrary to duty and in the latter whatever is allowable within a given context or in light of some pre-given end (in accordance with the 'rules of the game').[47] Presently, however, we are concerned merely with the conditions of the justification of the desire or interest based maxims of transcendentally free rational agents, that is, agents for whom the choice of such maxims both requires rational justification and is attributed to an act of freedom. Given these constraints, it is apparent that permissibility cannot be construed as a function of desires or interests, even the most fundamental ones. In other words, we are not looking for a rule or set of rules which determine what is permissible within the framework of some presupposed end. On the contrary, what must be determined is the rule or set of rules governing the pursuit of any end at all, including desire or interest based ends. In view of the 'transcendental' function of such a rule or set of rules (its function with respect to end setting *überhaupt*), it is also apparent that it must be both universal and 'formal' in the specifically Kantian sense. That is, it must not only apply to all transcendentally free rational agents, it must also apply to them regardless of what desires or interests they may happen to have. But such a rule or set of rules is precisely what Kant understands by a practical law. Consequently, it must either be denied that the maxims of transcendentally free agents can be justified at all (which amounts to a denial of rationality) or it must be acknowledged that conformity to practical law is the criterion governing the selection of the maxims of such agents. Combining this result with the further claim that the moral law is the required principle, we have the Kantian argument for the 'analytic' connection between transcendental freedom and the moral law.

Since the above analysis turns largely on the distinction between the rationality and the freedom of an agent, it might itself seem problematic as Kantian exegesis. Such a conclusion, however, would be erroneous. Although Kant only makes this distinction fully explicit in *Religion within the Limits of Reason Alone*,[48] it is implicit in his thought from the *Groundwork* on.[49] Admittedly, only a rational agent can be free in the transcendental (or even the practical) sense, but an agent is not free in the transcendental sense simply in virtue of being rational.

At least freedom in this sense cannot be derived from rationality; and, therefore, neither can the validity of the moral law. Unfortunately, the whole point is usually missed by Kant's critics. Starting with the reasonable assumption that a Kantian justification of morality must somehow demonstrate the irrationality of rejecting the categorical imperative, these critics tend to assume that the argument to this end must proceed simply from the concept of a rational being. This is not the case, but it is only by focusing explicitly on the Reciprocity Thesis that it becomes clear why it is not.

VI

Given the preceding analysis, we can now deal with the common objection that the Reciprocity Thesis, particularly as presented in the *Groundwork*, leads Kant to the devastating consequence that we are free only insofar as we act in obedience to the categorical imperative. This consequence is devastating not only because it entails that we are not responsible for either our immoral or our morally neutral actions, but also because it suggests that even our morally good actions (actions performed for the sake of duty) are due ultimately to a fortuitous lack of interference by nature (in the guise of sensuous inclination) with the autonomous workings of pure practical reason. After all, if a free will is defined as one governed by the moral law, and if, as Kant suggests, this is analogous to the way in which natural phenomena are governed by the laws of nature, then it would seem that a free will could no more violate the moral law than a falling body could violate the law of gravity. Correlatively, if a non-moral or heteronomous will is subject to the laws of nature, then there is no way to understand how a will that is not already moral could choose to become such. In short, by distinguishing so strongly between nature and freedom and by defining the freedom of the will in terms of its subjection to the moral law, Kant seems to have made it impossible to provide a coherent account of either immoral or moral action.[50]

The standard strategy for defending Kant against this line of objection is to admit that it applies to the *Groundwork* and to deny that it applies to the later treatment in *Religion within the Limits of Reason Alone*, where Kant offers an account of moral evil in light of the *Wille–Willkür* distinction.[51] The basic idea is that *Willkür*, as spontaneous, is free either to determine itself to act in accordance with the dictates of *Wille* (the stern call of duty) or to subordinate these dictates to the demands of inclination. The claim, in other words, is that what the *Groundwork* presents as heteronomy and opposes to autonomy is seen in *Religion within the Limits of Reason Alone* as itself an expression of freedom.

There can be little doubt that the account of freedom in *Religion within the Limits of Reason Alone* has a subtlety and depth that are lacking in both the *Groundwork* and the *Critique of Practical Reason*. We have already seen, however, that rather than precluding this conception of freedom, the Reciprocity Thesis, as formulated in these earlier works, requires it in the sense that it is only by construing freedom in this way that the argument can be made to work. Admittedly, this does not of itself prove that Kant actually held such a conception at that time, but it certainly suggests that he could have, and it puts the burden of proof on those who would deny it.

There appear to be three aspects of Kant's account in the *Groundwork* to which the critic can appeal in support of this denial. Since all three of them have already been noted, we need only recall them here. First and foremost is the language of the Reciprocity Thesis itself. By explicitly identifying a free will with a will under the moral law, Kant certainly seems to leave no room for any free action that does not conform to the law. Second, this impression is greatly reinforced by the unfortunate analogy between the moral law and a law of nature. Finally, there is the apparent identification of heteronomous action and action in accordance with (or governed by) the laws of nature. This identification suggests that a heteronomous will can be neither free nor morally responsible, and this, in turn, raises the perplexing question of how such a will could ever become either free or morally good. Although not free (because heteronomous) is it free to become free?

In dealing with the first two aspects, it is obviously crucial to determine with some precision the sense in which a free will is supposed to be subject to, or governed by, the moral law. As we have already seen, in the *Critique of Practical Reason* Kant maintains that only a formal principle (later identified with the moral law) is 'competent to determine it (a free will) necessarily.' This locution once again suggests the very problem currently under consideration. Being determined necessarily by the moral law seems to mean being subject to it in precisely the same sense in which a physical object is subject to the laws of nature. And this, of course, rules out the possibility of any deviation from the law. It is, however, not only unnecessary, it is also implausible to take Kant to be making any such claim. Since 'determine necessarily' means simply to possess a lawlike status for a free will (to be 'objectively necessary'), all that Kant is claiming here is that only a formal principle (the moral law) can serve in this capacity for a free will.

The question thus becomes what is involved in serving in this capacity and the answer is quite apparent. It can mean only that the law provides a norm or standard in terms of which the choices of a free will are justified before the bar of reason. Material practical principles cannot do the job because they presuppose an object of desire as the determining ground of the will and, as we have seen, a free will is (by definition) responsible for the selection of any such objects as its ends. it hardly follows, however, from the fact that the moral law is the norm or standard for a free will that such a will is not 'capable' of failing to live up to this norm. As Kant frequently insists, although 'objectively necessary,' the moral law is nonetheless 'subjectively contingent.'[52] Consequently, we are free to act heteronomously, to make the satisfaction of our desires the basis of our choice. In so doing we are, at least according to Kant's moral theory, misusing our freedom; indeed, we are misusing ourselves in that we are treating our 'higher' or 'proper self' [*das eigentliche Selbst*] merely as a means for the satisfaction of our 'lower' or sensuous nature. Nevertheless, this misuse of freedom is still very much an act of freedom, and there is nothing in Kant's theory that requires us to think otherwise.

Perhaps the single most important Kantian text bearing on this issue is the discussion in the Introduction to the *Metaphysics of Morals*. Kant there first defines freedom (the positive concept) as 'the power of pure reason to be of itself practical.'[53] Then, later, after introducing the *Wille–Willkür* distinction, and claiming that *Wille* cannot be properly regarded as either free or unfree since it deals with legislation rather than action, he writes

Freedom of choice, however, cannot be defined as the capacity for making a choice to act for or against the law (*libertas indifferentiae*), as some people have tried to define it, even though choice as a phenomenon gives frequent instances of this in experience. For freedom (as it first becomes known to us through the moral law) is known only as a negative property within us, namely, the property of not being constrained to action by any sensible determining grounds. . . . But we can see clearly that although experience tells us that man as a sensible being exhibits a capacity to choose not only in accordance with the law but also in opposition to it, yet his freedom as an intelligible being cannot be thus defined, since appearances can never enable us to comprehend any supersensible object (such as free choice is). . . . For it is one thing to admit a tenet (of experience) and quite another to make it both the defining

principle (of the concept of free choice) and the universal mark
distinguishing free choice from *arbitrio bruto s. servo*, since in
the first case we do not assert that the mark necessarily belongs
to the concept, which we must do in the latter case. Only freedom in relation to the internal legislation of reason is properly
a capacity; the possibility of deviating from it is an incapacity.
How, then, can the former be explained by the latter?[54]

Already Reinhold had objected to this formulation by presenting
a dilemma. According to Reinhold's analysis, if the only concept of
freedom derivable from the moral law is that of the self-activity
(*Selbsttätigkeit*) of reason, then the presumed 'capacity' to act immorally
is not only an incapacity but an impossibility. If, on the other hand, freedom is construed as the capacity of the *person* for self-determination,
then the 'capacity' to act immorally is not a mere incapacity but rather
the very same capacity without which moral action cannot be thought.[55]
Otherwise expressed, Reinhold's complaint seems to be that the proper
concept of freedom must be a morally neutral one, and that this is
incompatible with Kant's insistence that our understanding of freedom
is derived entirely from our consciousness of the moral law. Quite
recently, Gerold Prauss has raised similar objections. Prauss, however,
also claims that Kant's account of freedom in the passage currently
before us marks a regression from the standpoint of *Religion within the
Limits of Reason Alone*, where he at least attempted (albeit unsuccess-
fully) to provide an account of immoral action in terms of freedom, back
to that of the *Groundwork*, where such action is seen as a product of the
heteronomy of nature.[56]

We can readily accept Prauss's assertion of the agreement of the
account of freedom in this passage with that of the *Groundwork*,
although not his characterization of its as a 'regression,' and certainly
not his analysis of its implications. The key term in Kant's account is
obviously 'power' or 'capacity' (*Vermögen*). By the 'power of reason
to be of itself practical' Kant means first of all its capacity to provide
a binding law for the will.[57] Reinhold is correct in suggesting that if
this were all that Kant means by freedom, then the freedom to disobey
the law has not been established. There is, however, no need to accept
this result nor, therefore, the terms of Reinhold's dilemma. Since
ought implies can (at least for Kant), the capacity of pure reason to
be practical, that is, to provide a binding law, entails the capacity of a
free agent to obey the dictates of this law. This is precisely the point
that Kant makes when he remarks that through the moral law we are
aware of freedom as a 'negative property . . . of not being constrained

to action by any sensible determining grounds.' Thus, freedom is understood as the will's capacity to follow its own self-imposed laws, which requires an independence from constraint by any sensible determining grounds. In the preferred jargon of Kant's later moral philosophy, freedom is construed as the capacity of *Willkür* to obey the dictates of *Wille*. Once again, it should be obvious that the possession of such a capacity is perfectly compatible with the failure to actualize it. Kant acknowledges this, but he also insists that this 'capacity' to fail is really an incapacity (presumably because it cannot be ascribed to perfectly rational beings) and, therefore, should not be regarded as definitional of freedom. Reinhold and Prauss to the contrary, this does not at all entail that such failure is not itself an expression of freedom.

The third and final aspect of the problem concerns Kant's tendency, particularly in the *Groundwork*, to equate heteronomy with subjection to the laws of nature. In response to this it should suffice to note that there is no need to take the claim that the heteronomous will is 'subject' to the laws of nature to mean anything more than that the inclinations and desires upon which it bases its choice are themselves products of nature. Subjection to the laws of nature in this sense is perfectly compatible with the Kantian conception of freedom. It does not follow from the fact that the inclinations and desires on the basis of which one chooses to act are products of nature, that the act of choice itself, through which they are 'incorporated' into the maxim of the will, is likewise such a product.

VII

Even if sound, the argument offered here for the Reciprocity Thesis hardly suffices to establish the Kantian version of morality. It shows only that we cannot both affirm our freedom (construed in the transcendental sense) and reject the categorical imperative. In this respect it can be said to have established the price of moral skepticism. The problem, of course, is that this price (the rejection of transcendental freedom) is one that the moral skeptic (or the rational egoist) is more than willing to pay. This is particularly true in view of the notorious difficulties in Kant's attempt to reconcile this freedom with the universal sway of the principle of causality.

Nevertheless, the question of transcendental freedom must at least be faced by anyone who wishes to criticize the Kantian attempt at the justification of morality. This attempt cannot be dismissed in the casual manner of Philippa Foot, who contends that there is nothing irrational or inconsistent in the rejection of the categorical imperative, or, at least, that no one has ever shown that there is,[58] while also insisting elsewhere that 'a reason for acting must relate the action directly or indirectly to something the agent wants or which it is in his interest to have. . . .'[59] Foot is certainly consistent here, but in a way that sidesteps the main thrust of Kant's position. Given her conception of agency, it not only would not be irrational to reject the categorical imperative, it would be metaphysically impossible to obey it. Perhaps it is, but simply to assume this is the case, is to beg the whole question.

In the last analysis, then, Kant's moral theory stands or falls with the metaphysical doctrine of transcendental freedom. As the Reciprocity Thesis makes clear, this freedom is not only a necessary, it is also a sufficient condition of morality as Kant conceives it. Consequently, if this freedom be denied, nothing remains save a rather complex and convoluted analysis of the presuppositions of a set of illusory beliefs. If, on the other hand, it be granted, then the validity of the moral law follows. This same reciprocity, however, suggests that it might very well be impossible to establish either one without presupposing the other, which would mean that Kant's attempt to justify morality is caught in a vicious circle from which there is no escape. Kant himself raises the spectre of just such a circle in the *Groundwork*, but claims to be able to avoid it. Whether he is successful, either there or in his fresh treatment of the problem in the *Critique of Practical Reason*, is a larger issue, which cannot be dealt with here.

Notes

1 *Groundwork of the Metaphysics of Morals, Kants gesammelte Schriften*, Berlin: Königliche Preussische Akademie der Wissenschaften, 1901–1922, IV, 440.
2 For the distinction between two senses in which Kant speaks of a 'supreme principle of morality,' one of which applies to the categorical imperative and the other to the principle of autonomy, see Lewis White Beck, *A Commentary on Kant's Critique of Practical Reason* (Chicago: University of Chicago Press, 1960), p. 122 and T.C. Williams, *The Concept of the Categorical Imperative* (Oxford: Clarendon Press, 1968), pp. 33–35.
3 *Kants gesammelte Schriften*, IV, 445.
4 The fullest and most significant discussion of this issue is by Dieter Henrich, 'Die Deduktion des Sittengesetzes,' in *Denken im Schatten des Nihilismus*, ed. Alexander Schwan (Darmstadt: Wissenschaftliche Buchgesellschaft, 1975), pp. 55–112.
5 *Kants gesammelte Schriften*, V, 42–50.
6 For a recent discussion of the 'Reversal Thesis,' which includes an excellent account of the whole debate, see Karl Ameriks, 'Kant's Deduction of Freedom and Morality,' *Journal of the History of Philosophy* 19 (1981), pp. 53–79.

7 See *Kants gesammelte Schriften*, IV, 447; V 29–31.

8 This point is noted by Henrich, 'Die Deduktion des Sittengesetzes,' pp. 89–90.

9 *Kants gesammelte Schriften*, IV, 446. *Groundwork of the Metaphysics of Morals*, Eng. trans. H.J. Paton (New York: Harper and Row, 1956), p. 114.

10 *Kants gesammelte Schriften*, V, 29.

11 Ibid., p. 30.

12 Ibid., pp. 93–94.

13 *Kants gesammelte Schriften*, VI, 35, *Religion within the Limits of Reason Alone*, Eng. trans. T.M. Greene ed., Hoyt Hudson (New York: Harper and Row, 1960), p. 30. See also *Reflexion 7202*, XIX: 281.

14 H.J. Paton, *The Categorical Imperative* (London: Hutchinson & Co., 1958), p. 211. A similar view is expressed by Sir David Ross, *Kant's Ethical Theory* (Oxford: Clarendon Press, 1954), pp. 70–71.

15 Rüdiger Bittner, *Moralisches Gebot oder Autonomie* (Freiburg/Munich: Verlag Karl Alper, 1983), pp. 119–134, claims that the argument of the third part of the *Groundwork*, particularly the Reciprocity Thesis, is vitiated by this slide, which is, in turn, based on a confusion of two senses of 'autonomy'. A similar line of objection is also developed by Gerold Prauss, *Kant über Freiheit als Autonomie* (Frankfurt: Vittorio Klostermann, 1983). Prauss insists upon the need for distinguishing between a morally neutral and a specifically moral sense of 'autonomy' and criticizes Kant for a failure to be clear on this point.

16 I have claimed that the above account is based on Kant's implicit definitions because his official definitions of these notions are notoriously confusing. Thus, in some places he simply identifies a practical law with an objectively valid principle (for example, *Critique of Practical Reason* §1, *Kants gesammelte Schriften*, V, 19); while in others he seems to regard practical laws as constituting a subset of objectively valid practical principles (for example, *Kants gesammelte Schriften* V, 20 and *Groundwork, Kants gesammelte Schriften*, IV, 416, 420). This, in turn, is connected with Kant's equally notorious confusion of laws and imperatives. Since all imperatives are objectively valid (in contrast to maxims) I take the latter position to be the one to which Kant is committed. For a further account of some of these issues, see Beck, *A Commentary*, pp. 79–84 and 121–122.

17 *A New Exposition of the First Principles of Metaphysical Knowledge*, Proposition IX. *Kants gesammelte Schriften*, I, 398–405.

18 *Kants gesammelte Schriften*, IV, 412.

19 Ibid.

20 Ibid., p. 446.

21 *Kants gesammelte Schriften*, IV, 400n and 420n; V, 19; and VI, 225.

22 For a useful discussion of this point and, indeed, of the whole topic of Kant's view of maxims see Onora Nell, *Acting on Principle* (New York and London: Columbia University Press, 1975), pp. 34–42.

23 This, again, is a fairly common line of criticism. A good formulation of it is provided by Marcus Singer, *Generalization in Ethics* (New York: Alfred A. Knopf, 1961), pp. 245–46.

24 On this point see Beck, *A Commentary*, p. 78, and Rüdiger Bittner, 'Maximen,' *Akten des 4. Internationalen Kant-Kongresses*, Mainz, 1974, ed. G. Funke and J. Kopper (Berlin: de Gruyter, 1974), pp. 485–498.

25 In *Eine Vorlesung über Ethik*, ed. Paul Menzer (Berlin: Rolf Hesse, 1924), pp. 52–53, Kant refers to the universalizability of the intention (*Intention*) of an action, thereby treating intentions much as he later does maxims. The problem is complicated for the English reader, however, by the fact that, in his translation of the *Critique of Practical Reason*, Beck frequently renders '*Gesinnung*', as 'intention'.

26 Onora Nell, *Acting on Principle*, p. 40.

27 Ibid., p. 41.

28 J.L. Austin, 'Three Ways of Spilling Ink,' *The Philosophical Review* 75 (1966), pp. 427–440, esp. 437–438.

29 Marcus Singer, *Generalizations in Ethics*, p. 57.

30 I am obviously ignoring the whole problem of specifying 'relevantly similar circumstances,' which is a critical issue in its own right. I think, however, that I am here in agreement with the analysis provided by Singer, *Generalizations in Ethics*, pp. 17–33.

31 Concise versions of this criticism are given by A. W. Wood, 'Kant on the Rationality of Morals,' *Proceedings of the Ottawa Congress on Kant in the Anglo-American and Continental Traditions* Held October 10–14, 1974, edited by P. Laberge, F. Duchesneau, B. C. Morrisey (Ottawa: The University of Ottawa Press), 1976, pp. 94–109; and by Gilbert Harman, *The Nature of Morality* (New York: Oxford University Press, 1977), pp. 76–77. In Harman's case, however, there is absolutely no attempt to connect the criticism to the Kantian texts.

32 *Groundwork of the Metaphysics of Morals*, *Kants gesammelte Schriften*, IV, 412.

33 *Kants gesammelte Schriften*, VI, 126 note. Eng. trans. p. 21.

34 One of the few recent commentators to grasp this point is Thomas E. Hill, Jr., 'The Hypothetical Imperative,' *The Philosophical Review* 82 (1973), pp. 429–450. In discussing the syntheticity of the principle which Kant attempts to justify in *Groundwork* III, Hill correctly notes that subjection to the moral law cannot be derived analytically from the concept of a rational person, but that the freedom of the person plays an essential role in the argument. In fact, Hill states clearly that Kant's argument rests on two poles. 1) The claim that any person that is negatively free is also positively free (which is supposed to be a matter of conceptual analysis). 2) The claim that every rational being is also negatively free (which is not a matter of conceptual analysis). I am in complete agreement with Hill regarding the structure of Kant's argument in *Groundwork* III. My concern here is to provide an argument in support of the first of these two poles, that is, to provide the required conceptual analysis, which is something that Hill does not attempt to do.

35 Admittedly, the above account of Kant's First Critique theory of practical freedom is grossly oversimplified. In particular, it ignores the fact that Kant explicitly connects such freedom with the capacity to act on the basis of imperatives (for example, A534/B562, A547–48/B575–76, A802/B830). This, in turn, has led many commentators to assume that, even here, Kant understands freedom in explicitly moral terms. In reality, however, in his First Critique account Kant does not focus exclusively, or even primarily, on moral imperatives. He is rather concerned with the presentation of the outlines of a general theory of rational agency. For a fuller account of my

views on this topic see 'Practical and Transcendental Freedom in the *Critique of Pure Reason*,' *Kant-Studien* 93 (1982), pp. 271–290, and *Kant's Transcendental Idealism: An Interpretation and Defense* (New Haven and London: Yale University Press, 1983), Chapter 15.

36 See *Critique of Pure Reason*, A533/B561, A803/B831; *Critique of Practical Reason*, *Kants gesammelte Schriften*, V, 97, Eng. trans. p. 100.

37 For an interesting recent formulation of this line of criticism see Terence Irwin, 'Morality and Personality: Kant and Green,' in *Self and Nature in Kant's Philosophy*, edited by Allen W. Wood (Ithaca and London: Cornell University Press, 1984), pp. 31–56.

38 The most detailed and scholarly of these attempts is by Rolf Meerbote, who interprets Kant in explicitly Davidsonian terms. See his reply to Irwin, 'Kant on Freedom and the Rational and Morally Good Will,' *op. cit.*, pp. 57–72; and 'Kant on the Nondeterminate Character of Human Actions,' *Kant on Causality, Freedom, and Objectivity*, edited by William A. Harper and Rolf Meerbote (Minneapolis: University of Minnesota Press, 1984), pp. 138–163. Many other contemporary philosophers, most notably Thomas Nagel, present quasi-Kantian accounts of agency while rejecting Kant's indeterminism.

39 Although I am no longer happy with all the details of my earlier analyses of this issue in 'Practical and Tanscendental Freedom in the *Critique of Pure Reason*' and *Kant's Transcendental Idealism*, I still contend that, as far as the interpretation of Kant is concerned, much depends on how one construes Kant's remark in the Canon:

> Whether reason is not, in the actions through which it prescribes laws, itself again determined by other influences, and whether that which, in relation to sensuous impulses, is entitled freedom, may not, in relation to higher and more remote operating causes, be nature again, is a question which in the practical field does not concern us (A803/B831).

Taken in connection with Kant's subsequent statement that 'we thus know practical freedom to be one of the causes of nature, namely, to be a causality of reason with respect to the will,' this suggests that, in the Canon, at least, Kant held that practical freedom would stand even if there were no transcendental freedom. Since transcendental freedom is, by definition, a non-compatibilist or indeterministic conception of freedom, the clear implication is that the detachable conception of practical freedom is not. Thus, one arrives at a compatibilist reading of practical freedom, albeit at the cost of a contradiction between the Canon and the Dialectic. Both the contradiction and the compatibilist reading of practical freedom can be avoided, however, if we keep in mind that the transcendental freedom to which Kant refers in the Canon is construed explicitly as a 'causality of reason.' As Kant himself states, 'transcendental freedom demands the independence of this reason – in respect of its causality, in beginning a series of appearances – from all determining causes of the sensible world' (A803/B831). Denying the 'independence' of the causality of reason in this sense would not seem to be equivalent to denying indeterminism; but it would clearly commit one to the view that the will is ineluctably heteronomous. I take

Kant's position in *The Critique of Pure Reason* to be an agnosticism with respect to the latter issue, which has nothing directly to do with the determinism-indeterminism question. In order to show that Kant's conception of practical freedom requires indeterminism, it would be necessary to consider his account of 'intelligible character,' a task that is obviously beyond the scope of this paper.

40 The point here is simply that a fundamental drive or impulse is a 'standing condition' rather than a cause in the sense of the Second Analogy. The latter, for Kant, is always an event from which another event (the effect) follows *necessarily and in accordance with an absolutely universal rule* (A91/B124). For my analysis of the Second Analogy, see *Kant's Transcendental Idealism*, Chapter 10.

41 I argue, however, in 'The Concept of Freedom in Kant's Semi-Critical Ethics' (forthcoming in *Archiv für Geschichte der Philosophie*) that it is perfectly compatible with Kant's moral philosophy at the time of the First Edition of the *Critique of Pure Reason*. The key point is that in 1781 Kant had not yet developed his doctrine of autonomy.

42 Kant develops this doctrine at length in *Religion within the Limits of Reason Alone* in connection with his account of 'radical evil.'

43 Lewis White Beck, 'The Fact of Reason: An Essay on Justification in Ethics,' *Studies in the Philosophy of Kant* (Indianapolis: Bobbs-Merrill, 1965), pp. 200–214, provides the best discussion, from a Kantian point of view, of the problems involved in the justification of fundamental practical principles.

44 There are obvious affinities between this line of argument and those which appeal to the is–ought distinction and the 'naturalistic fallacy.' For an important discussion of the relevance of such arguments to Kant's own position see Karl-Heinz Ilting, 'Der naturalistische Fehlschluss bei Kant,' *Rehabilitierung der praktischen Philosophie*, I, edited by Manfred Riedel (Freiburg: Rombach, 1972), pp. 79–97.

45 See *Groundwork*, *Kants gesammelte Schriften*, IV 438, and the *Metaphysics of Morals*, VI, 422.

46 For a discussion of the issue see Paton, *The Categorical Imperative*, pp. 141–142, and Beck, *A Commentary*, p. 122.

47 Kant himself suggests such a distinction in the *Critique of Practical Reason, Kants gesammelte Schriften*, V. 11n.

48 Kant's clearest statement on this point occurs in connection with his account of the distinction between the predisposition (*Anlage*) to *humanity* in man, 'taken as a living and at the same time a *rational* being' and the predisposition to *personality* in man, 'taken as a rational and at the same time accountable being,' *Kants gesammelte Schriften*, VI, 26–28.

49 I take this distinction to be implicit in the distinction which Kant suggests in the *Groundwork* between rational beings *simpliciter* and rational beings possessed of a will. *Kants gesammelte Schriften*, IV, 448–459. The same distinction is also operative in the *Critique of Practical Reason, Kants gesammelte Schriften*, V, 32. For a discussion of the significance of this distinction see Dieter Henrich, 'Die Deduktion des Sittengesitzes,' esp. pp. 91–100.

50 The most detailed and powerful formulation of this line of criticism in the recent literature is by Prauss, *Kant über Freiheit als Autonomie*, esp. pp. 60–115. Versions of it are found, however, in a large number of

commentators. Indeed, as Prauss points out, it can be traced back to Kant's own contemporaries.

51 See Silber, 'The Ethical Significance of Kant's Religion,' LXXXV, CXXVII–CXXVIII.

52 See *Kants gesammelte Schriften*, IV, 413–414.

53 *Kants gesammelte Schriften*, VI, 214, Eng. trans. *The Metaphysical Principles of Virtue*, translated by James Ellington (Indianapolis, New York: Bobbs-Merrill), 1964, p. 12.

54 Ibid., p. 226. Eng. trans. p. 26.

55 Karl Leonhard Reinhold, 'Einige Bemerkungen über die in der Einleitung zu den "Metaphysischen Anfangsgründen der Rechtslehre" von. I. Kant aufgestellten Begriffe von der Freiheit des Willens,' in *Materialen zu Kants 'Kritik der praktischen Vernunft,'* edited by Rüdiger Bittner and Konrad Cramer (Frankfurt am Main: Suhrkamp Verlag, 1975), pp. 310–323.

56 Prauss, *Kant über Freiheit als Autonomie*, p. 112. Prauss also offers a critique of Reinhold's own account, pp. 84–92.

57 For a similar analysis of this text and its relevance to the general problem of the possibility of free and yet non-moral action for Kant see Nelson Potter, Jr., 'Does Kant have Two Concepts of Freedom?' *Akten des 4. Internationalen Kant-Kongresses*, 590–596.

58 This is the central thesis of her influential paper, 'Morality as a System of Hypothetical Imperatives,' *The Philosophical Review* 81 (1972), pp. 305–316. Reprinted in *Virtue and Vices and Other Essays in Moral Philosophy* (Berkeley and Los Angeles: University of California Press, 1978), pp. 157–178.

59 'A Reply to Professor Frankena,' *Virtues and Vices*, p. 179. It should perhaps also be noted here that Foot defends an essentially Humean theory of agency, including a version of compatibilism in several of the essays included in this volume. This is not, of course, to say that she is wrong in this regard, but only that the question of the cogency of Kant's analysis of morality is inseparable from the question of the cogency of his theory of agency.

KANT'S THEORY OF MORAL SENSIBILITY: RESPECT FOR THE MORAL LAW AND THE INFLUENCE OF INCLINATION

Andrews Reath

This paper is concerned with two parallel topics in Kant's moral psychology – respect for the Moral Law as the motive to moral conduct and the influence of inclinations on the will. I explain some of Kant's views about respect for the Moral Law and its role in moral motivation, and this leads to a consideration of the sensible motives that respect for the law limits, as well as the more general question of how Kant thinks that inclinations affect choice. It turns out that these two topics are best understood in relation to each other. When we look at the motives that respect for the law must oppose, certain facts emerge about how it determines the will. By the same token, when we consider how respect limits the influence of inclinations, we are forced to artic-ulate a clearer picture of how inclinations influence the will. In considering these questions together, one can begin to outline an inter-pretation of Kant's general theory of motivation and choice, which provides the common ground between sensible and rational motives that is needed to explain how they interact.[1] I begin in section I with some background, and in section II turn to Kant's account of respect.

I

Kant's most complete discussion of respect occurs in the third chapter of the *Critique of Practical Reason*, entitled 'The Incentives of Pure Practical Reason.'[2] To place it in context, we should recall that a central aim of the second *Critique* is to show that pure reason is practical, and that Kant undertakes this project in order to answer a question left unresolved by the *Foundations*. The first two chapters of the latter derive a statement of the Moral Law from the concept of practical reason, but do not establish its validity for us. Kant thinks that this gap is closed by showing that pure reason is practical. If pure reason is 'sufficient to determine the will, then there are practical laws' – i.e., laws that apply validly to us (*Kr. d. p. V.* 17/19). This issue, in turn, is resolved through the doctrine of the Fact of Reason. Kant holds that our ordinary moral consciousness shows us that we do recognize the authority of the Moral Law and can act from its principles.[3] Since the Moral Law is an expression of pure practical reason, this suffices to show that pure reason is practical.

By the third chapter of the *Critique*, Kant has established that the Moral Law can influence the will, or in his phrase, functions as an 'incentive' (*Triebfeder*). One purpose of this chapter is to explore the effects of the moral consciousness on the faculty of desire. Here Kant outlines what might be called a theory of moral sensibility, in that he is led to a set of topics that concern the interaction between practical reason and our sensible nature which marks out the experience of the Moral Law peculiar to us.[4] This includes, first, the account of respect both as the moral incentive, and as the feeling which arises when the Moral Law checks the inclinations. Second, there is a discussion of virtue as a condition in which one successfully masters motives that are contrary to duty. Kant closes by considering the elevating side to the experience of respect, which leads us to see certain elements of our nature as worthy of esteem. The very fact that the Moral Law can check the inclinations and 'humiliate' the pretensions of our sensible nature reveals our responsiveness to rational principles, and independence from the natural order. Respect points out certain of our limitations; but when we realize that this law has its source in our own reason, it also reveals the 'higher vocation' which is the source of our dignity.[5]

Since the concept of an incentive is a technical term for Kant, it deserves comment. He defines it as 'a subjective determining ground of a will whose reason does not by its nature necessarily conform to the objective law' (*Kr. d. p. V.* 74/72). It is a *subjective* determining ground in the sense that it is that in the subject which determines the will on a particular occasion. Thus, an incentive must be a kind of determining ground of the will, or kind of motivation from which human beings can act. The sense of the concept, as understood by Kant, presupposes a contrast between different kinds of motivation that may be effective at different times. Though incentives are 'subjective' in the above sense, they can include reasons that are objectively valid: respect for the law is the operative incentive in morally worthy conduct, and hence its 'subjective determining ground.'[6]

II

In a footnote to the *Foundations*, Kant offers apparently different characterizations of respect, which all re-appear in the second *Critique*. First, it is a 'feeling . . . (which) is self-wrought by a rational concept.' Second, it is 'the direct determination of the will by the law, and the consciousness of this determination.' And third, Kant calls it 'the conception of a worth that thwarts my self-love.'[7] The second remark conveys what I shall view as the primary notion of respect as the proper moral incentive, or form of moral motivation. Respect for the Moral Law, in this sense, is the immediate recognition of its authority, or the direct determination of the will by the law. To be moved by, or to act out of, respect is to recognize the Moral Law as a source of value, or reasons for action, that are unconditionally valid and overriding relative to other kinds of reasons; in particular, they outweigh the reasons provided by one's desires. Respect is the attitude which it is appropriate to have towards a law, in which one acknowledges its authority and is motivated to act accordingly. I will refer to this attitude as the 'intellectual' aspect of respect.[8] One can also display this attitude towards individuals. This could be in an honorific sense, as when one respects a person's merits or accomplishments by acknowledging the value of what he or she has achieved. Or one can show respect for humanity in the broadly ethical sense defined by the second formula of the Categorical Imperative. Here it involves the recognition that humanity (in oneself or in others) has an absolute value which places limits on how it is permissibly treated.[9] But in addition to its intellectual aspect, Kant also makes it clear that respect has an 'affective' side: it is a feeling or emotion that is experienced when the Moral Law checks the inclinations and limits their influence on the will.[10]

Though the intellectual and the affective aspects of respect at first seem quite different, Kant does not keep them apart. In fact he seems to devote effort to showing that they are the same thing. An understanding of the phenomenon in question requires that we first distinguish them, and then see how they are related and why Kant thinks that they coincide in us. The existence of the affective aspect of respect also raises special questions in the context of Kant's theory. How can there be a 'moral feeling' and what is its role in moral motivation? We will see that it is the intellectual aspect which is active in motivating moral conduct, while the affective side, or feeling of respect, is its effect on certain sensible tendencies. I will begin by looking at what Kant says about the moral feeling of respect.

This feeling is most easily explained as the experience of constraints which the Moral Law imposes on our inclinations. Thus, Kant stresses that it originates as a 'negative effect' of our moral consciousness. When the Moral Law determines the will, it frustrates the inclinations, and 'the negative effect on feeling . . . is itself feeling' (*Kr. d. p. V.* 75/73). In short, the feeling of respect is an emotion that is the effect of, and follows from, the determination of the will by the Moral Law, when the latter limits the inclinations. Kant also tries to spell out a sense in which this feeling is an incentive in moral conduct by showing how this originally negative effect is at the same time a positive source of motivation. In us the inclinations present obstacles which we must control, or overcome, when we act morally. Respect promotes the satisfaction of our moral interests by counteracting these obstacles. Kant holds that it is an incentive towards good conduct in that it offsets the influence of contrary motives, and thus moves us toward something that we must at some level find good. This point is made in the following passage:

> For any diminution of obstacles to an activity furthers this activity itself. . . . Therefore, respect for the Moral Law must be regarded also as a positive but indirect effect of the law on feeling, insofar as this feeling (of respect) weakens the hindering influence of the inclinations through humiliating self-conceit; consequently, we must see it as a subjective ground of activity, as an *incentive* for obedience to the law (*Kr. d. p. V.* 82/79. Cf. also 78/75).

However, Kant's attempt to show how the *feeling* of respect can be an incentive is somewhat misleading. Strictly speaking, he should not say that this feeling is what weakens the influence of inclinations. Since, as we shall see, it is the experience one has when the inclinations are weakened by a superior motive, it presupposes that the inclinations have already been weakened. This point emerges from a clarification which Kant himself adds to his discussion of the moral incentive. In attempting to explain how the feeling of respect is an incentive in good conduct, he stresses that it is not 'an antecedent feeling tending to morality' (*Kr. d. p. V.* 78/76). In other words, Kant is careful to make it clear that he is not adopting any sort of moral sense theory. Since his aim is to show that the will is directly responsive to practical reason, and thus autonomous, he must avoid a view which makes use of a natural desire, or disposition, that moves us toward moral conduct, and provides morality with its content. He cannot explain our ability, or interest, in acting morally as a feature of our psychological constitution, or by introducing any motivational factor beyond the recognition of the validity of the Moral Law. Such a view would in effect grant that pure reason is not practical. Thus, respect can be neither a source of motivation, nor a standard of moral judgment, which is independent of our recognition of the Moral Law.[11]

Such considerations underlie the following important, if obscure, remark:

> Thus respect for the law is not the incentive to morality; it is morality itself regarded subjectively as an incentive, inasmuch as pure practical reason, by rejecting all rival claims of self-love, gives authority and absolute sovereignty to the law (*Kr. d. p. V.* 78 f./76).

Here Kant means to say that respect is not an incentive that exists prior to, or independently of our recognition of the Moral Law, but is simply this recognition itself as it functions as an incentive in us.[12] All of this suggests that the *feeling* of respect is an incentive only in an attenuated sense. It is indeed the inner state of a subject who is moved by the Moral Law, but the active motivating factor is always the recognition of the Moral Law. Thus the moral incentive, properly speaking, is what was distinguished above as the intellectual aspect of respect. The affective aspect is the experience of one's natural desires being held in check by the moral consciousness, and as such, an effect that occurs after, or in conjunction with, the determination of the will by the Moral Law. At times a subject may feel as though these sensible motives are being overpowered by a higher order emotion, which, so to speak, clears the way for one to act morally – so that a specifically moral emotion would be operative as a motive force. But this is not correct, on the model Kant means to propose. One's inclinations are held in check simply by the recognition of the Moral Law (the intellectual aspect of respect), and this interaction between practical reason and sensibility gives rise to the feeling of respect (the affective aspect). The resulting moral emotion ends up being something like the way in which we experience the activity of pure practical reason.[13]

It turns out that there is a tight connection between these two aspects of respect, due to certain facts about our nature, and this explains why Kant tends to treat them as identical. Our sensible nature is a source of motives that conflict with the moral disposition – specifically, because it includes the tendencies to give priority to our inclinations which Kant terms self-love and self-conceit. Kant thinks that these motives and tendencies are always present to some degree. Thus, whenever the Moral Law is effective, it must overcome contrary motives that originate in sensibility, and will thus produce some feeling. The determination of the will by Moral Law will always be accompanied by an affect. Moreover, though distinguishable, these aspects of respect need not be phenomenologically distinct, but would be experienced together. As a result, the immediate recognition of the Moral Law and the feeling which it produces represent connected aspects of what is in us a single phenomenon.

This discussion brings out a further point of some importance: Kant does not think that the Moral Law determines the will through a quasi-mechanical or affective force.[14] Such a view is implied by his remark that respect is not an 'incentive *to* morality,' but the Moral Law itself regarded as an incentive. This qualification to the account of respect is added to make it clear that moral motivation does not require, or occur through any feeling that exists independently of the moral consciousness. In addition, we saw that, while an affect is produced when the Moral Law determines the will, it is not this affect that motivates. The picture underlying these ideas is that, in acting from respect, the simple recognition of an obligation determines or guides one's choice. This is to be opposed to a model which would understand the moral motive to operate by exerting a force on the will. More general grounds for this interpretation are supplied by Kant's conception of the freedom of the will. According to his 'principle of election,' an incentive never determines the will directly, but only through a choice made by the individual which can be expressed as the adoption of a maxim.[15] This would seem to rule out the idea that the will is determined solely by the force that an incentive might have, or that actions should be understood as resulting from the balance of forces acting on the will. In short, it suggests that Kant's conception of choice should not be understood on the analogy of a sum of vector forces (or of mechanical forces acting on an object). Kant can allow an incentive to have an affective force of some sort, but the role assigned to such force in motivation and the explanation of action must be limited so as to leave room for the notion of choice. Thus, we may think of respect for the law as one incentive in competition with others, against which it sometimes wins out. But rather than prevailing against its competitors by exerting the greater force on the will, its influence comes from providing a certain kind of reason for choice.

This is a point of interpretation, but there are deeper reasons for thinking that it should be Kant's view. If the Moral Law determines choice by exerting a force that is stronger than the alternatives, moral conduct will result from the balance of whatever psychological forces are acting on the will. The issue is whether this model permits us to sustain the idea that it is autonomous and the product of will. To see this, we might first consider why Kant cannot turn to a moral sense theory to explain moral motivation. If the moral motive were based on a natural desire or disposition that could be directed and refined in various ways, moral conduct would be the outcome of different drives and natural desires that are present in our psychology. Morality would then become an empirically explainable natural phenomenon; and one would lose the notion that pure reason is practical, since one could account for moral conduct entirely in terms of natural desires. (Whatever the merits of this view, it is certainly one that Kant wants to avoid.) Furthermore, it is not clear that this model leaves room for any real notion of will or choice. The determination of action rests on the ways in which competing forces support each other, or cancel out, so that individuals act morally when the desires moving in the direction of moral conduct are stronger than the alternatives. Now consider a model on which the recognition of the Moral Law motivates by exerting a force on the will. Reason might still determine the will, but it is difficult to see how it does so through a choice by the individual. The moral motive would still be one psychological force among others, which is effective when it is the stronger, or when favored by the balance of psychological forces. What is missing from this model is the idea that the subject's action stems ultimately from a choice made on the basis of reasons.

The concerns raised in this section lead to two further lines of inquiry, which I will pursue in the remaining sections. First, we have seen that our experience of the activity of pure practical reason has a subjective character, due to the sensible motives with which it interacts. This suggests that we can broaden our understanding of respect by exploring the character of the motivational tendencies which it offsets (Section III). Second, to fully understand how the Moral Law functions as an incentive, one must see how it limits the influence of inclinations. But we will not understand that until we see how inclinations influence the will. At this point Kant's views about specifically moral motivation begin to have implications for his general theory of motivation. Once we grant that the Moral Law does not become an incentive by exerting a force on the will, it becomes harder to see how it can counteract inclinations, though Kant surely thinks that it does.

Asking how this can occur leads us to look for an account of how inclinations influence the will that allows for this possibility. In short, on the assumption that respect for the Moral Law does counteract the influence of inclination, we need a model of both that explains how this is possible (Section IV).

III

In the following passage Kant provides a catalogue of different kinds of motivational tendencies that respect for the law counteracts:

> All inclinations taken together . . . constitute *self-regard* (solipsismus). This consists either of *self-love*, which is a predominant benevolence toward oneself (*philautia*) or of self-satisfaction (*arrogantia*). The former is called, more particularly, *selfishness*; the latter, *self-conceit*. Pure practical reason merely checks selfishness . . . But it strikes down self-conceit (*Kr. d. r. V.* 76/73).

Here self-regard (*Selbstsucht*) refers to the rationally guided interest in the satisfaction of one's inclinations, which is indifferent to the happiness of others.[16] In this section I will offer an interpretation of the two kinds of inclinations that it comprises: self-love (*Selbstliebe*), or selfishness (*Eigenliebe*), on the one hand, and self-conceit (*Eigendünkel*).[17] Self-conceit in particular is pertinent to an understanding of respect. The points to bear in mind are that self-love is a 'predominant benevolence towards oneself', while self-conceit is termed 'satisfaction with oneself,' and later, the 'opinion of personal worth' (*Kr. d. p. V.* 81/78). Furthermore, the Moral Law responds to these attitudes in different ways. It 'checks' selfishness, which, when 'restricted to the condition of agreement with the law,' is called 'reasonable self-love' (*Kr. d. p. V.* 76/73). But it 'strikes down' and 'humiliates' self-conceit. Or as Kant later says, the Moral Law 'excludes the influence of self-love from the highest practical principle,' but 'forever checks self-conceit' (*Kr. d. p. V.* 77/74). While one may at times act on selfish inclinations, this is never true of self-conceit, and this difference requires an explanation.

The distinction between self-love and self-conceit is mentioned briefly in the discussion in the *Doctrine of Virtue* of *love* and *respect* as different kinds of concern that one can have (or fail to have) toward others.[18] The object of love is a person's welfare (*Wohl*) or the satisfaction of a person's ends, while respect is concerned with worth, dignity, or how a person is regarded by others. As selfishness and self-conceit are forms of these attitudes directed at the self, we may interpret the distinction as follows. Selfishness is the interest in one's own welfare and in the satisfaction of one's own desires. It contains inclinations directed at ends outside the self, such as those that bring well-being, satisfying activities, the means to such ends, etc. On the other hand, the object of self-conceit is best described as personal worth or esteem, or importance in the opinions of others. It is a desire to be highly regarded, or a tendency to esteem oneself over others. It should be stressed that it is a natural inclination, specifically for a kind of esteem that depends on the opinions either of oneself or of others, and on one's standing relative to others. It turns out for this reason to be a form of value which one only achieves at the expense of others – e.g., by surpassing them, or by being perceived to surpass them in certain qualities. Briefly, the object of self-conceit is a form of esteem or personal importance which you can only achieve when you deny it to some others.[19]

A further dimension to this distinction appears when self-love is called 'a propensity to make oneself, according to subjective determining grounds of one's choice (*Willkür*), into an objective determining ground of the will (*Wille*) in general.'[20] When self-love 'makes itself legislative and an unconditional practical principle, it can be called self-conceit', it 'decrees the subjective conditions of self-love as laws' (*Kr. d. p. V.* 77/74). Provisionally we may take self-love (or selfishness) as a tendency to take one's inclinations to provide sufficient reasons for one's actions, which would justify them to others. In making self-love 'legislative,' self-conceit goes a step further in being a tendency to treat *your* inclinations as providing reasons for the actions of *others*, or to take your desires as sources of value to which they should defer. To put the point another way, self-love tends toward a form of general egoism: I take my inclinations as sufficient reasons for my actions, but can view the inclinations of others as sufficient reasons for theirs, so that all would be permitted to pursue their own interests as they see fit. In contrast, self-conceit would produce a form of first person egoism, in which I act as though *my* inclinations could provide laws for the conduct of *others*: it expresses a desire that they serve or defer to my interests.[21]

People naturally place a special importance on themselves, and often make a concern for others conditional on its congruence with their own interests. As Kant understands it, self-conceit tries to get others to accord the same priority to your interests that you give them, by putting your desires forward as conditions on the satisfaction of their own. Though aimed at increasing one's welfare, it does so by claiming a certain kind of value for one's person relative to others. How could you possibly get other rational individuals, with desires of their own, to treat your desires as reasons for their actions? Self-conceit attempts to get others to defer to your interests by ranking yourself higher, and by claiming a special value for your person. In this way, it seeks a kind of respect that moves in one direction. When you treat a person with respect, you attribute a value to his or her person which limits how you may act. Self-conceit would have others act as though your interests outweigh theirs, and refuses to return the respect which it demands. This indicates that it is at root a desire to dominate and manipulate others. It is an outgrowth of self-love in that those who are able to manipulate others in this way both protect their own interests, and increase the means available for getting what they want.

We can now say why the Moral Law only restricts selfishness, but strikes down self-conceit. Selfishness is a concern for well-being which modifies an inclination only when it conflicts with one's overall happiness. It is opposed to the moral disposition, not due to the inclinations involved, but because it recognizes no moral restrictions. The inclinations may be good in that they can ground morally permissible ends, when properly limited. But in recognizing no moral restrictions, selfishness makes the Moral Law a subordinate principle. In the language of the *Religion*, by reversing the moral ordering of incentives, it is a propensity to evil.[22] It follows that what is bad about selfishness can be corrected when restricted by moral concerns. In this case, many of the original inclinations may be retained and their ends adopted, though now on different grounds. It is in this sense that the Moral Law need only check self-love, and 'exclude its influence from the highest practical principle.' When it does, self-love can become good.

In contrast Kant claims that inclinations for personal importance can never be made acceptable. He says that 'all claims of self-esteem which precede conformity to the Moral Law are null and void' and that any presumption to personal worth which is prior to the moral disposition is 'false and opposed to the law' (*Kr. d. p. V.* 76/73). The view to consider is that no claims to self-esteem are acceptable unless grounded in the consciousness of one's moral capacities. As Kant says, the Moral Law opposes the tendency to seek self-esteem 'so long as it only rests on the sensibility' (*Kr. d. p. V.* 76/73).

First we must clarify when a morally grounded claim to self-esteem, or demand that others respect you, is acceptable. One could claim what we earlier called honorific respect, out of a belief that one has acted well in some significant way, and some people might think this would entitle you to preferential treatment. Or one could claim broadly ethical respect from others – i.e., demand that you be treated as an end. It is hard to see how one could legitimately make a claim of the former kind on one's own behalf.[23] Others may offer you this form of respect; but you cannot demand it, and it would not entitle you to special treatment. But it is certainly acceptable to demand ethical respect from others when it is being denied, and to think that one's interests ought to be regarded as important. This is an example of a claim to be worthy of respect which is grounded in the moral consciousness; it is justified simply by one's possession of rational and moral capacities, and not by anything in particular which one has done with them.[24] Of course, this form of respect is mutual and reciprocal: giving it to one person, or claiming it for oneself, will not be prejudicial to the interests of anyone else.

Self-conceit is a claim to deserve priority (resembling a demand for honorific respect) that implicitly treats your inclinations as special sources of value. It seeks a form of personal worth attainable only at the expense of others, which is oriented towards domination and manipulation. Since such desires seek to use others as a means, they are incompatible with ethical respect for others. They are bad inclinations, unacceptable in all forms, and for this reason, the Moral Law opposes claims to self-esteem based on inclination. It is interesting to note how the moral flaws of self-conceit can be located in certain features which it very nearly shares with the proper moral attitude. It is as a distortion of a moral attitude that it is fundamentally opposed to true respect. Self-conceit is a desire for a kind of respect, that claims something like an absolute value for oneself. But this is thought to ground preferential treatment from others; it is not reciprocal; and the purpose is to further the satisfaction of one's inclinations.[25] It is as though you take your inclinations to confer a value on your person that sets you above others. This prevents you not only from recognizing their humanity, but your own as well, in that you have taken inclinations, rather than rational nature, as the ultimate source of value in your person.

IV

The preceding section discussed different kinds of inclinations and motivational tendencies which respect for the law must counteract. In this section I will turn to the more general question of how inclinations influence the will. I have interpreted self-love as the tendency to treat one's inclinations as sufficient reasons for one's actions, and, following Kant's usage, have freely referred to the 'claims' made by both self-love and self-conceit. The interpretation of Kant's understanding of motivation and choice that I develop should make it clear why this language is appropriate.

In section II, I argued that the moral incentive does not influence choice by exerting a quasi-mechanical or affective force on the will. Among other reasons, this was supported by the fact that the motive to moral conduct is the intellectual aspect of respect, or the immediate recognition of an obligation, rather than any feeling which it produces, or which exists independently. This interpretation is also required by the model of free choice expressed by Kant's 'principle of election.' But as Kant's view is that *no* incentives (including sensible incentives) determine the will directly except through a choice by the individual, similar considerations should apply to actions done from inclination. That is, while inclinations can have an affective force, it cannot be through this force that they ultimately influence the will. Furthermore, if inclinations could determine the will solely by their affective force, it is hard to see how they could be offset by respect for the Moral Law, as Kant clearly wants to hold is possible. Consider for a moment that counteracting an inclination consisted only of setting up an opposing psychological force which cancels it out. That leaves no way to explain how respect for the law limits the influence of inclinations, since it exerts no such force. This indicates the need for a different account of how inclinations influence choice. There must be enough common ground between motivation by inclination and moral motivation to show how the moral incentive can limit the influence of non-moral incentives. Here we can see how Kant's views about specifically moral motivation have important implications for his overall theory of motivation. If the moral incentive does not operate by exerting a force on the will, then it seems that, in general, a 'balance of forces model' of the will is not appropriate to Kant's theory of motivation.

How then do inclinations influence choice? Kant's view, I want to argue, is that one chooses to act on an incentive of any kind by regarding it as providing a sufficient reason for action, where that is a reason acceptable from the standpoint of others, not just that of the agent. Simply stated, inclinations influence choices by being regarded as sources of reasons which can be cited in some form to make your actions acceptable to others. Their influence on choice comes not simply from their strength or affective force, but from the *value* which the agent supposes them to have. This view needs certain qualifications. First, it does not suppose that inclinations do provide sufficient reasons for actions. It is enough that the individual is prepared to regard them in this way, and here lies the appropriateness of referring to the claims made by self-love. Typically the person moved by self-love claims a value, or justifying force, for the inclinations that they do not have; yet it is by being viewed in this way that they influence choice. Second, it is not necessary for the agent to view his inclinations as sources of reasons that will make the action acceptable to *all* others, or to those most directly affected by the action. Rather, they must be viewed as reasons which would justify or explain the action from a point of view which individuals other than the agent can take up (e.g., the members of some community). Thus, the interpretation proposed is that all choice occurs on quasi-moral grounds, or proceeds from reasons that resemble moral reasons in form. How the Moral Law checks inclinations may be explained roughly as follows. Since inclinations influence the will through the value which the agent supposes them to have, the Moral Law can limit their influence by showing that they do not have this value, and by presenting a higher form of value. This is not a question of countering one kind of affective force by another that is stronger. The appropriate metaphor is rather that of a struggle between two parties for something like legal authority or political legitimacy.[26]

This conception of choice presupposes that all action carries an implicit claim to justification.[27] To explore its ramifications, we should bear in mind that the principle of election characterizes choice as the adoption of a maxim. That is, all action proceeds from maxims which the agent in some sense adopts or decides to act on. How does this conception apply to action done from inclination? Schematically, we can say that inclinations are produced as sensuous affections and that, in response, an agent formulates a maxim of acting in a certain way – for instance, performing the action that will best satisfy the inclination. Here the role of the maxim is to express the reason for action in a form which can be assessed and cited to others. But I would argue that the principle of election implies further that a maxim is only adopted if it is regarded as a principle with justifying force, which others can accept. It is a necessary feature of free choice that it involve regarding one's action as good, at some level. If incentives become effective through the adoption of maxims, then maxims are always chosen on the supposition that they express sufficient reasons for action. As well as being objects of choice, they carry the burden of justification, and serve as principles that explain your actions to others. To put the point another way, we always choose maxims that we suppose could be made universal laws.

This feature of action can be taken as an aspect of the Fact of Reason – i.e., of our recognition of the Moral Law in everyday life. One element of ordinary moral consciousness is a readiness to submit your actions to public scrutiny and to supply reasons and explanations of a certain kind. On Kant's view, this procedure is initiated by citing the maxim of your action, which commits you to view it, at least initially, as a sufficient explanation for what you did. The presumption is that someone who understands your maxim can at some level accept your way of acting. Such dialogue might have the structure of rudimentary universality arguments. Others might agree that if they were in the same situation, they might have done the same thing, or acted from your principle. This acknowledgement on their part might lead them to view your action as a reasonable thing to have done, and might bring them to some sort of understanding with you. But if individuals do acknowledge the burden of accounting to others, this will not occur only after choices are made, but must inform the procedure of choice itself. Choice and action must occur within some framework of sufficient reasons from the start.

The direct textual support for attributing to Kant the view that all action carries an implicit claim to justification is limited. But it can be seen in the characterization of self-love discussed above, and in a passage from the *Foundations*. Regarding the first, Kant writes that

> we find our pathologically determined self, although by its maxims it is wholly incapable of giving universal laws, striving to give its pretensions priority and to make them acceptable as first and original claims, just as if it were our entire self. This propensity to make oneself, according to subjective determining grounds of one's choice, into an objective determining ground of the will in general can be called self-love (*Kr. d. p. V.* 77/74).

Here self-love is described as the tendency to treat subjective grounds of choice as objective reasons. That is, one's inclinations, which may provide valid reasons to the subject, are treated as reasons that can be valid for anyone, and could thus lead others to accept the action. The context permits the reading that the subject, when acting from a sensible motive, views the maxim as suitable for universal law (whether or not it is). The passage from the *Foundations* claims that even in 'transgressions of duty' we acknowledge the validity of the categorical imperative. In such cases, he suggests that we view the action as a permissible exception to a principle that we otherwise hold valid. This could be done by regarding one's action as a departure warranted by exceptional circumstances; or by restricting the principle so that it will not apply to this case.[28] Thus he is claiming that the agent will continue to regard the action as consistent with principles acceptable to others, and as an instance of a maxim that could be universalized.

These passages bring out the fact that this model of choice applies equally to actions that are not morally acceptable. The claim is not that maxims of inclination do provide sufficient reasons for action, but only that they are adopted by regarding them in this way. It is in this sense that it conceives all choice to occur on quasi-moral grounds, or to proceed from reasons that resemble moral reasons in form.[29] The role which this allows to rationalization in choice may be significant for Kant's view as a whole.[30] It is central to his moral doctrine that we always act with some recognition of the requirements of the Moral Law. But this assumption leaves the problem of what to say about conduct that is contrary to duty – specifically about conduct in which we ignore our duty, or act against our better judgment. While Kant generally says only that conscience condemns one on such occasions, his theory is better served by taking stock of the distorted forms in which moral consciousness can surface in public behaviour. A recognition of the need to account to others is exemplified as much as anywhere in the rationalizations and disingenuous explanations that individuals are prone to engage in. One can acknowledge the propriety of public scrutiny through the pretense of submitting to it, and this occurs in many ways. Individuals often skew the perceptions of their circumstances so as to favour their private interests, or protect their reputations. Nor is it unusual for people to support their actions with principles that they do not really accept, and would not accept from others. These are everyday forms of dissemblance and self-deception in which the appearance of moral dialogue lends the impression of legitimacy to self-interested motives. Such behaviour underhandedly reveals a recognition of the authority of moral concerns. How else are we to understand these particular forms of dishonesty?

In self-regarding conduct, individuals make the principle of self-love their highest maxim, and act from reasons that are only subjectively valid (valid only for the subject). But this fact must be obscured if choice proceeds from reasons taken to be acceptable to others. In short, on Kant's view subjectively valid motives must be viewed as though they were objective reasons if they are to influence choice. In this way, self-regarding conduct seems to require a discrepancy between the individual's actual maxim and the maxim that is avowed, or between the actual value and the value claimed for the maxim. There are numerous forms that this could take, some disingenuous, others more straightforward. Where individuals recognize that self-love by itself cannot count as a principle with justifying force, they will hide or disguise their motives. The result will be to act under the guise of a principle that is acceptable, but which may have little bearing on, or will tend to obscure their actual motive. In such cases, subjective motives are treated as objective reasons by disguising them. On the other hand, self-love is sometimes cited as a principle with justifying force – for example, out of an impoverished view of the self, or confusion about the nature of moral reasoning. Someone who believes that the will is moved exclusively by empirically given motives will view self-interest in some form as a justifying reason, simply because there are no alternatives. Here it is not a question of disguising one's motives, but of attributing a value to them which they do not have. In cases where individuals make a permissible exception for themselves from a principle that they otherwise accept, they need not be treating self-interest as a generally sufficient reason. But they may claim that special circumstances obtain, so that in this case it counts as a reason with something like moral force.

When Kant refers to treating the subjective grounds of choice as objective reasons, there need be no single phenomenon that he has in mind. But the different tendencies which this description fits might share the feature of being sustained by some set of false or impoverished beliefs. These could range from beliefs about one's motives or the relevant features of one's situation, to beliefs about the moral capacities of the self, or the nature of moral reasoning. For this reason it seems appropriate to say that the influence of self-love on the will is sustained by an ideology of sorts, which enables individuals to view their maxims as objectively acceptable reasons. In the passage just cited, Kant says that the 'pathologically determined self . . . strives to give its pretensions priority and to make them acceptable as first and original claims, just as if it were the entire self . . .' (*Kr. d. p. V.* 77/75). Beliefs to the effect that natural inclinations and empirical practical reason exhaust our practical capacities support the view that inclinations are the only source of value, or that they provide sufficient reasons under selected circumstances. In a similar way, disguising or misdescribing a maxim of self-love allows the individual to claim to be acting from a maxim that is a good reason. In all of these cases, some false or impoverished beliefs serve to hide the gap between the actual value of one's maxim and its asserted value, and prevent the individual from openly assessing his motives. This seems particularly noteworthy. The claims to value made by self-love can only be sustained in the absence of any comparison of its maxims with the Moral Law. Ideological beliefs support the influence of self-love in this way: they enable the individual to regard inclinations as sources of sufficient reasons by obstructing any comparison of their value with the value of the Moral Law.

V

We can now add a few details to our account of respect. Respect for
the law limits the influence of inclinations by exposing the claims of
self-love and undermining its pretensions to being a source of sufficient reasons. Perhaps the main point to be made is that it operates
by effecting a devaluation of the inclinations in the eyes of the subject.
It shows that maxims of self-love do not have the value, or justifying
force, that they are initially taken to have. Given what we have seen,
we might distinguish two aspects to this process. Some analysis seems
needed to expose any discrepancies between the actual value of the
agent's maxim and the value which the agent takes it to have. Roughly,
the overall process is initiated by bringing the actual maxim into the
open, so that it can be seen for what it is. Second, the texts indicate
that this leads up to the comparison of the value of the maxim to the
value of the Moral Law which had previously been obstructed by
the agent's beliefs and rationalizations. At one point Kant says that
'the moral law inevitably humbles every man when he compares the
sensuous propensity of his nature with the law' (*Kr. d. r. V.* 77/74).
His view is that when maxims of self-love are placed side by side with
moral maxims, we cannot help but acknowledge the superiority of the
latter. The Moral Law always presents a higher form of value which
diminishes the value of inclinations in comparison, so that they can no
longer appear to be sources of sufficient reasons. When this occurs,
maxims of self-love will be withdrawn, because the condition of their
adoption is seen not to hold.

Kant says that the Moral Law becomes an object of respect when
it checks selfishness and strikes down self-conceit. We have seen that
these are tendencies to exercise the power of choice that, in different
ways, give priority to the inclinations. Kant thinks that these motivational tendencies are so deeply rooted in our nature that they are always
present, and must be held in check whenever one acts from a moral
motive. Thus the immediate recognition of the Moral Law is always
the recognition of a form of value that entails a devaluation of the
inclinations. As Kant says in the *Foundations*, respect is a 'conception
of a worth that thwarts my self-love.'

The model of choice outlined in the previous section should explain
how interaction between sensible and rational motives is possible, as
well as making clear the arena in which it takes place. Even though

these kinds of motives may originate in different parts of the self, they affect choice within the same framework of reasons (in each case, by being regarded as sources of sufficient reasons). Here we should note that the 'sensible tendencies' which respect for the law checks are tendencies to view inclinations as providing certain kinds of reasons, and to value a certain part of the self. This fact has a bearing on the character of the feeling of respect. We can now see that this is the feeling that results when the agent recognizes that inclinations are not sources of justifying reasons, and represent only a subordinate form of value. We underestimate this experience if we understand it simply as the frustration that might result from electing to leave certain inclinations unsatisfied. More than anything, respect is thought to show that claims about the value of the inclinations that the agent is prepared to advance are unwarranted. In many instances what is at stake here will be the agent's self-worth, and ability to view his or her actions as justified from the point of view of others. It is for this reason that Kant often associates respect for the law with a lowering of the agent's self-esteem. It may be most interesting to consider this point in relation to self-conceit. Respect for the law is thought to have an intimate connection with the negation of self-conceit, which Kant specifically describes as a form of humiliation. We have seen that self-conceit attempts to place a kind of absolute value on one's person, which sets one apart from and above others. Respect produces humiliation in striking down this tendency, because it denies an excessive esteem or personal importance that one seeks for oneself. It effects a devaluing not just of particular desires, but of a part of your person. It seems particularly appropriate that Kant should tie respect to the feeling that results from the frustration of this particular tendency. And as Kant suggests, it is the capacity to strike down self-conceit which makes the Moral Law an 'object of greatest respect' (*Kr. d. p. V.* 76/73).[31]

Notes

1 Citations to Kant's works will give the page in translation followed by the page in the Prussian Academy edition of Kant's *Gesammelte Schriften.* References to the *Critique of Practical Reason* are included in the body of the paper. The translations used are as follows: *Foundations of the Metaphysics of Morals,* tr. Lewis White Beck (Indianapolis: Bobbs-Merrill, 1959). *Critique of Practical Reason,* tr. Lewis White Beck (Indianapolis: Bobbs-Merrill, 1956). *Critique of Judgment,* tr. J.C. Meredith (Oxford: Clarendon Press, 1952). *The Doctrine of Virtue: Part II of the Metaphysic of Morals,* tr. Mary J. Gregor (Philadelphia: University of Penna. Press, 1964). *Religion Within the Limits of Reason Alone,* tr. T.M. Greene and H.H. Hudson (New York: Harper & Row, 1960).

2 Though Beck laments that this is 'the most repetitious and least well-organized chapter of the book,' he stresses its importance, and I have drawn on his treatment. See *A Commentary on Kant's Critique of Practical Reason* (Chicago: University of Chicago Press, 1960), pp. 209–236.

3 See *Kr. d. p. V.* 31/31, 43/42, 47 ff./46 ff., and 94 ff./91 ff. Here I draw on John Rawls' series of lectures, *The Fact of Reason* (unpublished, 1983). See also Beck's *Commentary*, ch. X.

4 Kant suggests that this discussion be called the 'aesthetic of pure practical reason' (*Kr. d. p. V.* 93/90).

5 Cf. *Kr. d. p. V.* 89/86–87, 90/87, 91/88; and also *Kr. d. p. V.* 105 ff./257, 123/271.

6 Beck makes this point in his *Commentary*, p. 217. See also pp. 90 ff., and generally, pp. 215–225. It is not immediately obvious why Kant holds that 'no incentives can be attributed to the divine will' (*Kr. d. p. V.* 74/72), since incentives can include objectively valid reasons. The explanation as to why human conduct is characterised by incentives must be that, in us, reasons and sensibility provide different grounds for choice. Since human beings do not by nature act from the moral law, those occasions when an individual does must be due to some fact about his or her state at that time. Since a divine will acts only from objectively valid motives, there is no variation in the character of its choices, and thus no sense to talking about the kind of motivation from which it acts. Thus, the idea of a 'subjective determining ground' – one which is effective due to its state at a particular time – is out of place in a description of its will.

7 *Foundations* 17 n/401 n. For a discussion of the role of respect in the *Foundations*, see Nelson Potter's The Argument of Kant's Grundlegung, Chapter 1, *Canadian Journal of Philosophy*, Suppl. No. 1 (1974), pp. 89–91. – For some German commentary on the notion of respect for the law, see e.g., Bruno Bauch, *Immanuel Kant* (Berlin und Leipzig: de Gruyter & Co., 1921), pp. 317–319; and Hans Reiner, *Pflicht und Neigung* (Meisenheim: Verlag Anton Hain, 1951), pp. 22–28. While many commentators have explored the relationship between reason and sensibility within Kant's theory of motivation, this paper is concerned with an aspect of this issue not usually addressed. The tendency has been to focus on the differences between motivation by respect for the law and motivation by inclination, and on the question of how the presence of an inclination, or of an end in an agent's maxim, bear on an action's moral worth. Thus, Bauch, in explaining why Kant thinks that ethics cannot properly be given an empirical grounding, views material practical principles as empirical psychological principles that describe actual motivational and behavioural tendencies. He views them as a species of natural law, which for that reason can have no implications for how one ought to act (308–311). This leads him to claim that heteronomous action involves a kind of compulsion in that, in acting for the sake of a desired end, the will is determined by external material conditions (317). (I discuss why the latter is inadequate as an account of Kant's view of motivation at the end of section II, and in section IV below.) Bauch also goes to some length to explain that the fact that the good will is determined by the general form of law in a maxim, in abstraction from its material, does not imply that such a will can have no object (314–316). Reiner is concerned with the relationship between

inclination and duty, specifically with the issue raised originally by Schiller of whether the presence of supporting inclinations undermines the moral worth of actions done from duty, and of the proper understanding of moral virtue. He notes that since respect is a moral feeling, sensibility must play some role in morality; but the feeling of respect must be sharply distinguished from feelings of inclination, in that the former is not grounded originally on a feature of sensibility that operates contingently, but on rational considerations which are determinable a priori, and therefore universally valid (23–24). Reiner goes on to point out that though duty requires a subordination of inclination to the moral law in cases of conflict, acting from duty does not preclude acting with accompanying inclinations (but only acting from inclination). He argues that a concurrence of the two is possible since they affect the will on essentially different principles (26–27). However, this paper takes up the different question of how moral motives and sensible motives interact, and how respect counteracts the influence of inclination; I am concerned to develop a theory of motivation that provides the common ground between these two types of motive that is needed to explain how such interaction is possible.

8   It is 'intellectual' in that it involves an attitude that one displays towards a person, or a form of value, as a result of practical reasoning. This term will not be too misleading as long as we bear in mind that this is a practical attitude which guides, and is displayed in, one's actions. My aim in introducing this term is to distinguish this aspect of respect from the 'moral feeling' of respect.

9   Kant discusses 'honorific respect' for individuals (my terminology) at *Kr. d. p. V.* 79 ff./77 ff. He explains it as respect for their moral qualities and accomplishments (a 'tribute we cannot refuse to pay to merit'), and thus as respect for the principles which they exemplify – 'really for the law, which [their] example holds before us' (*Kr. d. p. V.* 81/78). For a discussion of 'broadly ethical respect' see, of course, *Foundations* 46–49/428–431, among other places. There is also a brief reference to ethical respect for humanity in this chapter of the second *Critique* – see *Kr. d. p. V.* 90/87.

10 The honorific attitude towards merit will also have an affective aspect, which Kant describes as the experience of feeling humility before the talents of another, or the example which he or she has set. This is a distinctive moral emotion, whose explanation will be the same as for the feeling of respect for the Moral Law.

11 Cf. *Kr. d. p. V.* 79/76.

12 Kant makes the same point in an equally obscure discussion of the 'predisposition to personality' in the *Religion*, pp. 23/27–28.

13 Kant may create an unnecessary difficulty for himself in these passages (Cf. *Kr. d. p. V.* 77 ff./75 ff., 81 ff./79 ff.). He seems concerned to explain how the feeling of respect can be a legitimate moral incentive, which moves us in some positive direction by winning out against competing motives (but without viewing it as an impulsion that would end up being heteronomous). In doing so he may have had the following schema in mind. The recognition of the Moral Law produces the feeling of respect; this feeling then neutralizes opposing non-moral motives, thereby allowing the original recognition of the Moral Law to become practical and take

effect. The need for such a model might rest on the assumption that the affective obstacles posed by inclinations can only be controlled by a greater affective force – i.e., an assumption that one might find in Hume or Spinoza. If this was how Kant reasoned in certain passages, then it seems to me that he was not completely clear about the distinctive force of his own account of motivation, as I shall try to show. Kant does want to say that inclinations pose obstacles which must be controlled, and indeed that this involves controlling their affective force. But this would be accomplished through our recognition of the authority of the Moral Law, and not by an emotion which this recognition produces. This is a part of the force of claiming that pure reason is practical in us – in fact, it is what it is to have a will, on Kant's view. Thus, it adds an unnecessary step to say that a morally produced emotion is necessary to offset the influence of inclinations, as in the model just sketched.

14 In this paper I will occasionally refer to the concept of an 'affective force' (or an 'affect'), by which I mean the force (or excitation) carried by a psychological state such as a desire, emotion or drive, which provides a stimulus to action in a subject. It is appropriate to think of an affective force as moving or inclining the subject towards a course of action. I take this to be a notion for which an intuitive characterization will suffice.

15 Cf. *Religion* 19/23–24. I get the phrase 'principle of election' from Rawls; see note 3 above.

16 In the second *Critique*, Kant tends to treat all inclinations as self-regarding, in a way that suggests an egoistic conception of happiness. Cf. his 'Theorem II,' which holds that all action from inclination falls under the principle of 'self-love' (*Kr. d. p. V.* 20 ff./22 ff.). But this seems inconsistent with his recognition that we can have sympathetic inclinations, directed at the welfare of others. I discuss these issues in my Hedonism, Heteronomy and Kant's Principle of Happiness (*Pacific Philosophical Quarterly* 70, No. 1, 1989), where I argue, among other things, that the 'principle of self-love' is simply the principle of acting from the strongest desire, and that action done from 'self-love' need not be egoistical. But in this paper, I leave these problems aside.

17 Kant's distinction between *Eigenliebe* and *Eigendünkel* seems to derive from Rousseau's distinction between *amour de soi* and *amour propre*, of which he was certainly aware. However, space does not permit me to explore the precise relationship in any detail. For a discussion in Rousseau see *Discourse on the Origin of Inequality*, in *On the Social Contract*, tr. Donald Cress (Indianapolis: Hackett Publishing, 1983), pp. 133, 214 (*Discours sur l'Origine de l'Inégalité*, Première partie, in *Œuvres Complètes*, III, Paris: Gallimard, 1964, p. 154 and especially note XV).

18 Cf. *M. d. S.* 115–145/448–473.

19 This can be seen in specific examples of self-conceit, such as the vices of pride, calumny, and mockery. All attempt to gain esteem for oneself by trying to improve one's standing relative to others – either by claiming a higher standing for oneself (pride), or by humiliating others so that one will look better in comparison (calumny, mockery). In general, self-conceit is connected with the failure to give others the respect which they are due. Thus, in the *Doctrine of Virtue*, Kant calls it a 'lack of modesty in one's claims to respect from others,' or what amounts to the same thing, the

failure to limit one's esteem for oneself by the dignity of others (*M. d. S.* 131/462, 116 f./449).

20 I have altered Beck's translation here at the suggestion of Stephen Engstrom.

21 The distinction between general egoism and first person egoism is discussed by Rawls in *A Theory of Justice* (Cambridge: Harvard University Press, 1971), p. 124.

22 Cf. *Religion* 25/30, 31/36.

23 This is for a variety of reasons. One is Kant's view that, in general, we cannot know when an individual has acted with true moral worth, and that, in particular, one is a bad judge of one's own case on this matter. There is also the question as to whether one would lose title to the honorific form of respect by trying to claim it publicly. In this paragraph I am indebted to a comment of the referee which led me to clarify my initial analysis.

24 Cf. *Foundations* 56/437–8, 58/440.

25 This is to suggest that if self-conceit were made universal, reciprocal, and focused on rational nature, it would develop into true ethical respect.

26 Some readers may reject my interpretation on the grounds that Kant often discusses motivation in terms that suggest the metaphor of mechanical force. For example, Kant says that respect 'increases the weight of the Moral Law by removing, in the judgment of reason, the counterweight to the Moral Law' (*Kr. d. p. V.* 78/76). For other instances of the image of opposing physical forces, see, e.g., *Kr. d. p. V.* 81/78, 91/88, and *M. d. S.* 13/216, 37/380. However such metaphors are consistently embedded in discussions in which the dominant theme is a struggle for authority, sovereignty, superiority, etc., in which it is claims or pretensions that are being opposed to each other. This holds even for the remark just quoted, in that the 'counterweight' is removed 'in the judgment of reason' through a 'representation of the superiority [*Vorzug*] of its objective law over the impulses [*Antriebe*] of sensibility' (*Kr. d. p. V.* 78/75). I believe that a close reading of this chapter of the second *Critique* shows that legal and political metaphors dominate.

27 This must be understood in light of the qualifications introduced in the previous paragraph. The 'claim to justification' need only be something which the agent is prepared to advance, and need not be universal in scope.

28 *Foundations* 42/424. Cf. also 21/405.

29 Questions of interpretation aside for a moment, while many people find this view plausible, others find it extremely implausible. However it is harder to find unarguable exceptions to this model than those not initially inclined to accept it might realize. While it is not my aim to fully endorse this conception of choice here, I will indicate briefly how it might handle difficult cases. One such case is weakness of the will. But here one may say that the agent's will crumbles at that point when he says to himself that he will perform the action 'just this once,' or will do better on the next similar occasion. That is, weakness of will can be handled as cases of making a permissible or (unimportant) exception for oneself on a particular occasion. A second difficult kind of case includes those of harm to another, in which an action seems clearly wrong from the public point of view, and unacceptable to the recipient. Here one would look for a rationalization to attribute to the agent which might make the action seem acceptable to

some, though not all others – perhaps to a special community of which the agent, but not the recipient, is a part. As an example, the agent might view the action as forced on him by his circumstances, and claim that the recipient might be forced to the same action in similar circumstances. Here it should be noted that it is consistent with the view being proposed that often the agent can expect at best a limited understanding with others through his rationalization of the action. After understanding the agent's rationale, the recipient might still try to resist the action. ('You've got your reasons, but I have mine too.') Or observers who understand the agent's rationale need not fully approve of the action, or see it as something they would have done. But this is to be expected when the principle used to justify an action is one of self-interest.

30 A similar interpretation is developed by Alexander Broadie and Elizabeth Pybus in their Kant and Weakness of the Will. See *Kant-Studien* 73 (1982), pp. 406–412, where they discuss the role which self-deception might play in actions contrary to duty. For a general discussion of this idea see T.M. Scanlon, *Contractualism and Utilitarianism* in Amartya Sen and Bernard Williams, *Utilitarianism and Beyond* (Cambridge: Cambridge University Press, 1982), pp. 115–119, esp. p. 117.

31 I would like to thank Christine Korsgaard for discussion and many helpful comments during the writing of this paper. I am also indebted to the referee for *Kant-Studien*, whose comments led to several changes in the final version. Versions of this paper were presented to the departments of philosophy at the University of Chicago (October 1984) and at the University of Massachusetts at Amherst (October 1986). I also had the opportunity to discuss the paper with the members of the Center for Philosophy and Public Policy at the University of Maryland, and with the department of philosophy at Mount Holyoke College.

KANT'S THIRD ANTINOMY AND ANOMALOUS MONISM

Hud Hudson

According to Kant, at any moment of time, the entire world at that time and the laws of nature together determine a unique future, i.e. causal determinism obtains. Also, according to Kant, the human will, independent of pathological necessitation, is capable of both autonomous and heteronomous spontaneity of action, i.e. the human will is free.[1]

Kant gives his official reconciliation of the apparent incompatibility of causal determinism and human free will in his discussion of the Third Antinomy in the *Critique of Pure Reason*. In his resolution to the Third Antinomy, Kant intends to show that the interests of practical reason which are committed to the popular dogmatist Thesis that there is a causality of reason (or transcendental freedom) can be satisfied along with the interests of speculative reason which are committed to the empiricist Antithesis that the only causality is that of nature. His strategy for accomplishing this daunting task involves drawing a distinction between things in themselves and appearances, a distinction which will permit him to maintain the possibility of the truth of both the Thesis and the Antithesis – i.e. both may be true, provided that they are interpreted under the different senses provided by the distinction [A531–A532/B559–B560].[2]

Unfortunately, however, Kant never seemed to be satisfied with his exposition of the Third Antinomy and its resolution. In almost every major work after the *Critique*, he endlessly repeated his solution, rephrased it, then summarized it, rehearsed it in numerous footnotes, and tugged and pulled at all its corners until he succeeded in shrouding it in more obscurity than ever. In his obsession not to be misunderstood on this topic, he commented so often on his achievement that he gave critics and sympathizers alike several apparently conflicting statements in his later works to hurl at one another in their attempts to attack or defend his position.

In this chapter, I give a reading of the Third Antinomy and of its resolution. In the first and second sections, I address three traditional interpretations of the Third Antinomy, and I argue that they are unsuccessful, though instructive, for a proper reading. In the third section, I present what I take to be Kant's compatibilistic resolution to the problem of free will and causal determinism. Finally, in the fourth section, I address one significant point of contact between the Kantian view and certain positions in contemporary philosophy of mind that I see as essentially Kantian in character.

Wood on Kant's compatibilism

Kant motivates his discussion of compatibilism with a conditional statement of incompatibilism from the first *Critique*: if one does not distinguish between things in themselves and appearances, then one 'could not, therefore, without palpable contradiction, say of one and the same being, for instance the human soul, that its will is free and yet is subject to natural necessity, that is, is not free. For I have taken the soul in both propositions in one and the same sense' [Bxxvii]. And again, in the second *Critique*, 'if one takes the attributes of the existence of things in time for attributes of things in themselves, which is the usual way of thinking, the necessity in the causal relation can in no way be united with freedom. They are contradictory to each other' (V, 94).[3] Kant vouches for the truth of the conditionals, but is not committed to the consequent since he denies the antecedent. That is to say, Kant does distinguish between things in themselves and appearances, and he locates freedom in the former and causal determinism in the latter.

Allen Wood puts his view of the distinction as follows: 'Kant's compatibilism, however, is based on the aggressively metaphysical distinction between phenomena and noumena; far from unifying our view of ourselves, it says that freedom and determinism are compatible only because the self as free moral agent belongs to a different world from that of the self as natural object.'[4] Under this two-worlds hypothesis, then, Wood assigns the causality of reason to the intelligible world and the causality of nature to the sensible world. Let us call this metaphysical or ontological interpretation a two-selves or two-worlds reading of Kant's distinction. We might also note that it is a plain, textual, fact that in many of those passages where Kant draws his distinction, he seems to speak in just the sort of metaphysical language which suggests an ontological reading. The question, then, will be whether this two-worlds hypothesis is ultimately the best way to interpret Kant's distinction, both with a view to consistency against the rest of the Kantian corpus, and with a view to the philosophical merit of the resulting position.

Now, Kant's primary question throughout the resolution of the Third Antinomy is 'whether freedom [as a causality of reason] is completely excluded by this inviolable rule [namely, the principle of the Second Analogy], or whether an effect, notwithstanding its being thus determined in accordance with nature, may not at the same time be grounded in freedom' [A536/B564]. In other words, Kant wants to show the mere logical compatibility of the two senses of causality. Wood, however, goes on to attribute a much stronger view to Kant. Wood proposes that whereas empirical causes are real, and not merely apparent, causes, nevertheless they are not complete or self-sufficient causes. His idea is that without a free act of the will, certain events would not come into being, their natural causes being insufficient in themselves to produce their effects. He expresses this idea by suggesting that 'empirical causality regarding human actions is an effect of intelligible causality', and that the causal efficacy behind the production of our actions is to be found only in the intelligible world.[5] This view is stronger than Kant's professed aim in as much as it makes transcendental freedom necessary for the production of certain events, not just that it is possible to think its coexistence along with natural necessity. After presenting the final aspect of Wood's interpretation, I return to this difficulty.

In locating the human agent and causal efficacy in the ontologically distinct intelligible world, Wood also attributes to Kant the hypothesis that human beings are timeless beings and that they engage in timeless agency. Wood believes that the doctrine of timeless agency also will permit Kant to defend an additional thesis which Wood (correctly) believes Kant to have maintained: that an agent can do otherwise than the agent in fact does. According to Kant's hypothesis (on Wood's view), human beings engage in a timeless choice of character through which the empirical character, or man as appearance, is wholly fixed, and through which the empirical character is exhibited in the course of nature. A being could have done otherwise with respect to some specific empirical action, then, by having made a different timeless choice concerning the character he has. One's timeless choice, then, restricts the number of possible worlds which might become actual, since it guarantees that one will do certain things and avoid others. Finally one's timeless choice is to be appropriately connected to one's empirical actions by being 'considered simultaneous with each act as it occurs in the temporal order.'[6] This, then, serves as the basis for Wood's reading of the passages in which Kant declares that our free actions are not themselves determined in the time-order of appearances, and thus are not causally conditioned.

Here, then, is one reading of Kant's compatibilism. As I have reconstructed it, the interpretation is characterized by three theses:

(i)   Kant's distinction between things in themselves and appearances is an ontological two-worlds thesis;
(ii) the intelligible cause is the source of causal efficacy, and the empirical cause, which is the effect of the intelligible cause, is not self-sufficient for its effect in the world of appearance;
(iii) human beings participate in timeless agency.

It is worth noting that on Wood's view Kant is not committed to the truth of (i)–(iii), but rather only to the coherence of the hypothesis characterized by (i)–(iii). In other words, Wood suggests that if Kant can demonstrate the coherence of this hypothesis and if Kant can show that no one could ever be in a position to refute that coherent hypothesis, then Kant will have all he needs in order to protect from incompatibilist opponents his doctrines regarding freedom, even if it should turn out that our actions are determined by natural causes. Nevertheless, if these were Kant's views, he would be in trouble, for they not only conflict with his other views, but are internally inconsistent.

With respect to thesis (iii), we are offered a truly incredible doctrine: although intelligible acts of choice are timeless, in order to connect the choice of the agent with the empirical event it is supposed to condition (say, my rising from my chair now – rather than the Lisbon earthquake), we are forced to regard the choice as simultaneous with the relevant empirical event. However, it is difficult to see this as anything but an outright contradiction: no two objects are simultaneous if one is wholly without temporal location or duration. In short, to purchase compatibilism at the price of ignoring the incoherence of timeless choices which are also simultaneous with empirical events seems an awfully high price to pay.

Moreover, this strategy would wreak havoc on much of Kant's moral philosophy. For example, choosing actions to perform and choosing a character are clearly temporal processes, and nowhere does Kant give an analysis of a non-temporal sense of 'choice' which allows us to conclude that he thought otherwise. On the contrary, he emphasizes repeatedly how one's choices are always pathologically affected but not necessitated. On Wood's view, these passages cannot be adequately accommodated. 'Being pathologically affected' is another temporal relation, and, worse yet, one that certainly cannot occur if the senses belong to a being in one world, but the choice is made by an agent in another. Hence, Wood's account cannot make sense of Kant's discussions of moral failure or moral evil; barring any affection by the senses upon the act of choice, one cannot give a coherent account of how the agent might be sensuously inclined to adopt them into his maxim and thus transgress the moral law. Furthermore, as Wood himself points out, this creates difficulties for the possibility of moral improvement, for the notion of human striving and for a number of other themes intimately related to Kantian ethics.

In conclusion, let us simply note that there is no external textual support for the thesis of timeless agency, and let us also note that what Kant does commit himself to, namely the claim that the content of a description of transcendental freedom does not involve its object in conditions of possible experience or time-determination, does not serve as evidence for timeless agency either. In other words, one should not draw inferences from the atemporality of the content of a description to the atemporality of the object which falls under that description.

With respect to thesis (ii), as already pointed out, it commits Kant to a necessity claim where he believes himself to have established only a thinkability or possibility claim, and this, as it turns out, is untenable for the following reasons. If an empirical cause were not itself sufficient for its effect, the argument of the Second Analogy would be forfeited, and Kant's causal determinism would be in ruins. According to Kant, an empirical cause is not only sufficient for its effect in the sense of producing it, but necessitates its effect under an empirical law of nature. But if an empirical cause is sufficient for its effect after all, then either Wood is mistaken or Kant is inconsistent when he resolves his Third Antinomy. Since Wood's construal of Kant's hypothesis commits Kant to a weaker view of the efficacy of empirical causes than Kant has argued for, and since it is the weaker view which is responsible for the problems just noted, I suggest that it is Wood who is here mistaken.

Furthermore, it is unclear in what sense we are to understand the term 'effect' in the proposal 'intelligible causality has as its effect empirical causality'. As I show below, Kant does have a way of relating an intelligible cause to an empirical effect which does not violate his condition that the only proper relata of cause and effect connections in nature are empirically given natural events, but I do not see how that relation can be defended when the relata are taken not to be events, but rather to be the types of causality themselves. Finally, if Wood means by the insufficiency of empirical causes simply that there must be something 'behind' the appearances (namely that there must be something appearing), and if he intends to locate transcendental freedom merely in this fact, then it would turn out that, on Kant's view, everything is the product of such freedom. Everything would be free, because every appearance is conditioned by noumena in this minimal fashion. Thus we will discover that it is not simply in virtue of having a noumenal counterpart that an action is free, but rather in having the right sort of thinkable determining ground for the action, which, as it turns out, is subject to a description which shares important features with other noumenal descriptions.

Lastly, with respect to thesis (i), is Kant's distinction an ontological one? There is a great (largely German) tradition of interpretation in favor of this thesis.[7] Since it is reasonable to suppose that thesis (i) leads naturally (as evidenced by Wood's article) to theses (ii) and (iii), we might argue that (i) is to be rejected because (ii) and (iii) are. But this (perhaps illegitimately) begs the question of Kant's consistency. So, let us investigate this thesis on its own as well.

We may begin by contrasting it with its rival, a two-aspects or two-descriptions, methodological or epistemological reading of the distinction. On the two-worlds interpretation, we have ontologically distinct kinds of objects, and we have two levels of reality in which they reside. The two-descriptions interpretation differs from Wood's precisely in the respect that there are not two selves and two worlds to put them into, but one self and one world, a self and a world which admit of different types of description. These descriptions, one concerned with intelligible aspects and the other with sensible aspects of their mutual object, can comprise two self-contained worlds only metaphorically; i.e., they are isolated realms only in that, although their descriptions refer to the same object, no inference is permitted from an instance of one type of description to an instance of the other type.

Now is such a reading plausible, or is Kant stuck with a hopeless ontologically motivated two-worlds view? One defence of a methodological or an epistemological reading is suggested by Gerold Prauss in his remarks on the German constructions Kant uses for drawing his distinction. Prauss argues that the terms 'in itself', 'for itself', 'itself', etc., are used adverbially, modifying a manner of consideration or reflection, rather than substantively, such that the distinction should be drawn between the thing considered in itself and the thing considered as appearance.[8] The obvious, but crucial, point is that one and the same thing is at issue: specifically it is one and the same object/event multiply described.

Another compelling defence of an epistemological reading has been offered by Henry Allison in a discussion of the problem of the thing in itself in his commentary on the first *Critique*. Allison interprets the distinction between an appearance and a thing in itself simply as a function of the two ways in which we can consider one and the same object in transcendental reflection: first, in relation to conditions of human cognition, and then, apart from any relation to conditions of human cognition.[9] In his clear treatment of this issue, Allison considers (and rejects) a causal reading and a semantic reading of the distinction, but then modifies the semantic interpretation, bringing it into line with the position articulated by Prauss. I refer the reader to that discussion.[10]

Furthermore, the epistemological reading is reinforced in most of the passages where Kant draws the distinction by his explicit insistence on the sameness or identity of the referent involved in each case. Neither is his commitment to this version of the distinction a correction of some earlier and failed attempt to make a two-worlds reading work. Rather it is fully evident in the Preface[11] and in the Analytic[12] of the first *Critique*; it is repeated in the *Foundations* where Kant rightly points out that the concept of duty or obligation makes sense only under a two-descriptions view and not under a two-worlds view;[13] it is confirmed in the second *Critique* where Kant continually insists on the sameness of the subject in two different relations.[14]

But, most importantly, it is the very reading he himself gives to the distinction while invoking it in the resolution of the Third Antinomy: Kant asks, 'is it truly a disjunctive proposition to say that every effect in the world must arise either from nature or from freedom; or must we rather not say that, in one and the same event, in different relations, both can be found?' [A536/B564]. In answering, as Kant does, this question with the latter alternative, he commits himself to a two-descriptions theory, and thus we can turn to an investigation of his compatibilism which begins with that interpretation, and we can turn away from the ontological two-worlds approach with its doctrine of timeless human agency.

Beck and Butts on Kant's compatibilism

Lewis White Beck and Robert E. Butts are two commentators who endorse a version of the non-ontological reading of Kant's distinction. Beck, however, endorses the view for reasons quite different from those just presented. According to Beck, Kant is driven from a two-worlds view to a two-descriptions view because of a problem which supposedly arises when Kant attempts to hold both that freedom does not infringe on the mechanism of nature, but nevertheless is adequate to the needs of ethics.[15] As Beck rightly points out, Kant maintains that all an agent's actions, as events, are fully determined, and that if we knew all of the empirical facts and natural laws, the agent's actions could be predicted with perfect certainty [See A549–A550/B577–B578; and also V, 99]. Beck condenses his criticism by posing a dilemma for Kant, a dilemma which straightforwardly advances an incompatibilist sentiment: 'if the possession of noumenal freedom makes a difference to the uniformity of nature, then there is no uniformity; if it does not, to call it "freedom" is a vain pretension'.[16] This dilemma, then, is what forces a two-descriptions approach to resolving the Antinomy in Beck's opinion.

As is clear from the structure of his dilemma, Beck believes that the possession of noumenal freedom is inconsistent with the uniformity of nature (i.e. with the claim that those phenomenal events which are free actions are subject to causal determination through the laws of nature). His idea seems to be that genuine freedom requires the ability to choose from among alternative courses of action, but that the uniformity of nature (i.e. the strict ordering of nature in accordance with natural laws) would unacceptably restrict the range of alternatives in every case, leaving only whatever action the agent is causally determined to perform. Possession of genuine freedom, Beck implies, would (sooner or later) lead to the actual performance of some action which was not in accordance with the history of the phenomenal world and the natural laws which govern it. In other words, if we possess genuine freedom, the thesis of the uniformity of nature is false.

In this spirit, the proposition corresponding to the second horn of the dilemma states that 'if the possession of noumenal freedom does not make a difference to the uniformity of nature, to call it "freedom" is a vain pretension'. But, although initially attractive, this proposition is quite simply mistaken. It is mistaken because it conflates possessing an ability with exercising that ability. Even if the exercise of such an ability would falsify a natural law, we have no reason to assume that the uniformity of nature will be disrupted by a being possessing such a fantastic ability, unless possessing an ability commits one to exercising it. But since there is clearly no such commitment, it is not a vain pretension to term such an ability 'freedom'. Hence, as originally formulated, the dilemma is not successful.

Perhaps someone will think that I am missing the point of the real dilemma, though. Suppose we replace the words 'makes a difference' with 'can make a difference' in the hopes of re-establishing the dilemma. But then the proposition corresponding to the first horn is false, since it would now say that 'if the possession of noumenal freedom can make a difference to the uniformity of nature, then there is no uniformity'. And this, too, is false since it also patently conflates the possession of an ability with the exercise of that ability.

Finally, someone might attempt to convey the point of Beck's critique by simply advancing the claim that motivated the dilemma in the first place: namely 'genuine freedom requires the ability to do otherwise, and if an agent's actions are causally determined, then he lacks the ability to do otherwise; accordingly, to maintain that such an agent is free is nothing more than a vain pretension'. Now, suppose we concede that freedom requires that an agent can do otherwise than the agent in fact does (or is causally determined to do), but that we want to deny that his so acting would violate the uniformity of nature. Accordingly, in response to the objection noted above we may argue that either the agent could make a difference to the manner in which nature is uniform or he could make a difference to which nature is uniform. Let me explain: two schools of compatibilism have surfaced in recent debate, and they have been classified according to a particular strategy they adopt when responding to certain incompatibilist arguments. Theorists known as 'divergence-miracle' or 'altered-law' compatibilists will attempt to tell a plausible story in which if freedom were to make a difference to the uniformity of nature it would do so by making a difference to the manner in which nature is uniform, by making a difference in the set of actual empirical laws. Theorists known as 'altered-past' compatibilists will attempt to tell a similarly plausible story in which if freedom were to make a difference to the uniformity of nature it would do so by making a difference to which nature is uniform, by making a difference in the events of the past. Furthermore, in order to defend their respective positions, neither sort of compatibilist is constrained to endorse the obviously false claim that an agent can perform some action which has as a causal consequence a change in the laws of nature or in the events of the past. The point is simply that there are ways to make a difference to the uniformity of nature which are not tantamount to violating the uniformity of nature.[17]

It is significant that the dilemma fails, because Beck believes that once even the first version is granted there is 'only one way out of the dilemma', and that belief leads Beck to assign the two theses to Kant which comprise his, Beck's, interpretation of Kant's resolution to the Third Antinomy. The first thesis is that Kant held the two-descriptions rather than the two-worlds theory. The second thesis is that both freedom and natural necessity are to be read as regulative Ideas, rather than freedom's being subordinate to the constitutive principle of natural necessity.[18] Beck's first thesis is in accidental agreement with my discussion against Wood's two-worlds interpretation, but the pseudo-dilemma which led him to this thesis also leads him to the second, which I first reconstruct and then attempt to give further reasons for abandoning.

Beck's second thesis requires a fundamental restructuring of our ordinary views of the epistemology of the *Critique of Pure Reason*. 'Specifically, it requires that the sharp distinction between constitutive category and regulative Idea be given up, that even the categories be regarded as devices for the regulation of experience and not as structures necessarily given in a fixed constitution of our experience of nature.'[19] Beck notes that the only evidence we possess that indicates this is Kant's view is section 70 of the *Critique of Judgment* where Kant presents an antinomy which Beck believes Kant solves in the way he ought to have solved the Third Antinomy. Beck's interpretation of that later resolution of the Antinomy of Teleological Judgement serves as a model for the Third Antinomy as follows: Kant could have interpreted the thesis and antithesis in the Third Antinomy as regulative principles which correspond to maxims governing our investigations in two fields. Our two maxims would then be:

(a) 'Always (in science) search for mechanical causes and allow no non-natural causes to enter into the explanation of natural phenomena'; and

(b) 'Always (in ethics) act as if the maxim of the will were a sufficient determining ground of the conduct to be executed or judged.'[20]

Note the advantages of such a reading: neither of the maxims makes an ontological claim committing Kant to a two-worlds view. Both retain their *a priori* structure, and can make a defensible claim to cover all of the relevant experience. And, finally, neither of the maxims makes a declarative statement, and thus the principles do not conflict with one another, since they lack truth-values (i.e. this is one way to solve the Antinomy). Beck considers the remaining type of conflict which is characterized by the command to pursue two incompatible courses of action, but argues that even that sort of conflict will never arise with respect to maxims (a) and (b) above.

Robert E. Butts also opts for such a reading of the Third Antinomy, but he makes a stronger claim regarding it than does Beck. Beck's position is that Kant was a two-worlds theorist in the first *Critique*, did not appreciate the paradoxes regarding his solution to the Third Antinomy when invoking that desperate ontological move, finally came to a realization in the third *Critique* of the improvements available through a two-descriptions view, and changed his mind about the constitutive character of his categories in order to accommodate his new discovery. Hence, Beck's real reading of the Third Antinomy is that Kant fails as a two-worlds theorist; his charitable reading is that Kant can be saved in the manner of the third *Critique*.[21] Butts claims that the regulative reading of the Thesis and Antithesis is already present in the first *Critique*, and that Beck's way of resolving the Third Antinomy by noting that such rules are non-propositional and thereby cannot conflict is Kant's early view as well.[22] Butts explicitly supports Beck's motivational dilemma but adds to Beck's solution that 'the one way out' which he believes leads to the regulative reading of the categories is already present in Kant's Dialectic from the first *Critique*.[23]

Here, then, are two slightly different readings of Kant's compatibilism. Interestingly, they are both prompted by a straightforward incompatibilism. For reasons already given, though, Beck's dilemma is unsuccessful, and there is more than 'only one way out'. However, this simply shows that Beck and Butts are incorrect in thinking that Kant must adopt this reading of his compatibilism in order to remain self consistent. That is important, but it does not by itself show that Kant did not take just this approach; i.e. it does not by itself show that he is not permitted to have resolved his problem in this fashion. So, with reference to the latter claim, is this a proper reading of Kant's compatibilism?

Beginning with the stronger reading first, Butts's claim that this is already Kant's view in the first *Critique*, we can oppose his single citation from the Antinomies with an overwhelming number of passages. Throughout the Preface, Introduction, Aesthetic and Analytic of the first *Critique*, Kant argues that we bring a structure to our experience such that we legislate, through the nature of our understanding, *a priori* constitutive principles of our experience, which he later contrasts with the regulative Ideas of reason. Perhaps, given the location of Butts's evidence, though, we are to understand that certain conclusions reached in the Dialectic are to be read back into those earlier sections containing the positive epistemology of the first *Critique*. Even strictly confining ourselves to the Dialectic, though, we can find passages which cannot plausibly be interpreted as being consistent with a regulative reading of the category of causality. For example, from the resolution to the Third Antinomy, Kant writes, 'that all events in the sensible world stand in thoroughgoing connection in accordance with unchangeable laws of nature is an established principle of the Transcendental Analytic, and allows of no exception' [A536/B565]; and, again, 'the thoroughgoing connection of all appearances, in a context of nature, is an inexorable law' [A537/B565]; and, again, 'this law is a law of the understanding, from which no departure can be permitted, and from which no appearance may be excepted' [A542/B570].

Butts faces another difficult problem. On his view, the Thesis and Antithesis when not reinterpreted as regulative are in inescapable conflict: when reinterpreted as regulative, they do not conflict because they do not, as maxims, have truth-values at all. But if they do not have truth-values at all, then Butts attributes to Kant a resolution of his Third Antinomy which contradicts what Kant says about how he will resolve the problem in the text of the Third Antinomy: Kant claims that given a certain distinction, both Thesis and Antithesis may be true [A531–A532/B559–B560]; Butts's reconstruction of the resolution allows neither to be true.[24] Butts slightly anticipates this objection when he declares that 'they both can be "true", that is, reasons can be given for adopting one in this context, the other in another context.'[25] Butts's hesitancy reveals itself in his use of scare-quotes, however, and it seems fairly unlikely that this is the sense of 'truth' Kant appeals to in this regard. To make it a plausible reading, Butts needs to provide us with some further reason for believing it to be Kant's usage. For instance, is there a similarly diluted sense in which both Thesis and Antithesis in the mathematical Antinomies are 'false'?

Let us now examine Beck's reading. Beck does not have to answer the questions of internal consistency in the Dialectic which Butts faces, since Beck believes Kant to be a confused two-worlds theorist in the first *Critique*. But, as I have argued, it is not clear that Kant ever endorsed the two-worlds theory in his first *Critique*. It is understandable how a sympathetic and incompatibilist critic, such as Beck, who believes that there is only 'one way out' of the dilemma, might attribute an unsuccessful ontological distinction to Kant (since he can see no other way to accommodate Kant's obvious compatibilistic desires in the first *Critique*), and then, armed with a story of philosophical development and Kant's more mature texts, attempt to correct the philosopher's earlier views with the help of his later ones. But despite the fact that there is more than one way out of the dilemma, it remains to be seen if the proposal really solves the antinomy after all, and if so, at what cost.

Recall that the proposal in question requires that we regard moral and natural laws as coordinate, rather than the former subordinate to the latter in experience. Then we are to raise the question of freedom or natural necessity with respect to some action or event either within the context of an investigation into ethics or within the context of an investigation into nature, but not both. (In fact, Beck goes so far as to argue that we are incapable of simultaneously ascribing causal necessitation and freedom to the same event, but must first ascribe one, and then change the context and ascribe the other.)

Now the driving force behind this revision is just the familiar incompatibilist worry about whether any event is ever a proper subject of both types of description, and Beck remains firmly incompatibilist when he explains that if he knew what empirical cause produced some action, he 'would no longer say (with Kant) that this action was a free one and the defendant was responsible for it'.[26] I take it, that this is because he believes that causation interferes with our freedom in some important way (most probably, with our ability to do otherwise than we in fact do). But unless a defence can be offered for that presupposition, something beyond Beck's dilemma (which simply assumes it), we need not be led to that form of incompatibilism, and neither do we need to invoke this approach, so opposed to Kant's project in the first *Critique*, in order to rescue Kant from any untenable position.

Finally, a brief comment about the price of such a revision in Kant's epistemology is in order. The consequences are staggering. On this regulative interpretation, we are to understand that only those actions which are uncaused are free and also that there are such actions, i.e. that some events do not, in fact, have a sufficient natural cause.[27] In short, to grant this revision is to reject the main task of the first *Critique*. There is no longer any justification for metaphysical, synthetic, *a priori* judgments, since without the full strength of the categories as constitutive principles these judgments lose their claim to strict necessity and universality. Also, Kant's causal determinism would be in shambles, since it depends on the universality and necessity of this causal principle. Lastly, Kant would be landed in exactly the kind of scepticism he repudiates, since his account of the empirical knowledge of events, which also depends on the full strength of the principle of the Second Analogy, would be forfeited. For an unnecessary revision, that price is too high.

Kant's compatibilism reconsidered

Merely cautioning against taking certain paths to interpreting Kant's compatibilism, however, does not also show us which path to take instead, or even if there is a path which leads to a coherent reconstruction of his view. On the face of it, there are serious obstacles to our reaching such a reconstruction. The following four problems attest to this. Taking a two-descriptions reading as fixed, we need to discover whether Kant contradicts himself by stating

(i) that events which are free human actions are causally determined, and yet arise from a will with the freedom of independence from pathological necessitation;

(ii) that they are members of a series in which every member follows from some other member and a strict law, and yet have their absolute beginning in a determining ground (or causality of reason) which is such that it does not follow from some other member in that series and a strict law;

(iii) that they are one and all in time and subject to conditions of time-determination, and yet are related to a merely intelligible ground which is not subject to the conditions of time-determination at all;

(iv) that they are fully explicable and predictable as events in nature, and yet rise from unknowable and incomprehensible grounds.

For convenience let us refer to these four problems as the problems of independence, of absolute beginnings, of atemporality and of incomprehensibility, respectively.

Before addressing these problems, a preliminary investigation will be worthwhile. As I argue momentarily, Kant's theory of human agency can be adequately represented by Donald Davidson's pro-attitude belief model of human agency. Under this model, an agent selects from among alternative means–end relations, furnished by pure or empirical practical reason, the selection being dependent upon a belief in the propositional representation of the means to some end which has been conceptualized by the agent and for which the agent has some (rational or sensuous) desire. This, then, provides us with one sense of the phrase 'being determined to act'; i.e. an agent's actions are determined by his belief in the proposition expressing a relation of means to some end which is an object of desire for that agent. This sense of 'determination', however, does not appear to be of the nature of a competitor to the sense of 'determination' applicable to natural events under the scope of the Second Analogy.

In the case of what we might call pro-attitude propositional determination (what Kant would term 'the determination corresponding to an intelligible cause'), if an agent S in performing action x is determined by something y, then y is S's practical reason for performing x, and y consists in the conjunction of a desire for some end and a belief in a proposition expressing means to that end. Whereas such determination is necessary, but not sufficient, for its outcome (for reasons which I discuss below), that is, whereas some agent's having a practical reason for performing some action is not invariably followed by a performance of that action, the sense of 'determination' at work in the Second Analogy differs in precisely that regard. In the case of what we may call empirical causal determination (the only case which Kant allows as a productive or efficacious usage of the term), if an event x is determined by something y, then y is an event which, together with a causal law, necessitates the occurrence of x.

A commentator on Kant must admit that in addition to saying that events determine other events he says that actions determine events and that acts of will are themselves determined by the causality of reason. But we need not convict him of a confusion if we recognize that sometimes he uses his term in the one way and sometimes in the other. Accounting for some action's being determined by the causality of reason would involve us in the task of providing reasons for that action utilizing some story concerning propositional representations, beliefs and desires, but it does not introduce a new productive force into nature. Rather, since Kant holds the identity theory of actions and events, any free action which is subject to this determination of the causality of reason is token–token identical with some event which is determined (in the strong sense of empirical causal necessitation) by some antecedent event and a natural law. Hence, in thinking about the determination of a causality of reason, we do not introduce any supernatural productive forces into nature, and (owing to the identity theory) nor do we lose an account of the efficacy of the causal connection.[28]

On that reading, then, intelligible causes do not determine natural events at all, but this claim must be understood only as a denial of a sense of 'determination' which is both distinct from determination of causes under the principle of the Second Analogy and sufficient for an account of causal efficacy. (Kant nowhere provides an account of a productive sense of 'determination' which is not empirical causal determination.) Nevertheless, whereas a free action is productive (i.e. brings consequences into being) only by being token–token identical to an event which is the effect of some natural cause, it also can be regarded as being determined by the causality of reason in our sense of pro-attitude propositional determination.

That the efficacy of intelligible causes is due to their being identical to natural events is Kant's own conclusion as well in a very important footnote in the *Critique of Judgment*: 'even the causality of freedom (of pure and practical reason) is the causality of a natural cause (the subject regarded as a human being and hence as an appearance) subject to [the laws of] nature'.[29] And again in the text of the third *Critique*, 'it is true that when we use the word cause with regard to the supersensible, we mean only the basis that determines natural things to exercise their causality to produce an effect in conformity with the natural laws proper to that causality'.[30]

Now according to Kant, reason is such a supersensible faculty in agents, and (in its practical employment) it is the intelligible cause which determines the agent's will [A546–A547/B574–B575]. Moreover, Kant maintains, that we regard our reason as having causality is clear from the imperatives which are constructed when we employ pure or empirical practical reason in the hopes of attaining some desired end [A547/B575]. This causality is distinct in type from that at issue in the Second Analogy, since these imperatives are always formulated with an 'ought' (a term which has no place in empirical descriptions or natural law). Thus we have the form of the propositional representations required in Kant's analysis of human agency.[31] That is to say, when one is determined by the causality of reason, Kant maintains that one believes in something equivalent to a statement of the form 'if I desire end x, I ought to do action y', and one, in fact, desires x. An agent who then performs y might well adduce his desire and belief in that proposition as his (practical) reason for doing y. All of this is consistent though with regarding y as token–token identical with an event which is the effect of a natural cause, i.e., which has been determined in the strong sense that Kant regards as productive of events in the world.

An agent's ability to determine himself in this manner through the causality of reason by representing means–end relations (i.e., to act on reasons or in accordance with a conception of laws) is regarded by Kant as the mark of a rational being, or an intelligence (V, 125), or of a being with personality (V, 87). Moreover, he tells us that 'so far as we consider a being (man) entirely according to this objectively determinable reason, he cannot be considered as a being of sense; this property is a property of a thing in itself'.[32] Here, as elsewhere, we do not take a different referent in making the switch from 'a being of sense' to 'a thing in itself', but rather take the same object but considered apart from the conditions of our knowledge of it, that is, considered apart from conditions of spatial or temporal determinations of it through which we could connect it to other appearances in nature and thereby come to make empirical knowledge claims concerning the object in question.

So, Kant is here telling us that in so far as we regard the human subject as an intelligible cause through reason, in so far as we entertain the notion of a transcendentally free agent, we apply descriptions which are of such a nature that they cannot be used in generating any empirical knowledge concerning their object. It is absolutely vital to understand that this is not to say that no descriptions exist which, if applied to the same object, would be of a sort to yield empirical knowledge of that object; of course, such empirical, natural descriptions are available. It is merely to say that empirical knowledge is not forthcoming while restricting oneself to the intelligible descriptions concerning an ordering not of the way things are, but of the way they ought to be, i.e. an ordering thought in the employment of free human agency.

In addition to its providing the token–token identity thesis, we now begin to discover Kant's further use of the two-description theory through an inquiry into the nature and limitations of the types of description in question. To that extent, Beck and Butts are right to look to the third *Critique* for clues in interpreting the Third Antinomy from the first *Critique*. For it is in that work that Kant carefully crafts the distinction between the intelligible descriptions appropriate to a thing considered in itself, and the natural descriptions appropriate to a thing considered as a being of sense, which he employs in his resolution of the Third Antinomy. Without reducing the category of causality from a constitutive principle to a regulative Idea, we can benefit from Kant's treatment of regulative principles in the third *Critique*. As Ralf Meerbote has recently argued, 'the concepts of a purpose and a reason for an action are ideas [i.e. Ideas of reason, in Kant's technical sense], and descriptions of agents acting on reasons are descriptions in a language of regulative principles'.[33] His point is that the purposive activity of human beings, the activity requiring the use of reason, and thus, as Kant tells us, the activity which is described as belonging to a thing considered in itself rather than to a thing considered as a being of sense, admits of noncausal teleological descriptions. Meerbote identifies these as 'nondetermining descriptions', meaning thereby descriptions which are not determining in the sense of empirical causal determination. We may adopt this terminology, provided that we remember that some subclass of nondetermining descriptions, in Meerbote's sense, may yet be such that they are determining in our sense of pro-attitude propositional determination.

By saying that action descriptions are nondetermining descriptions, one maintains, at the very least, that such descriptions afford neither causal inferential connections between the action and the events which precede and follow it, nor determination of their objects in space or time. Consequently, to say that a person employs transcendental freedom (i.e. exercises a causality of reason with its attendant pro-attitude propositional determination) is to apply a nondetermining description to that person. Such nondetermining descriptions (which in these contexts are used to express the purposes and reasons for action) are, of course, not reducible to any determining descriptions, owing in part to the presence of the irreducibly intelligible term 'ought' which occurs in them essentially, and in part to their failing to supply information necessary to ground claims to empirical knowledge concerning their objects.

Making exactly that point seems to be Kant's intention when he applies his distinction between things in themselves and appearances (to man as agent) in his resolution of the Third Antinomy [A545–A547/B573–B575]. After reaffirming the full strength and scope of the principle of the Second Analogy, he draws the distinction between types of character along the lines of how descriptions express the information in virtue of which an object is experienceable or knowable for us. His result, the empirical contrasted with the intelligible character of an agent, is just the result of contrasting determining with nondetermining descriptions of one and the same object.

Specifically, then, the Kantian compatibilist can claim to have located the empirical cause of an action with a determining description regarding a certain belief–desire pair functioning as a reason for action (i.e., in a certain neurophysiological event which tokens the reason), but also claim to have satisfied the Kantian demand for an intelligible character of the action in virtue of the applicability of a nondetermining description to that token, a description expressing a practical reasons connection. The empirical character of the action, then, can serve an explanatory role in empirical causal contexts, and the intelligible character can serve a regulative function in the conception of ourselves as rational agents by providing nonempirical grounds for imputational and justificatory contexts. Consequently, the action of such an agent is free (i.e. admits of noncausal, nondetermining, descriptions which concern a pro-attitude propositional determination of the agent's will by practical reason), and is causally determined (i.e. is token–token identical to an event in nature which is necessitated as the effect of an antecedent event and a causal law).

With the present account of Kant's compatibilism in hand, let us return to the four problems I mentioned at the outset of this section. Our task is now to determine whether or not the problems of independence, of absolute beginnings, of atemporality and of incomprehensibility still present us with any obstacles to reconstructing a satisfactory interpretation of Kant's compatibilism.

HUD HUDSON

The problem of independence

How can Kant say both that actions are causally determined and yet belong to an agent with the freedom of independence from pathological necessitation? To some extent, we can provide the beginning of an answer to this problem if we note that the absence of pathological necessitation is not absence of all types of determination, in as much as pathological necessitation limits itself to sense and imagination. According to Kant, something which is pathologically necessitated 'cannot be determined save through sensuous impulses' [A802/B830]. A rational agent, on the other hand is not such a being precisely because he can be determined 'through motives which are represented only by reason' [A802/B830]. Determination, so considered, is our pro-attitude propositional determination, and Kant's claim that this is independent of causal determination can now be read as follows: an imperative can determine the will in the sense of providing the propositional component of a practical reason for an agent's action, and such pro-attitude propositional determination is not expressed with causal, determining, descriptions. Significantly, this commitment does not count against the resulting free action's being token–token identical to a natural event. Consequently, Kant in granting the freedom of independence is still able to preserve the scope and force of the principle of the Second Analogy, while simultaneously providing an account of the efficacy of actions in producing their consequences.

This independence which Kant insists on has extremely important consequences. Since he thereby denies type–type reducibility, then unless he also adopted a token–token identity theory, he would be committed to a much stronger thesis about the type of determination involved in the causality of reason. In other words, he would have to make reasons efficacious, not by being identical to some event which is a natural cause, but by construing the relation as lawlike between an agent's having a practical reason for performing some action x and his subsequent performance of x. That, of course, would effectively make nonsense of his discussions of deliberating about competing means–end relations, and of his account of the possibility of moral failure and moral evil, which depend on a plurality of such practical reasons in an agent, only one of which is acted upon. Similarly, Meerbote has argued that treating reasons as efficacious leads to lawlikeness, which leads to integration or reducibility of mental descriptions to physical descriptions (the nondetermining to the determining), which, in turn, leads to a rejection of the freedom of independence as I have just described it.[34] As we have seen, though, Kant accepts a

252

token–token identity thesis and denies a type–type reducibility thesis, and thereby preserves the freedom of independence without violating the causal determinism to which he is committed.[35]

The problems of absolute beginnings and of atemporality

How can Kant say both that any action is a member of a series in which every member is subject to conditions of time determination, and in which every member follows from some other member and a strict law, and yet has its absolute beginning in a causality of reason which is not subject to conditions of time determination, and which beginning does not follow from any other member and a strict law? (Given Kant's view concerning the intimate relation between causality and time determination, it is fitting that these two problems stand together.)

Kant states that 'the absolutely first beginning of which we are here speaking is not a beginning in time, but in causality' [A450/B478]. His theory of causality commits him to as much, since any happening is temporal and thus has only a relative beginning in the causal series. With this clue, though, we can introduce our distinction once again to read these passages. As Kant writes in the *Prolegomena*, 'every beginning of the action of a being from objective causes regarded as determining grounds is always a first beginning, though the same action is in the series of appearances only a subordinate beginning' in accordance with the principle of causality.[36] His reason for regarding the event as having a first beginning under its action description is that the relation expressed between an action and its intelligible determining ground is not a temporal and, *a fortiori*, not a causal relation. 'The action in so far as it can be ascribed to a mode of thought as its cause does not follow therefrom in accordance with empirical laws', since 'pure reason, as a purely intelligible faculty, is not subject to the form of time, nor consequently to the conditions of succession in time' [A551/B579]. In other words, the intelligible cause is not orderable in time nor locatable in an empirical causal chain in so far as it falls under nondetermining intelligible descriptions. Therefore, in so far as we regard it under such a description, the pro-attitude propositional determination of the causality of reason does not follow from any natural law, and in this independence from nature can itself be regarded as a first beginning. Alternatively, as Kant explains in his *Religion Within the Limits of Reason Alone*, a first beginning 'is the derivation of an effect from its first cause, that is, from that cause which is not in turn the effect of another cause of the same kind'.[37] The causality of reason obviously can be considered a first beginning in this sense as well, since such an intelligible cause, unlike a natural cause, does not follow from any cause of its same type.

In saying all of this, however, 'we should not be asserting that the effects in the sensible world can begin of themselves' [A541/B569]. Rather, the token–token identity thesis allows us to say of that causally unconditioned, absolute beginning that it is tokened by an event which always has merely a subordinate beginning. Hence, the atemporality and lack of information relevant to establishing empirical causal connections between events, which characterizes the content of action descriptions, does not lead, as is often thought, to the atemporality or to the causally unconditioned nature of the objects which fall under those descriptions.

Our present analysis also leaves us with a way to deal with a notoriously difficult passage in the *Critique of Practical Reason*, the 'wretched subterfuge' passage. I have here suggested that (as in his early *Nova dilucidatio*) Kant locates freedom in the type of the determining ground of an action which is also causally necessitated. Specifically, he locates freedom in the applicability of a nondetermining description concerning a pro-attitude propositional determination of a will through imperatives furnished by practical reason, which, as it happens, is token–token identical to some natural event.

Apparently against exactly this, Kant now writes, it is 'a wretched subterfuge to seek escape' with reference to 'the kind of determining grounds of [an agent's] causality.' He labels this notion the concept of a 'free-effect', meaning 'that of which the determining natural cause is internal to the acting thing'. Even worse, along these very same lines, Kant seems to argue against freedom as determination by laws of reason, as well: 'if these determining conceptions themselves have the ground of their existence in time, and more particularly, in the antecedent state . . . then it is natural necessity after all and not transcendental freedom' (V, 96–7). This wretched subterfuge, he maintains, yields only the freedom of a clock, a projectile, or a turnspit; i.e. provided that it is wound up, launched or cranked, it carries out its further motions without influence from any other external forces.

In this passage (V, 97) Kant argues against a Leibnizian theory of freedom (or, at least, against what he takes to be a Leibnizian theory of freedom), but careful attention to his text will show that what he says is not also a rejection of the view which I have attributed to him. What he objects to in this passage is the claim that freedom obtains when 'the determining natural cause is internal to the acting thing'. On the present reconstruction, though, freedom is not accounted for in terms of natural causes at all, whether internal or external to the acting thing. Rather it is found in the applicability of an intelligible cause, independent from natural causes. Again, he objects to the view of freedom's consisting in being determined by reason, 'if these determining conceptions themselves have the ground of their existence in time . . . in the antecedent state'. But the present reconstruction, as shown in our answers to the problems of absolute beginnings and atemporality, denies just this. Nondetermining descriptions of the sort appropriate for the pro-attitude propositional determination of the causality of reason do not yield temporal determination of their objects, and therefore no 'antecedent state' or law is such as to determine the causality of reason (see V, 97–8).

Nevertheless, misreadings of the wretched subterfuge passage have been quite successful in supporting rejections of the sort of compatibilism which I have attributed to Kant. One recent example which deserves special mention and some extended discussion is Henry Allison's attack on compatibilist readings of Kant. In his treatment of Kant's theory of freedom, Allison repeatedly advances the thesis that the concept of transcendental freedom is an explicitly incompatibilist conception of freedom, and therefore that Kant cannot properly be read as adhering to a compatibilism between freedom and causal determination of the Humean, Leibnizian, or even the contemporary Anglo-American stripe.[38] He acknowledges that Kant does argue for a reconciliation of some sort, though, and Allison follows Allen Wood's description of this project by saying that Kant wants 'to establish the compatibility of compatibilism and incompatibilism'.[39] (In other words, on Allison's view, Kant wants to hold both a genuine compatibilism between freedom and causal determinism and, in some sense, an 'incompatibilist' theory of freedom.)

The problem with such an approach is that Allison repeatedly and mistakenly treats 'indeterminist' and 'incompatibilist' synonymously in the descriptions he uses to characterize Kant's conception of transcendental freedom. Allison rightly argues that the concept of transcendental freedom is a nonempirical or indeterminist one precisely because it involves an act of (practical) spontaneity performed by the agent which, in so far as it is regarded as an expression of intelligible character, is nonexperienceable, unknowable and thus indeterministic. Nevertheless, one may respond that this indeterminist conception can make for an incompatibilist conception only to the extent that a given compatibilist theory depends on a notion of freedom which is determinist in that sense (e.g. the one we have just seen Kant attribute to Leibniz, in which freedom is located in the right kind of natural determining cause, internal to the acting thing).

As should now be clear, though, not all of the types of compatibilist theory which Allison hopes to rule out of consideration as approximating Kant's view do depend on such a determinist conception of transcendental freedom, thereby identifying it with a special kind of empirical or natural cause. In brief, Allison is mistaken to group together the Humean, Leibnizian, and various contemporary Anglo-American compatibilist positions. His arguments work only against ascribing to Kant a compatibilism which takes an empirical or determinist conception of freedom (i.e. they work against an ascription of Leibnizian compatibilism to Kant), but they say nothing against a compatibilism which takes a nonempirical or indeterminist conception of freedom.

When Allison considers these contemporary approaches, he suggests that they presuppose a 'naturalistic framework' and that they try to show that rational agency can somehow be 'naturalized'.[40] In other words, according to Allison, such views suggest that rational agency is to be explained on the familiar belief–desire model, with the resulting reason for action being identified with the empirical cause of the rational activity. But that achievement, Allison would protest, addresses only the empirical character of rational agency by identifying the empirical psychological causes (i.e. some belief–desire pair) of action, and hence fails altogether to address the intelligible character of rational agency. As we have seen, however, stating that a reason is identical to a cause is not at all equivalent to stating that reason descriptions are identical or even reducible to empirical or causal descriptions.

Hence, once again, the contemporary compatibilist can claim to have located the empirical cause of an action with a determining description regarding an agent's coming to have a certain belief–desire pair functioning as a reason for action (i.e. in a certain neurophysiological event which tokens the reason), but also claim to have satisfied the Kantian demand for an intelligible character of the action in virtue of the applicability of a reason description to that token, a non-determining description which employs a nonempirical indeterminist conception of transcendental freedom, complete with its notion of (practical) spontaneity. Furthermore, since reason descriptions are not a species of empirical or causal description, spontaneity, the ground of imputation, is not thereby analysed in a naturalistic causal framework, and neither is the freedom which is signalled by such spontaneity accounted for in terms of any special kind of natural determining ground. Thus the present view is not subject to Allison's criticism.

The problem of incomprehensibility

How can Kant say both that actions are fully explicable and predictable as events in nature, and yet rise from unknowable and incomprehensible grounds? This problem is slightly easier to deal with than are the others. Actions are tokened by natural events which we could predict with certainty, if we knew all of the relevant empirical facts and the causal laws [see V, 99; A549–A550/B577–B578], since nature is subject to a thoroughgoing causal determinism. Nevertheless, we may still regard them as arising from intelligible causes, causes which are thought apart from conditions of spatial and temporal determination, and which, to that extent, are not regarded as objects of experience or as knowable for us, since they are not subject to any intuition in the absence of these conditions (V, 56–7). For Kant, if an object is unintuitable, it is unknowable as well. The unknowability or incomprehensibility of these grounds, however, does not cast any doubt on their status as intelligible causes. Instead it simply underscores a traditional Kantian thesis: only natural causality produces explanations (V, 30). Or, as Kant declares in the *Foundations*, 'we can explain nothing but what we can reduce to laws whose object can be given in some possible experience'.[41] Put simply, then, the ground of any action is knowable and explicable as an event under an empirical determining description, but is unknowable (but nonetheless thinkable) under an intelligible nondetermining description.

In conclusion, our reconstruction of Kant's compatibilism has not been obstructed by the four problems which have led commentators to incompatibilist readings, to two-worlds distinctions and to dubitable rescue attempts such as calling upon the doctrine of timeless agency or that of the reduction of constitutive, categorial principles to regulative Ideas. On the strength of a two-descriptions interpretation of Kant's distinction between things in themselves and appearances, that is, on the strength of his theory of token–token identity and type–type irreducibility, we have a compatibilistic reading which accommodates the various texts often thought to threaten any imputation of a serious compatibilism to Kant, and we have elucidated an interesting philosophical thesis: whereas, at any moment of time, the entire world at that time and the laws of nature together determine a unique future, the human will, independent of pathological necessitation, is capable of both autonomous and heteronomous spontaneity of action. Or, if one prefers, human action is both causally determined and transcendentally free.

Anomalous monism

As the previous section makes clear, I believe that Kant developed a compatibilist position which is philosophically sophisticated, but it is a position which has probably found better expression (in both lucidity and detail) in its descendants. Moreover, I think we do Kant a service, if we admit (when it is true) that his views resemble certain contemporary views in certain respects, and if we treat them as the sort of thing which can be improved upon and refined in the light of contemporary analysis, without thereby doing violence to his original intentions, rather than treating them merely as wonders to be unearthed and marvelled at. Accordingly, in this final section, I offer a few remarks on some of the current work in philosophy of mind which I see as Kantian in character.

One prominent figure in contemporary philosophy of mind who has his share of Kantian sympathies is Donald Davidson. In a series of papers on freedom, agency, event theory and the philosophy of psychology, Davidson has sketched a theory of action and a relation between mind and body that, while distinct in several aspects, nevertheless, bears remarkable similarity to Kant's own view. I have already had occasion to compare Kant to Davidson with reference to how we are to understand Kant's theory of human agency and with reference to how we are to understand the pro-attitude propositional determination which belongs to a proper analysis of the causality of reason. Davidson treats the relation between the reason for performing an action and the action itself (under one type of description) as a species of causal explanation. Also, like Kant, he construes such a reason, a 'primary reason', as composed of the union of a propositional representation of a means–end connection with a desire for the end in question. Davidson, then, advocates a theory of action in which the primary reason on the basis of which an action is performed is its cause.[42] Furthermore, again like Kant, he sees causation as a relation between individual events (i.e. unrepeatable dated particulars with a determinate location in time and space), and he argues that a particular causal connection requires some causal covering law which is instantiated by some correct descriptions of the events related as cause to effect.[43] For both Kant and Davidson, then, an important consequence of these views is that whereas causality is a relation between events however described, the instantiation of a causal law is a relation between events relative to a description. These common views contribute to a version of the token–token identity theory which Davidson advances in his paper 'Mental Events', and which he terms 'anomalous monism'.[44] To this influential thesis we may now briefly turn.

Davidson begins his classic paper 'Mental Events'[45] with a quotation from Kant and with an expression of agreement with the content of the quoted passage which suggests that philosophical study will reveal a compatibilism between freedom and determinism. As is customary in the contemporary discussion, however, Davidson argues for the compatibility of the existence of various sorts of mental events which act as causes (of which the employment of free will is a species) with the anomalousness of mental events in general (which is a feature of free will as well as of rememberings, perceivings, regrettings, etc.).

This Kantian optimism is directed specifically at a reconciliation of three theses which Davidson identifies as follows:

(i)   principle of causal interaction (PCI): 'at least some mental events interact causally with physical events'.
(ii) principle of the nomological character of causality (PNCC): 'events related as cause and effect fall under strict deterministic laws'.
(iii) anomalism of the mental (AM): 'there are no strict deterministic laws on the basis of which mental events can be predicted and explained' (ME, 208).

The apparent worry is that these principles might form an inconsistent triad, since PCI and PNCC seem to imply that AM is false. Davidson suggests that the three theses can be shown to be consistent, though, and he points out that such a demonstration is 'essentially the Kantian line' (ME, 209).

He is more correct than he might have guessed. Davidson simply assumes the truth of PCI and of PNCC as 'undeniable facts', and argues in favor only of AM. Kant, on the other hand, attempts to offer argument for all three, and a brief reminder of the nature of those arguments will reveal how serious the issue is for him. When Kant offers his theory of rational agency, he commits himself to PCI, i.e. to the view that some mental events cause physical events. In fact, he is committed to a stronger series of theses as well: when he opens the first *Critique* by referring to occasions when objects affect our senses [A19/B33], he also acknowledges that some physical events cause some mental events (e.g. our coming to have sensations). And when he writes that having sensations 'stirs the understanding', i.e. prompts the activity of concept formation and application, he admits that some mental events cause other mental events. Also Kant's proof of the Law of Universal Causation in the Second Analogy has as a corollary that the causal connection is generalizable, i.e. that there are covering laws, and that causal connections are not singular. Accordingly, I maintain that

Kant has reason to regard PNCC not merely as a regulative principle, but rather as a constitutive *a priori* principle governing the very possibility of experience. Finally, Kant's notions of transcendental and practical freedom require a sense in which the will is independent from nature. This requirement, which proves both to be an essential feature of his ethical theory and to play a crucial role in his compatibilistic analysis, also involves a clear affirmation of AM. (I will mention some other means by which Kant may defend AM below.) Davidson is right, then, to note that he and Kant are working on the same problem, Davidson with its general form and Kant with its specification, the relation of causal determinism to free will.

Davidson's project is to argue from PCI, PNCC and the absence of any psychophysical laws (which justifies AM) to the truth of a token–token identity theory which he classifies as anomalous monism. He hints that this argument is weak, since he does not offer any support for PCI and PNCC beyond their own self-evidence. As just noted, though, Kant believes the principles can be supported by argument. Kant's defence of these principles relies heavily on his causal theory of time, and whether or not one believes that theory to be well-developed in Kant's writings, at the very least Kant succeeds in showing the relevance of the theory to the truth of PCI and PNCC. Perhaps, then, in the contemporary advocates of a causal theory of time, Hans Reichenbach and Adolf Grünbaum, one could find grounds for a more compelling Kantian argument in favor of PCI and PNCC than Davidson offers himself.

Davidson's strategy in arguing for AM is to first argue for a position which (together with some other less problematic assumptions) entails it, namely that there are no psychophysical laws. This claim (i.e. AM), together with his token–token identity, captures the dual thesis of anomalous monism. Monism for Kant and Davidson is a version of token-physicalism, with any mental event being identical to some physical event, but it is a nonreductive version of token-physicalism. By the anomalousness of the mental, Davidson sometimes writes as if he just means a denial of psychophysical and correlation laws, but it would seem that he also intends (and needs) to deny strict psychological laws as well. As we will see, Kant is once again in agreement on both counts: as Davidson correctly points out, 'Kant believed freedom entails anomaly' (ME, 208), and, as is well known, Kant denied that psychology could be a science because it lacked both the requisite mathematical structure and the strict laws necessary for explanation and predictability of psychological occurrences.[46]

Before I consider the arguments against psychophysical and psychological laws further, it would be worthwhile to sketch the precise argument for the identity theory offered by Davidson in 'Mental Events' and elsewhere (ME, 223–4).[47] Some mental events interact causally with physical events [from PCI]. When a mental event stands in a causal relation with a physical event, there is some strict law which they instantiate [from PNCC]. But there are no psychophysical laws (i.e. strict laws subsuming a mental event and a physical event under mental and physical descriptions), nor are there any psychological laws (i.e. strict laws subsuming two mental events under mental descriptions), nor are there any bridge laws (i.e. claims to a necessary coextension between a mental and a physical predicate on the basis of which a reduction can be accomplished) [from AM]. So, by elimination, these events instantiate a strict physical law. Therefore, since the only events which instantiate strict physical laws are physical events, any mental event which interacts causally with a physical event is itself a physical event.

It is only fair to point out that this argument, if successful, establishes merely that all mental events which stand in causal relations with physical events are themselves physical events, and Davidson shies away from the prospect of showing that all mental events have such causal relations (ME, 224). But it also seems fair to point out that it establishes the identity thesis for those mental events which we are likely to care about. That is to say, although this leaves conceptual room for some special sort of being that has psychological states with no causal history or future in virtue of which they are related to the physical world (e.g. a being who does not perceive, etc.), we are certainly not such beings ourselves. To borrow a line from Kant, for us 'there can be no doubt that all our knowledge begins from experience' [B1], and all of our subsequent mental events thereby possess the appropriate causal history, grounded in perceptual encounters, to be proper targets for the present argument. In addition to this, an alternative Kantian argument for the claim that all mental events stand in causal connections to physical events can be drawn from the fact that any two events (whether mental or physical) are temporally related, and this fact together with Kant's theory of the time-determination of events in the Second Analogy guarantees a thoroughgoing causal connectedness between the mental and the physical.

As before, the important move in Davidson's argument is from events as the relata of causal connections to events under certain descriptions as instantiating a strict physical law. In other words, whereas events, however described, are the relata of causal connections, only certain descriptions of those events are relevant for explaining the causal connection. Thus, instantiating a causal law is something which events undergo only relative to certain of their descriptions. Hence, we are to understand the two principles at work in this argument with the following important (italicized) qualifications: PNCC 'events related as cause and effect [*have descriptions in virtue of which they*] fall under strict deterministic laws', and AM 'there are no strict deterministic laws on the basis of which mental events can be predicted and explained [*which subsume events under mental descriptions*]'. Consequently, whereas AM seems to mean that we cannot 'explain and predict human behavior with the kind of precision that is possible in principle for physical phenomena' (PSY, 230), we can in principle predict and explain the occurrence of a human action, but only insofar as we can in principle predict and explain the physical event with which it is identical. What we cannot do with strict precision is explain or predict the event in terms of a mentalistic vocabulary (PSY, 230). I submit that this is also the reading to adopt with respect to Kant's own claim that human actions are as predictable as an eclipse of the sun or moon [A549–A550/B577–B578]. One should note that Kant claims that we can do the latter only when considering those actions in the field of appearance, i.e. as physical events under natural determining descriptions, and he explicitly contrasts this with predicting them as human mental actions, i.e. in their relation to reason and to man's intelligible character.

One may note that Davidson's argument strategy for the identity theory is employed also in Kant's compatibilistic resolution, and that we may substitute 'free will' for 'mental event' and draw the corresponding conclusion, that all instances of an exercise of free will are also physical events: Kant, who is committed to PCI due to his theory of action, to PNCC due to his argument for causal determinism, and to AM due to his views on psychology, and to his theory of a type of freedom essential for rational human agency, also argues to a token–token identity of actions and natural events in the resolution of the Third Antinomy.

Now the key premiss for both Kant and Davidson is the denial of strict psychophysical, psychological and bridge laws which prevents this version of token-physicalism from becoming a reductive materialism. Davidson defends the premiss by (i) denying strict psychophysical and psychological laws on the grounds that psychology is not a closed theory nor can it be nomologically reduced to a closed theory. In other words, psychology is not and cannot be reduced to a theory which, like physics, has no causes or effects which are not of the same type,[48] and by (ii) denying bridge laws on the grounds that there are irreducible differences in the constitutive principles characterizing the domains of psychological and physical predicates (PSY, 231).[49]

I will close these observations on Davidson's (Kantian) identity theory with a brief discussion of Kant's arguments for (i) and (ii), and the relation of those arguments to Davidson's defence of the same theses. Against psychological laws, Kant argues that psychology is not a science nor is it reducible to a proper science such as physics, precisely because it lacks the required mathematical structure to support lawlike generalizations subsuming events under mentalistic descriptions.[50] Moreover, psychology, unlike physics, offers no well-defined contrariety relations to support scientific investigation. Against psychophysical laws, Kant can also offer an argument grounded in his ethical views. In his so-called Reciprocity Thesis from the *Critique of Practical Reason*, Kant argues from a consciousness of the moral law, characterized as the necessary determination of the power of choice by pure practical reason, to a sense of freedom of the will involving independence from nature. Kant could, then, argue from that particular feature of his theory of free will to the absence of any psychophysical laws which would otherwise violate the sort of independence required for rational human agency. There is no circularity here, for though the absence of psychophysical laws is a necessary condition for Kant's compatibilism, which is a necessary condition for an attribution of freedom to a subject, on Kant's view, the argument for the denial of such laws begins with an independent justification for the moral law which, in turn, guarantees the freedom of independence with which Kant can deny such laws.

Finally, against bridge laws (i.e. against claims to the necessary coextension of a physical and a mental predicate) Kant would share with Davidson the approach which relies on distinguishing noninterchangeable constitutive principles of the physical and mental conceptual schemes, and noninterchangeable standards of application for the respective concept types. The argument, then, is that no bridge laws are possible, since the concepts from the two essentially different conceptual schemes, which would thereby be made necessarily coextensive, have incompatible standards of construction and application.[51] The constitutive principles in question occupy a normative role in concept formation and application, and those underlying the mental conceptual scheme are, in general, rationality requirements. Davidson writes: 'if we are to intelligibly attribute attitudes and beliefs, or usefully to describe motions as behavior, then we are committed to finding, in the pattern of behavior, belief, and desire, a large degree of rationality and consistency' (PSY, 237). These conditions express how one ought to behave and what one ought to believe, given certain background evidence and beliefs, in order to conform to the standards of rationality and consistency (PSY, 231). Since no principles underlying physical conceptual schemes can manage to do this, the conditions for mental concept formation and application cannot be stated with a purely physical terminology. In short, then, since mental concepts can have only rational conditions of application, and since physical concepts can have only nonrational conditions of application, and, since bridge laws would require that mental concepts would have nonrational conditions of application, there cannot be such laws.

Similarly, Kant believes that there are rational conditions of mental concept formation and application. Talk of purposes and reasons for action invoke teleological, nondetermining, reflective judgments which may be contrasted with those causal determining judgments required for empirical knowledge which do invoke concepts taken from the physical conceptual domain. In the specific subclass of such mental concepts that Kant is interested in, the conditions required for the application of action descriptions apply to expressions of the pro-attitude propositional determination at work in the causality of reason. And, as is now obvious, the nondetermining descriptions serving as the relevant action descriptions are not reducible to any determining descriptions. One sufficient reason for this, among others, is that the former offer no causal connections or determinability of their objects in space or in time, and the latter require such connections and determinability. Consequently, Kant would deny the existence of bridge laws for exactly the same reasons that Davidson offers, because any claim to a necessary coextension of a physical predicate and a mental predicate would require the lawlike union of concepts from essentially incompatible conceptual domains.

Notes

1 This chapter contains excerpts from the second and third chapters of my *Kant's Compatibilism* (Ithaca, NY: Cornell University Press, 1994).
2 References to the *Critique of Pure Reason* will appear in the text and are to the standard pagination of the first and second editions, indicated as 'A' and 'B', respectively.
3 *Critique of Practical Reason*, AK V:94. (In order to economize on footnotes, a Roman numeral followed by an Arabic numeral in the text represent the volume and page, respectively, of the Akademie Edition of the second *Critique*.)
4 Allen Wood, 'Kant's Compatibilism', in Allen Wood (ed.) *Self and Nature in Kant's Philosophy* (Ithaca, NY: Cornell University Press, 1984): pp. 73–101.
5 Wood, 'Kant's Compatibilism', pp. 86–9 (emphasis added).
6 Wood, 'Kant's Compatibilism', pp. 90–101.

7 But recent Anglo-American commentators endorse it as well: Jonathan Bennett in his *Kant's Analytic* (Cambridge: Cambridge University Press, 1966), and Robert Paul Wolff in his *Kant's Theory of Mental Activity* (Cambridge, Mass.: Harvard University Press, 1963).

8 Gerold Prauss defends the two-descriptions view in his *Erscheinung bei Kant* (Berlin: Walter de Gruyter, 1971), and again in *Kant und das Problem der Dinge an Sich* (Bonn: Bouvier Verlag H. Grundmann, 1974).

9 Henry E. Allison, *Kant's Transcendental Idealism* (New Haven, Conn.: Yale University Press, 1983); esp. chapters 1, 2 and 11.

10 Allison, *Kant's Transcendental Idealism*, pp. 237–42.

11 E.g. at Bxix, note; Bxx; Bxxi; Bxxii; and especially at Bxxviii–Bxxix.

12 E.g. at B55; B69; B186; B258; A249–A253; B306; B333.

13 E.g. at AK IV:453; and again at pp. 450; 451; 456; 457.

14 E.g. at AK V:6, note; and again at pp. 42; 43; 65; 87; 95; 114.

15 Beck, *A Commentary on Kant's Critique of Practical Reason* (Chicago, Il.: University of Chicago Press, 1960): pp. 190–1.

16 Beck, *Commentary*, pp. 191–2. He repeats a similar worry in 'Five Concepts of Freedom in Kant', in J.T.J. Srzednicki (ed.) *Stephan Körner: Philosophical Analysis and Reconstruction* (Hingham: Kluwer Academic Publishers, 1987), pp. 42–3.

17 I comment on these counter-intuitive proposals at some length in the third chapter of my *Kant's Compatibilism*, where I defend Kant's position from contemporary incompatibilist arguments.

18 Beck, *Commentary*, p. 192.

19 Beck, *Commentary*, p. 193.

20 Beck, *Commentary*, p. 193; 'Five Concepts of Freedom in Kant', p. 45.

21 See his 'Five Concepts of Freedom in Kant', pp. 44–5.

22 Robert E. Butts, *Kant and the Double Government Methodology* (Dordrecht: D. Reidel, 1984), pp. 262–3. Butts's discussion is found roughly between pp. 248 and 273.

23 Butts endorses Beck's dilemma on p. 260 and on pp. 271–2. The primary piece of evidence he cites for his reading is from the text of the Fourth Antinomy at A561–A562/B589–B590.

24 Ralf Meerbote raises this objection to Butts in a critical review of his book. See *Noûs* 13 (1989), 266–70.

25 Butts, *Kant and the Double Government Methodology*, p. 262.

26 Beck, 'Five Concepts of Freedom in Kant', p. 47.

27 Beck, *Commentary*, p. 193; 'Five Concepts of Freedom in Kant', p. 48.

28 Much recent work has been done on the prospects of identifying a given mental event with a particular physical event (or in Kant's case, of a free action with natural events that stand under causal laws) without thereby incurring a commitment to the distinct (and unwelcome) thesis that mental descriptions are reducible to physical descriptions (or that action descriptions are reducible to natural descriptions). For a recent and very accessible overview of this literature, see Cynthia MacDonald's *Mind–Body Identity Theories* (New York: Routledge, 1989). For a discussion of the thesis tailored to the Kantian case, see the section titled 'Token–token identity and type–type irreducibility' in my *Kant's Compatibilism*, pp. 60–4.

29 *Critique of Judgment*, p. 36, note [AK V:196].

30 *Critique of Judgment*, p. 36 [AK V:195].

31 As he does elsewhere, Kant expresses his view that the intelligible determining grounds of a will which are given through the causality of reason are always bound up with an 'ought' in *Prolegomena to Any Future Metaphysics*, AK IV:345. This is intimately connected with Kant's view that the activity of the human will is always mediated by a maxim, or that human agency essentially involves imperatives.

32 *Prolegomena to Any Future Metaphysics*, pp. 92–3 [AK. IV:345].

33 Ralf Meerbote, 'Kant on the Nondeterminate Character of Human Actions', in William Harper and Ralf Meerbote (eds) *Kant on Causality, Freedom, and Objectivity* (Minneapolis: University of Minnesota Press, 1984) p. 139.

34 Meerbote, 'Kant on the Nondeterminate Character of Human Actions', pp. 151–3.

35 It is this compound thesis, complete with the sense of independence just described, which has led Ralf Meerbote to call Kant's theory a version of anomalous monism, by way of comparing it to the view advocated by Donald Davidson. See his 'Kant on the Nondeterminate Character of Human Actions'. I will have much more to say about Kant's Davidsonian tendencies (or, rather, about Davidson's Kantian tendencies) in the remainder of this chapter.

36 *Prolegomena to Any Future Metaphysics*, p. 94 [AK IV:346; see also IV:347].

37 *Religion Within the Limits of Reason Alone*, trans. T.M. Greene and H.H. Hudson (New York: Harper & Row, 1960), p. 34 [AK VI:39].

38 Allison, *Kant's Theory of Freedom*, pp. 5, 28, 34, *passim*.

39 Allison, *Kant's Theory of Freedom*, p. 28; Wood, 'Kant's Compatibilism', p. 74.

40 Allison, *Kant's Theory of Freedom*, pp. 34, 81.

41 *Foundations of the Metaphysics of Morals*, p. 77 [AK IV:459].

42 See Davidson, 'Actions, Reasons, and Causes', and 'Freedom to Act', both reprinted in *Essays on Actions and Events*, pp. 3–19 and pp. 63–81, respectively.

43 See Davidson, 'Causal Relations', reprinted in *Essays on Actions and Events*, pp. 149–62.

44 Again, reprinted in *Essays on Actions and Events*, pp. 207–25. See also 'Psychology as Philosophy', together with comments and replies and 'The Material Mind', in the same collection, pp. 229–44 and pp. 245–59, respectively.

45 References in the text followed by a page number refer to Davidson's papers, 'Mental Events' (ME) and 'Psychology as Philosophy' (PSY) in the collection *Essays on Actions and Events*.

46 See the Preface to the *Metaphysical Foundations of Natural Science*, AK IV:467–79.

47 In this regard, Brian McLaughlin's essay 'Anomalous Monism and the Irreducibility of the Mental', in Ernest LePore and Brian P. McLaughlin (eds) *Actions and Events: Perspectives in the Philosophy of Donald Davidson* (New York: Basil Blackwell, 1985), pp. 331–68, is remarkably helpful in its clear summarization and reconstruction of the views Davidson offers in several of his papers.

48 See McLaughlin, 'Anomalous Monism and the Irreducibility of the Mental', Sections VI–VIII, pp. 342–52, for a comprehensive discussion.

49 Again, see McLaughlin, 'Anomalous Monism and the Irreducibility of the Mental', section IX, pp. 352–9, for an extended discussion.
50 *Metaphysical Foundations of Natural Science*, AK IV:467–79.
51 This specific argument is analysed at some length in McLaughlin, 'Anomalous Monism and the Irreducibility of the Mental', pp. 354–9. What follows is partially drawn from that discussion.

SELECT BIBLIOGRAPHY

Allison, Henry E., 'The Concept of Freedom in Kant's "Semi-Critical" Ethics', *Archiv für Geschichte der Philosophie*, vol. 68, 1986, 96–115.

—— 'Morality and Freedom: Kant's Reciprocity Thesis', *Philosophical Review*, vol. 95, 1987, 393–425.

—— 'Justification and Freedom in the *Critique of Practical Reason*' in Eckhart Forster (ed.) *Kant's Transcendental Deductions in the Three 'Critiques' and the 'Opus postumum'* (Stanford, Calif.: Stanford University Press, 1989), pp. 114–30.

—— 'The Hidden Circle in *Groundwork* III' in G. Funke and Th. M. Seebohm (eds) *Proceedings: Sixth International Kant Congress* (Washington: University Press of America, 1989), pp. 147–58.

—— 'Kant's Preparatory Argument in *Grundlegung* III' in Otfried Höffe (ed.) *Grundlegung zur Metaphysik der Sitten: Ein kooperativer Kommentar* (Frankfurt am Main: Vittorio Klostermann, 1989), pp. 314–24.

—— *Kant's Theory of Freedom* (Cambridge: Cambridge University Press, 1990).

—— 'On a Presumed Gap in the Derivation of the Categorical Imperative', *Philosophical Topics,* vol. 19, 1991, 1–15.

—— *Idealism and Freedom: Essays on Kant's Theoretical and Practical Philosophy* (Cambridge: Cambridge University Press, 1996).

Ameriks, Karl, 'Kant's Deduction of Freedom and Morality', *Journal of the History of Philosophy*, vol. 19, 1981, 53–79.

—— 'The Hegelian Critique of Kantian Morality' in Bernard den Ouden and Marcia Moen (eds) *New Essays on Kant* (New York: Peter Lang, 1987), pp. 179–212.

—— 'Kant on the Good Will' in Otfried Höffe (ed.) *Grundlegung zur Metaphysik der Sitten: Ein kooperativer Kommentar* (Frankfurt am Main: Vittorio Klostermann, 1989), pp. 45–65.

—— *Kant and the Fate of Autonomy* (Cambridge: Cambridge University Press, 2000).

Aune, Bruce, *Kant's Theory of Morals* (Princeton, New Jersey: Princeton University Press, 1979).

Baron, Marcia W., *Kantian Ethics Almost Without Apology* (Ithaca, New York: Cornell University Press, 1995).

Beck, Lewis White, *A Commentary on Kant's Critique of Practical Reason* (Chicago: University of Chicago Press, 1960).

—— *Studies in the Philosophy of Kant* (Indianapolis: Bobbs-Merrill, 1965).

—— *Early German Philosophy: Kant and His Predecessors* (Cambridge, Mass.: Harvard University Press, 1969).

—— 'Five Concepts of Freedom in Kant' in J.T.J. Szrednicki (ed.) *Philosophical Analysis and Reconstruction* (Dordrecht: Martinus Nijhoff, 1987), pp. 35–51.

Bittner, Rüdiger, 'Maximen' in Gerhard Funke (ed.) *Akten des Internationalen Kant-Kongresses* (Berlin: Walter de Gruyter, 1974), pp. 485–98.

Broadie, Alexander and Pybus, Elizabeth M., 'Kant's Concept of Respect', *Kant-Studien*, vol. 66, 1975, 58–64.

—— 'Kant and Direct Duties', *Dialogue*, vol. 20, 1981, 60–67.

—— 'Kant and Weakness of Will', *Kant-Studien*, vol. 73, 1982, 406–12.

Carnois, Bernard, *The Coherence of Kant's Doctrine of Freedom*, trans. David Booth (Chicago: University of Chicago Press, 1987).

Cummiskey, David, *Kantian Consequentialism* (Oxford: Oxford University Press, 1996).

Davidson, Donald, 'Mental Events' in Donald Davidson, *Essays on Actions and Events* (Oxford: Clarendon, 1980), pp. 207–27.

Donagan, Alan, 'The Structure of Kant's Metaphysics of Morals', *Topoi*, vol. 4, 1985, 61–72.

—— 'The Relation of Moral Theory to Moral Judgments: A Kantian Review' in Baruch A. Brody (ed.) *Moral Theory and Moral Judgments in Medical Ethics* (Dordrecht: Kluwer, 1988), pp. 171- 92.

Duncan, A.R.C., *Practical Reason and Morality: A Study of Immanuel Kant's 'Foundations for the Metaphysics of Morals'* (London: Thomas Nelson, 1957).

Eggerman, Richard, 'Kantian Strict Duties of Benevolence', *Southwest Philosophy Review*, vol. 6, 1990, 81–8.

Engstrom, Stephen, 'Conditional Autonomy', *Philosophy and Phenomenological Research*, vol. 48, 1988, 435–53.

—— and Jennifer Whiting (eds) *Aristotle, Kant and the Stoics: Rethinking Happiness and Duty* (Cambridge: Cambridge University Press, 1996).

Flynn, James R., 'The Logic of Kant's Derivation of Freedom from Reason', *Kant-Studien*, vol. 77, 1986, 441–64.

Foot, Philippa, 'Morality as a System of Hypothetical Imperatives', *Philosophical Review*, vol. 81, 1972, 306–16.

Galvin, Richard F., 'Does Kant's Psychology of Morality Need Basic Revision?', *Mind*, vol. 100, 1991, 221–36.

—— 'Ethical Formalism: The Contradiction in Conception Test', *History of Philosophy Quarterly*, vol. 8, 1991, 387–408.

Genova, Anthony C., 'Kant's Transcendental Deduction of the Moral Law', *Kant-Studien*, vol. 69, 1978, 299–313.

Green, Michael K., 'Kant and Moral Self-Deception', *Kant-Studien*, vol. 83, 1992, 148–69.

Green, Ronald M., 'The First Formulation of the Categorical Imperative as Literally a "Legislative" Metaphor', *History of Philosophy Quarterly*, vol. 8, 1991, 163–79.

Gregor, Mary J., *Laws of Freedom*, (Oxford: Basil Blackwell, 1963).

Guyer, Paul, 'The Unity of Reason: Pure Reason as Practical Reason in Kant's Early Conception of the Transcendental Dialectic', *Monist*, vol. 72, 1989, 139–67.

—— 'Kant's Morality of Law and Morality of Freedom' in R.M. Dancy (ed.) *Kant and Critique: New Essays in Honor of W.H. Werkmeister* (Dordrecht: Kluwer, 1993), pp. 43–89.

—— 'Duty and Inclination' in *Kant and the Experience of Freedom: Essays on Aesthetics and Morality* (Cambridge: Cambridge University Press, 1993), pp. 335–93.

—— (ed.), *Kant's Groundwork of the Metaphysics of Morals: Critical Essays* (Lanham, Md.: Rowman & Littlefield, 1998).

Henrich, Dieter, 'Das Prinzip der Kantischen Ethik', *Philosophische Rundschau*, vol. 2, 1954–55, 20–38.

—— 'Die Deduktion des Sittengesetzes' in Alexander Schwan (ed.) *Denken im Schatten des Nihilismus* (Darmstadt: Wissenschaftliche Buchgesellschaft, 1975), pp. 55–112.

—— *Aesthetic Judgment and the Moral Image of the World: Studies in Kant* (Stanford, Calif.: Stanford University Press, 1992).

—— *The Unity of Reason: Essays on Kant's Philosophy*, ed. Richard Velkley, trans. Manfred Kuehn (Cambridge: Harvard University Press, 1994).

Herman, Barbara, *The Practice of Moral Judgment* (Cambridge, Mass.: Harvard University Press, 1993).

Hill, Thomas E., Jr, *Autonomy and Self Respect* (Cambridge: Cambridge University Press, 1991).

—— *Dignity and Practical Reason in Kant's Moral Theory* (Ithaca, New York: Cornell University Press, 1992).

—— *Respect, Pluralism and Justice* (Cambridge: Cambridge University Press, 2000).

Hinman, Lawrence M., 'On the Purity of Our Moral Motives: A Critique of Kant's Account of the Emotions and Acting for the Sake of Duty', *Monist*, vol. 66, 1983, 251–67.

Höffe, Otfried (ed.), *Grundlegung der Metaphysik der Sitten: Ein Kooperativer Komentar* (Frankfurt am Main: Vittorio Klosterman, 1989).

Hudson, Hud, '*Wille, Willkür* and the Imputability of Immoral Actions', *Kant-Studien*, vol. 82, 1991, 179–96.

—— *Kant's Compatibilism* (Ithaca, New York: Cornell University Press, 1994).

Korsgaard, Christine M., *Creating the Kingdom of Ends* (Cambridge: Cambridge University Press, 1996).

—— *The Sources of Normativity* (Cambridge: Cambridge University Press, 1996).

Louden, Robert, *Kant's Impure Ethics: From Rational Beings to Human Beings* (Oxford: Oxford University Press, 1999).

McCarthy, Michael, 'Kant's Application of the Analytic/Synthetic Distinction to Imperatives', *Dialogue*, vol. 18, 1979, 373–91.

—— 'Kant's Rejection of the Argument of *Groundwork* III', *Kant-Studien*, vol. 73, 1982, 169–90.

—— 'The Objection of Circularity in *Groundwork* III', *Kant-Studien*, vol. 76, 1985, 28–42.

—— 'Moral Conflicts in Kantian Ethics', *History of Philosophy Quarterly*, vol. 8, 1991, 65–79.

McCarty, Richard, 'Kantian Moral Motivation and the Feeling of the Respect', *Journal of the History of Philosophy*, vol. 31, 1993, 421–35.

—— 'Motivation and Moral Choice in Kant's Theory of Rational Agency', *Kant-Studien*, vol. 85, 1994, 15–31.

Meerbote, Ralf, '*Wille* and *Willkür* in Kant's Theory of Action' in M.S. Gram (ed.) *Interpreting Kant* (Iowa City: University of Iowa Press, 1982), pp. 69–84.

—— 'Commentary: Kant on Freedom and the Rational and Morally Good Will' in Allen Wood (ed.) *Self and Nature in Kant's Philosophy* (Ithaca, New York: Cornell University Press, 1984), pp. 57–72.

O'Neill, Onora [formerly Nell], *Acting on Principle: An Essay on Kantian Ethics* (New York: Columbia University Press, 1975).

—— *Constructions of Reason: Explorations of Kant's Practical Philosophy* (Cambridge: Cambridge University Press, 1989).

—— 'Reason and Autonomy in *Grundlegung* III' in Otfried Höffe (ed.) *Grundlegung zur Metaphysik der Sitten: Ein kooperativer Kommentar* (Frankfurt am Main: Vittorio Klostermann, 1989), pp. 282–98.

Paton, H.J., *The Categorical Imperative: A Study in Kant's Moral Philosophy* (London: Hutchinson University Library, 1947).

Potter, Nelson, 'Does Kant Have Two Concepts of Freedom?' in Gerhard Funke (ed.) *Akten des Internationalen Kant-Kongresses* (Berlin: Walter de Gruyter, 1974), pp. 590–96.

—— 'How to Apply the Categorical Imperative', *Philosophia*, vol. 5, 1975, 395–416.

—— 'Kant on Ends That Are at the Same Time Duties', *Pacific Philosophical Quarterly*, vol. 66, 1985, 78–92.

—— 'What Is Wrong with Kant's Four Examples?', *Philosophy Research Archives*, vol. 18, 1993, 213–29.

—— 'Kant and the Moral Worth of Actions', *Southern Journal of Philosophy*, vol. 34, 1996, 225–41.

Potter, Nelson, and Mark Timmons (eds) *Morality and Universality: Essays on Ethical Universalizability* (Dordrecht: D. Reidel, 1985).

Prauss, Gerold, *Kant über Freiheit als Autonomie* (Frankfurt am Main: Vittorio Klostermann, 1983).

Rauscher, Frederick, 'Pure Reason and the Moral Law: A Source of Kant's Critical Philosophy', *History of Philosophy Quarterly*, vol. 13, 1996, 255–71.

Rawls, John, 'Themes in Kant's Moral Philosophy' in Eckhard Forster (ed.) *Kant's Transcendental Deductions: The Three 'Critiques' and the Opus postumum* (Stanford, Calif.: Stanford University Press, 1989), pp. 81–113.

Reath, Andrews, 'Two Conceptions of the Highest Good in Kant', *Journal of the History of Philosophy*, vol. 26, 1988, 593–619.

—— 'The Categorical Imperative and Kant's Conception of Practical Rationality', *Monist*, vol. 72, 1989, 384–410.

—— 'Kant's Theory of Moral Sensibility: Respect for the Law and the Influence of Inclination', *Kant-Studien*, vol. 80, 1989, 284–302.

—— 'Hedonism, Heteronomy, and Kant's Principle of Happiness', *Pacific Philosophical Quarterly*, vol. 70, 1989, 42–72.

—— 'Legislating the Moral Law', *Noûs*, vol. 28, 1994, 435–64.

Reath, Andrews, Barbara Herman, and Christine Korsgaard (eds) *Reclaiming the History of Ethics: Essays for John Rawls* (Cambridge: Cambridge University Press, 1997).

Ross, W.D., *The Right and the Good* (Oxford: Clarendon Press, 1930).

—— *Kant's Ethical Theory* (Oxford: Clarendon Press, 1954).

Schlipp, Paul Arthur, *Kant's Pre-critical Ethics* (Evanston, Il.: Northwestern University Press, 1938).

Schmucker, Josef, *Die Ursprünge der Ethik Kants* (Meisenheim am Glan: Verlag, 1961).

Schneewind, J. B. (ed.) *Moral Philosophy from Montaigne to Kant*, 2 vols (Cambridge: Cambridge University Press, 1990).

—— 'Natural Law, Skepticism, and Methods of Ethics', *Journal of the History of Ideas*, vol. 52, 1991, 289–308.

—— *The Invention of Autonomy* (Cambridge: Cambridge University Press, 1998).

Sedgwick, Sally, 'On the Relation of Pure Reason to Content: A Reply to Hegel's Critique of Formalism in Kant's Ethics', *Philosophy and Phenomenological Research*, vol. 49, 1988, 59–80.

—— 'Can Kant's Ethics Survive the Feminist Critique?', *Pacific Philosophical Quarterly*, vol. 71, 1990, 60–79.

—— 'On Lying and the Role of Content in Kant's Ethics', *Kant-Studien*, vol. 82, 1991, 42–62.

Shell, Susan, *The Rights of Reason: A Study of Kant's Philosophy and Politics* (Toronto: University of Toronto Press, 1980).

Silber, John, 'The Copernican Revolution in Ethics: The Good Reexamined', *Kant-Studien*, vol. 51, 1959, 85–101.

—— 'Kant's Conception of the Highest Good as Immanent and Transcendent', *Philosophical Review*, vol. 58, 1959, 469–92.

—— 'The Importance of the Highest Good in Kant's Ethics', *Ethics*, vol. 73, 1962–63, 179–97.

—— 'Procedural Formalism in Kant's Ethics', *Review of Metaphysics*, vol. 28, 1974, 197–236.

—— 'The Moral Good and the Natural Good in Kant's Ethics', *Review of Metaphysics*, vol. 36, 1982, 397–438.

Singer, Marcus, 'The Categorical Imperative', *Philosophical Review*, vol. 63, 1954, 577–91.

—— *Generalization in Ethics* (New York: Alfred A. Knopf, 1961).

—— 'Reconstructing the *Groundwork*', *Ethics*, vol. 93, 1983, 566–78.

Stocker, Michael, 'The Schizophrenia of Modern Ethical Theories', *Journal of Philosophy*, vol. 73, 1976, 453–66.

Stratton-Lake, Philip, 'Formulating Categorical Imperatives', *Kant-Studien*, vol. 83, 1993, 317–40.

—— 'Kant and Contemporary Moral Theory', *Kantian Review*, vol. 2, 1998, 1–13.

—— *Kant, Duty and Moral Worth* (London: Routledge, 2000).

Sullivan, Roger, *Immanuel Kant's Moral Theory* (Cambridge: Cambridge University Press, 1989).

—— *An Introduction to Kant's Ethics* (Cambridge: Cambridge University Press, 1994).

Timmons, Mark, 'Contradictions and the Categorical Imperative', *Archive für Geschichte der Philosophie*, vol. 66, 1984, 294–312.

—— 'Kant on the Possibility of Moral Motivation', *Southern Journal of Philosophy*, vol. 23, 1985, 377–98.

Velkley, Richard, *Freedom and the End of Reason: On the Moral Foundations of Kant's Critical Philosophy* (Chicago: University of Chicago Press, 1989).

Ward, Keith, *The Development of Kant's View of Ethics* (Oxford: Basil Blackwell, 1972).

Wiggins, David, 'Categorical Requirements: Kant and Hume on the Idea of Duty', *Monist*, vol. 74, 1991, 83–106.

Williams, Bernard, *Problems of the Self* (Cambridge: Cambridge University Press, 1973).

—— *Moral Luck* (Cambridge: Cambridge University Press, 1981).

—— *Ethics and the Limits of Philosophy* (Cambridge, Mass.: Harvard University Press, 1985).

Williams, T.C., *The Concept of the Categorical Imperative: A Study of the Place of the Categorical Imperative in Kant's Ethical Theory* (Oxford: Clarendon Press, 1968).

Wolff, Robert Paul (ed.), *Kant: A Collection of Critical Essays* (Garden City, New York: Doubleday, 1967).

—— (ed.) *Foundations of the Metaphysics of Morals with Critical Essays* (Indianapolis: Bobbs-Merrill, 1969).

—— *The Autonomy of Reason: A Commentary on Kant's Groundwork of the Metaphysics of Morals* (New York: Harper & Row, 1973).

Wood, Allen W., *Kant's Moral Religion* (Ithaca, New York: Cornell University Press, 1970).

—— 'Kant on False Promises' in Lewis White Beck (ed.) *Proceedings of the Third International Kant Congress* (Dordrecht: D. Reidel, 1972), pp. 614–19.

—— 'Kant on the Rationality of Morals' in Pierre Laberge, Francois Duchesneau and Bryan E. Morrissey (eds) *Actes du congres d'Ottawa sur Kant* (Ottawa: University of Ottawa Press, 1976), pp. 94–109.

—— (ed.) *Self and Nature in Kant's Philosophy* (Ithaca, New York: Cornell University Press, 1984).

—— 'The Emptiness of the Moral Will', *Monist*, vol. 72, 1989, 454–83.

—— 'Unsocial Sociability: The Anthropological Basis of Kantian Ethics', *Philosophical Topics*, vol. 19, 1991, 325–51.

Yovel, Yirmiahu (ed.) *Kant's Practical Philosophy Reconsidered* (Dordrecht: Kluwer, 1989).

INDEX

competitiveness, 175–7
conformity, 162
consistency in action, 12
contentment, 25, 26–31
contradictions: in conception
(conceptual inconsistency), 162–8,
169–72; in will (volitional
inconsistency), 162–8, 172–7
Critique of Judgement 243, 248–9
Critique of Practical Reason, 13,
182–4, 201, 205, 211–28
Critique of Pure Reason, 6–9, 13,
195; Third Antinomy, 234–64

Darwall, xx, 99
Davidson, D., 247, 258–64
Descartes, R., 112
desire: and freedom, 4–5; for
happiness, 8–9; and moral
consciousness, 212
dignity, 67, 212
divine command theory, 9, 112,
128, 139–40, 142–3
Donagan, A., 99
duty, 11–14, 21, 67 of benevolence,
126, 136–7; canon of moral
judgement, 52–3; and the good
will, 28–31, 132–44; Hume's
Dilemma, 125–32, 143–4;
imperfect, 50–52; and inclination,
29; and moral worth, 159–61;
motive of, 28–31, 37–9, 121–44;
to others, 11, 29–30, 50–52, 58;
perfect, 50–52, 161, 169; and
practical reason, 105–6; principle
of, 31; to protect one's life, 29;
and reverence for law, 31–3,
137–44; and sympathy, 134–6; to
self, 30, 50–52, 57–8; *versus* self-
interest, 29

egoism: psychological, 3–4, 9;
rational, 193, 197, 204
ends, 55–7, 87, 102–5; Formula of
the End in Itself, 55–8; Formula
of the Kingdom of Ends, 61–7,

168; happiness as an end, 104–5,
114–17, 134; humanity as end in
itself, 114; and practical reason,
114–17; willing, 164
Epicurus, 6, 112
ethics (moral philosophy), 6, 19–22;
autonomous *see* autonomy;
development from rational
knowledge, 2–3, 25–36;
development into metaphysic of
morals, 37–71; heteronomous *see*
heteronomy; pure ethics, 20–22,
41, 54–5; universality tests, 154–78
External Law, 139–40, 142
externalism, 9, 121, 126, 131–2

Fact of Reason, 212, 223–4
false promise, 11–12, 33–4, 48–9,
51, 58, 140–41
feelings: *versus* cognition, 2–3; and
motivation, 7–9, 213–15; and
motivational internalism, 10; and
respect, 213–16; as warrant for
action, 11, 136–7
Foot, P., 103, 204–5
Formula of Autonomy, 59, 67
Formula of the End in Itself, 55–8
Formula of Humanity, 4, 12
Formula of the Kingdom of Ends,
61–7, 168
Formula of the Law of Nature, 50
Formula of Universal Law, 12, 33–4,
49–50, 52, 59–61, 124, 136–44,
154–78
free will and autonomy, 110–14; and
causal determinism, 234–64;
concept of, 39, 81–2;
subordination of everything to, 5
freedom, 1; to adopt or discard
maxims, 157; and autonomy of
will, 72–6, 78–80; and causal
determinism, 13–14, 234–64; and
the categorical imperative,
200–204; concept of, 72–3, 83–4;
and desires, 4–5; explanation of,
83–4; and the general will, 5; and

Reath, A., 2, 10, 211–28
reciprocity thesis, 13, 182–205
Reflexionen, 3, 4, 6
Reichenbach, H., 260
Reinhold, K.L., 203–4
Religion Within the Limits of Reason Alone, 136, 185–6, 194, 199, 200–201, 203, 220, 253
respect, 10; definition, 213; and feeling, 213–16; as incentive, 213–16; for Moral Law, 211–28; and self-esteem, 220–21; and self-love, 227
reverence, 63; for law, 31–3, 137–44
Ross, W.D., 130–32, 143
Rousseau, J., 3–5, 6–7
Rule Utilitarianism, 154

self-conceit (*Eigendünkel*), 218–21, 227–8
self-esteem, 220–21, 228
selfishness (*Eigenliebe*), 218
self-knowledge, 158
self-love (*Selbstliebe*), 218–21, 223–8
self-regard (*Selbstsucht*), 218, 225–6
sensible world, 76–80
sentimentalism: Kant's abandonment of, 6; moral knowledge, 2–3; and motivational internalism, 10; *versus* Wolffian rationalism, 5
Sentimentalists, 121–32
Shaftesbury, 6
Sidgewick, 192
Singer, M., 154, 192
slavery, 169–70, 171
Socrates, 34
stoicism, 5
suicide, 11, 12, 51, 57
Sulzer, J.G., 41
sympathy, 134–7

talents, 25; duty to further one's, 11, 51–2

theory of agency, 11
Third Antinomy, 234–64
transcendental freedom, 13, 194–6, 204–5
transcendental idealism, 13–14

Universal Prescriptivism (Hare), 154
universality, 7, 59; consistency/inconsistency, 162–9; Formula of Universal Law, 12, 33–4, 49–50, 52, 59–61, 124, 136–44, 154–78; tests, 154–78

vicious circle, 75–6
virtue, 55, 125–8, 212; dignity of, 62–3

will, 1; autonomy *see* autonomy; and choice (*Wille-Willkür* distinction), 189–91, 200–204, 219; contradictions in (volitional inconsistency), 162–8, 172–7; form of willing, 71; free *see* free will; general *versus* personal, 5; God's will, 9, 44, 68, 70, 142; good *see* good will; heteronomy, 68, 112, 201; and inclination, 211–28; Kant's definition, 184, 188; and lawfulness, 111–12, 187–91; lawless, 190–91; motivation to act morally, 6, 7–9; as practical reason, 42–3, 100–102; transcendental freedom, 13, 194–6, 204–5; and universal law, 59, 61–2; willing as such, 22
Wille-Willkür distinction, 189–91, 200–204, 219
Williams, B., 128
Wolff, C., 2–3, 5, 6–7, 11, 22, 123, 141
Wood, A., 235–40, 255